GOAL!

GOAL!

The Ultimate Guide for Soccer Moms and Dads

By Gloria Averbuch and Ashley Michael Hammond

Rodale Press, Inc.
Emmaus, Pennsylvania

Notice: This book is intended as a reference volume only. The information given here is designed to help you make informed decisions about your child's involvement in youth soccer. It is not intended as a substitute for any treatment that may have been prescribed by your doctor. You should seek your child's doctor's approval before beginning any exercise program.

There are more than 13.6 million American youths between the ages of 6 and 18 who play soccer, according to the Soccer Industry Council of America. Forty-two percent of them are girls. To reflect their participation, this book alternates between the usage of "he" and "she."

Printed in the United States of America on acid-free ∞, recycled paper ♻

Cover and Interior Design: **Tanja Lipinski-Cole**
Digital Imaging and Layout Design: **Dale Mack**
Illustrations (minivan): **Neverne Covington**

Library of Congress Cataloging-in-Publication Data

Averbuch, Gloria, 1951–
Goal! : the ultimate guide for soccer moms and dads / by Gloria Averbuch and Ashley Michael Hammond.
p. cm.
Includes index.
ISBN 1-57954-080-5 paperback
1. Soccer for children—United States 2. Parenting—United States. 3. Family recreation—United States. I. Hammond, Ashley Michael. II. Title: Ultimate guide for soccer moms and dads.
GV944.2.A94 1999
796.334'0973—dc21 99-24197

Distributed to the book trade by St. Martin's Press

2 4 6 8 10 9 7 5 3 1 paperback

Visit us on the Web at www.rodalebooks.com or call us toll-free at (800) 848-4735

OUR PURPOSE

"We inspire and enable people to improve their lives and the world around them."

To the Stampede, the 1997 and 1998 Mid-New Jersey Select U-10 and U-11 girls soccer team, whose laughter, passion, and guts taught me to love the game.

And to Grete Waitz—the most accomplished female distance runner in history—friend, counselor, and inspiration.

— Gloria

To my loving wife, Meg, for her patience, caring, and understanding;

to Andy Cole, for believing in me when I did not believe in myself;

to my mom and dad and my sisters, Sadie and Tansie, for their unconditional love and unerring support;

to Glen, for knowing me better than I know myself and for being the brother I never had.

— Ashley

acknowledgments

Thanks to those who made this book possible: First, our editor and stellar soccer-dad-in-training, John Reeser, for believing in this project from the beginning and making it happen; Pat Corpora, Debora T. Yost, Neil Wertheimer, and Jack Croft for taking our proposal seriously and giving us their full support; Ashley's Soccer Camp in Montclair, New Jersey, where I have learned the joys and heartaches (mostly joys) of working in youth soccer; my daughters—phenomenal, hardworking soccer players who inspire me daily—12-year-old Yael, for critically reviewing a large portion of this book like a pro and giving invaluable insights as a youth player; and 9-year-old Shira, for stapling, collating, copying, and putting her arms around me when I needed it most; my husband, Paul, for his expertise as a top athlete, world-class soccer dad and coach, and professional sports conditioning coach; our models, whose photographs appear in the book: Lucas Abbott, Shira Averbuch, Yael Averbuch, Andrew Goor, Annie Goor, Ryan Goor, Meg Hammond, Natasha Mottola, Justin Pack, Leroy Watkins, and Jon Claude Wells; Tanja Lipinski-Cole, who so artfully designed the book cover and interior; Erin McDonald and Peggy Lee and the staff of adidas soccer; Nancy Clark, M.S., R.D., my "nutrition muse"; Nancy Pierce, Program Specialist, United States Youth Soccer Association; Bob Vasser, coach, player, and educator; Grete Waitz, for her insights on parenting young athletes; orthodontist Ed Gold, D.D.S.; Beth Albert; Anson Dorrance, whose wise and wonderful soccer-coaching book inspired me to write one of my own; Melpomene, the Women's Sports Foundation, and Mona Shangold, M.D., for information on female athletes; Ed Decter, M.D., who condensed his significant youth soccer medical expertise into one chapter; and, last but not least, the many soccer parents whose ideas, support, and encouragement are reflected in this book.

— Gloria

Thanks to those who made it possible for me to co-write this book: the late Albert Dancy, boot room manager, and Tom Cheney, groundsman, of the Colchester United Football Club in England, who let me follow them around as a young boy; Bobby Roberts and Ray Hartford, Colchester coaches, for giving me a break; Rob Gilbert, Ph.D., Sue Schwager, Ph.D., Nancy Giardina, Ph.D., and Professor Tim Sullivan, all of Montclair State University in New Jersey, who guided me in becoming a youth educator; Camp Mah-Kee-Nac, Massachusetts, for seven great summers that taught me everything I know; the Bombers and manager Tom Roth, a team of soccer champions I loved and learned from; and the Martens, Hoffman, and Cherep families, for helping me to settle in the United States; Betty Ann Fazio, for guiding me; the Gordons, for so much help, and , finally, the numerous members of the Montclair United Soccer Club, past and present, and all of the children with whom I have been privileged to work.

— Ashley

adidas
adidas
adidas

foreword

Many years ago, as I was sitting in my recliner reading the evening paper, my six-year-old approached me. "Dad, I can be on the soccer team if you could be the coach." I had played a lot of sports, but soccer had been only a school recess game. I became my child's soccer coach, and thus began two decades of enjoyment in this great game. It would have been a big help if I had had this book then, as I learned a lot the hard way. The authors have done a wonderful job of explaining the game and making it "user-friendly" for you.

Now, I watch my two grandchildren play soccer. Over the years, I have been involved in all aspects of the game, from coaching and refereeing to holding top administrative posts in national soccer organizations. I have discovered that soccer is truly a family affair. Even major holiday celebrations are often planned around soccer tournaments. This intense involvement brings families closer together.

I encourage you to take advantage of that and to enjoy it. I know from personal experience the difficulty of commuting to practices and games, shuttling siblings, and braving all kinds of weather to cheer your children on. But in the final analysis, these are some of the best moments in life.

Soccer is about values. Parents are aware that the game teaches teamwork, fair play, patience, and honesty. Teamwork and fair play are self-explanatory. The game demands patience because players must learn skills, practice them, and understand that they cannot always go "straight to the goal." Adults need patience to let children make mistakes so that they may learn. Soccer also fosters honesty. Players know if their teammates are putting in an honest effort. Soccer involves every player on the team.

Soccer is not only fun, it is also healthy, safe, and full of action. It is an equal opportunity activity. That's why our motto at U.S. Youth Soccer is "The Game for All Kids." Regardless of gender or mental, physical, or socioeconomic status, there is a place for everyone at U.S. Youth Soccer.

I congratulate the authors of *Goal!* for taking a fresh approach to youth soccer. This is not just another soccer book but a complete guide for parents to understand the sport and support their children to the fullest so the entire family can have a positive and rewarding experience.

Always remember to keep the game fun and to have fun yourself. Encourage your children to play hard and to play fair. I'll see you on the field!

— Virgil Lewis, Chairman, U.S. Youth Soccer Association

preface

"They think it's all over. It is now."

– Television commentator immediately following
England's victory in the 1966 World Cup

Those words were spoken as Geoff Hurst netted his hat trick against Germany in the final of the 1966 World Cup. When I asked my parents when soccer became a passion for me, they relayed those words to me. My dad talks of almost stepping on me during the broadcast as I crawled around the floor in my diapers. He believes that it was then and there that my passion for soccer began. I like to believe it is true.

As a boy growing up in England, soccer was my life. My mates and I never thought twice about playing at every opportunity. We traded players' cards and watched longingly out of the schoolroom windows as friends played during gym or recess. Racing down to breakfast to grab the newspaper and check the team lineups for later discussion on the playground was as much a part of the school day as English or math. Wearing your team's colors on Monday if it won on the previous Saturday was as important as wearing your school tie. No wonder we all suffered the same depression when soccer season was over, hoping for a summer of World Cup or European Championship play to make the season more bearable.

I remember my first formal playing experience at age 10 for Hamilton Primary School. I scored 34 goals in the season and was awarded MVP (most valuable player). I went on to spend thousands of hours watching and playing for Colchester United Football Club in my hometown. Those many hours were the impetus behind my move to the United States, which allowed me the opportunity to spend my life running around a soccer field and passing on my love of the game to children. On attending university with a major in education, I developed an equal love of the teaching profession. The combination of soccer and teaching gave me a clear and confident vision for what I believe is necessary to be successful at American youth soccer.

I want the game for American children to be what it was for me: a time and activity away from the usual rigors of life, a chance to gain physical fitness and fulfill the desire to be involved in sports—and not just as a spectator. Finally, I want children who play soccer to know it as a passion, because it is so wonderful to be passionate about something.

I believe in American youth soccer so much that I built a company and my life on it. I am confident that this book communicates my love and knowledge of the game, and that it will help parents do the same for their children.

— Ashley Michael Hammond

introduction

My Life and the Beautiful Game is the title of a soccer classic, the autobiography of soccer's most famous player, Pelé. It is also a phrase that often ran through my mind while writing this book. Those words defined me and this project. They are the light that guided me. Devoted fellow soccer families understand, because those words define their lives as well.

What is this activity that so consumes the lives of millions of American families? How can we make it the best that it can be, for our children and for ourselves? How can we take what it is—a game—and make it an opportunity to share a deep family bond? These were the questions that I wanted to tackle as a writer, a soccer mom, a lifelong athlete, and a staff member of Ashley's Soccer Camp in Montclair, New Jersey, a professional youth training and coaching organization. I discovered the answers through watching and listening to the experts: coaches, players, parents, fans, and youth soccer administrators. They are Americans like me, for whom the youth soccer phenomenon is relatively new. And they are the English coaches I work with, who grew up in a culture of soccer, an activity that is an integral way of life.

Knowing the scope and passion of American youth soccer and the uncharted waters of this endeavor, the task ahead of me at times seemed enormous. So many parents had separate but legitimate questions and concerns, and so much about the subject was undocumented. Despite the difficulties, the mission was always clear: as the book title implies, to make each parent the ultimate soccer mom or dad. As I researched material for these pages, each revelation seemed more interesting and enlightening than the last. As a soccer mom, I knew that fellow soccer parents would benefit from this information as much as I did.

I realized in writing this book that in addition to being a great sport, soccer is an incredible opportunity to express the deepest aspects of parenthood. At its most basic, soccer is at the roots of being a complete parent. Through this seemingly simple yet complex activity, we can learn how best to support, protect, love, and encourage our children. We can take pleasure in developing their physical health and social development and cheer their personal accomplishments.

I wanted to give this perspective to the game by going beyond what any book had yet done. My hope is that this book, one of the first of its kind, will make you more knowledgeable about youth soccer and also a better parent. The beauty of youth sports is the deep and powerful relationships that they can create between parents and children. Each moment, every aspect of the game, is an opportunity for both parents and their children to teach, to learn, to grow. I know this through my own father, who gave me a sports experience that will last a lifetime.

When you watch your children play the game or, better yet, when you play soccer with them, it is my sincere hope that these pages will guide you. They are my gift to my own children and my promise to you of the wonderful journey that this sport has to offer. May you savor the joy and survive the heartaches that the game provides.

May you, too, come to understand—and to love—the beautiful game.

— Gloria Averbuch

1 THE PERFECT GAME

1. soccer on the rise 3
2. they play to have fun 9
3. soccer gear 15
4. programs and coaches 23
5. getting ready to play 30

2 SOCCER SKILLS

6. beginner 43
7. novice 49
8. intermediate 58
9. advanced 67
10. expert 78
11. goalkeeping 86

3 THE SOCCER LIFESTYLE

12. nutrition 97
13. cross-training and conditioning 108
14. injuries and safety 116

contents

4 SOCCER EXTRAS

15. levels of play 129
16. camps and special programs 136
17. serious soccer 143
18. parents as coaches 150

5 GIRLS' SOCCER

19. a recipe for success 161
20. guidance for girls 167

6 OFF THE PLAYING FIELD

21. the total soccer education 177
22. the soccer family 184

laws of the game 189
glossary 197
resource list 207
about the authors 211
index 213

adidas

1

THE PERFECT GAME

1. soccer on the rise 3
2. they play to have fun 9
3. soccer gear 15
4. programs and coaches 23
5. getting ready to play 30

CHAPTER 1

soccer on the rise

THE WORLD'S SPORT COMES TO AMERICA

No doubt about it, youth soccer is booming. The United States has finally been swept up in the passion that has long captivated the rest of the world. Youth soccer in the United States, though, isn't the same as youth play elsewhere, where professional soccer is a dominant part of cultures and serves as a model. Nor is youth soccer like other sports and fitness crazes that have swept this country. Exercise and fitness movements, such as running and aerobics, have traditionally been geared toward adults. The American fitness movement has largely left children behind, out of shape and out of touch with the pleasures of exercise and sports. Now comes a sport with the focus on them.

From commuting to the fields and watching the games to coaching and providing snacks, soccer is a sport that includes the entire family. This phenomenon is so broad and has risen so rapidly that the term *soccer mom* became a household word during the 1996 Presidential campaign. Another indicator of youth soccer's growing appeal can be seen in increasing numbers of advertising campaigns for everything from minivans to candy bars to sports drinks.

Little league baseball and football still symbolize American youth sports, but soccer—a sport that includes nonstop movement and more equal participation among all children—has nearly equaled them as the game of choice among young Americans. Soccer is fairly easy to learn, is relatively safe, can be played by those of all athletic abilities, and offers equal opportunities for boys and girls.

roots of a rising craze

Soccer (called football outside the United States) is the most popular sport in the world and traces its origins back to medieval English village life. All major developments in the history of soccer were English, such as international matches (between England and Scotland in 1872), the introduction of professional soccer (1885), and the first full-time league (1888). Soccer was brought to continental Europe, South America, and India by British sailors and settlers, and it immediately caught on. In

1908, the sport was made a regular event in the Olympic Games.

Soccer arrived in the United States during the late nineteenth century, but it did not become institutionalized until 1959, when the National Collegiate Athletic Association recognized it as an official collegiate sport. Soon after the formation of the North American Soccer League (NASL) in 1967, soccer became the fastest growing youth sport in the United States.

Youth soccer in the United States was given an early boost by the presence of a Brazilian by the name of Pelé. Probably the greatest player in the history of the game and certainly the most famous, Pelé joined the New York Cosmos of the NASL in 1975. Record numbers of fans came to see him, and young people were inspired to try the game. Other famous international players, such as Franz Beckenbauer, George Best, and Johan Cruyff, also played with Pelé on the Cosmos and added to the star quality of the team.

Despite the fact that the NASL folded after the 1984 season, fan appeal was rekindled by the creation of a similar league, Major League Soccer (MLS), in 1996, and the increasing television coverage of international soccer. Purists claim that unlike baseball's World Series, soccer's world competitions are truly international. Professional leagues on several continents play national competitions, after which the best teams take part in international cup, or tournament, play. This results in events such as the World Club Championship and, most notably, the World Cup.

By far, the most-watched sporting event in the world is the World Cup, contested every four years. Because of the growing popularity of soccer, every 1998 World Cup game was broadcast live or with only a slight delay in the United States. In a stunning breakthrough for women's sports, every game of the Women's World Cup in 1999 was shown on television.

NO SIGNS OF SLOWING DOWN

Soccer in America continues to grow every year, and there is no indication that it will slow down anytime soon. The Soccer Industry Council of America tracks the number of participants and reports that from 1987 to 1997, total U.S. participation climbed more than 18 percent, with the number of frequent participants (25 or more days per year) climbing by 43.4 percent. The latest numbers from the Council show that soccer's popularity in this country is being driven by our children.

More than 18 million people play soccer—60 percent male and 40 percent female—with 75 percent being kids ages 6 through 18. The youngest children, ages 6 through 11, make up nearly 50 percent of the mix.

two different worlds

There is a vast difference between soccer, especially youth soccer, in the United States and almost every other country worldwide. Most young people throughout the world grow up with soccer as a way of life. It is ingrained in the culture beyond comparison with anything in the United States, except perhaps the towns that are home to football or basketball dynasties.

Many of the experiences and insights of this book draw upon the soccer culture of England, where the game was invented. To understand the extent of this culture, consider that nearly every boy in that country plays on some level, even if it is only to kick a ball around on a playground. While numerous organized youth leagues exist on the local, regional, and even national level in the United States, that number is dwarfed by the thousands of youth teams and development programs in England. The current strength of the U.S. women's team is largely a result of a more-developed women's sports movement in the United States. Soccer in most other countries has traditionally been a male sport, but the number and quality of international women's teams is on the rise.

Even the best-organized U.S. youth soccer programs cannot compete with a culture in which soccer is a natural part of life, where entire countries shut down for competitions, and where women polish their nails with the design of the nation's flag during the World Cup. When a country plays a match in the World Cup, the population is mobilized into patriotic vigor. It is almost tribal, a kind of war readiness. The economy, politics, family relations—all are directly affected by the outcome of these games. Despite having a negative reputation for some violent fan behavior, most of the world views soccer as an exciting, passionate pastime.

In some countries—perennial soccer power Brazil is a frequently cited example—youth soccer has its roots in less wealthy, or even impoverished, areas. Like inner-city playground basketball, a hotbed of American talent, theories abound as to why these areas serve as a breeding ground for talented athletes with intense desires to work their way to the top of the sport's ladder.

In the United States, youth soccer has traditionally been a more suburban sport, with less participation in urban areas. Despite a long-standing national program, "Soccer in the Streets," which introduces the game to inner-city youths, American soccer administrators realize that there is still a shortfall and are taking action to get youth soccer into the cities. The U.S. Youth Soccer Association (USYSA) revamped its Soccer Start program, providing grants for disadvantaged children, and the U.S. Soccer Federation has announced its intention to provide money to inner-city clubs. Additionally, at least one major shoe company has begun plans to sponsor soccer events in urban neighborhoods.

American youth soccer has some strong positive elements. For one, the activity is not an isolated one. Entire communities are mobilized, with the numerous leagues comprising families, volunteer coaches, referees, and administrators who, in turn, work with town administrators. There are strong financial resources behind the sport, either from individual families, communities, or soccer organizations. And, very important, the size of the country and the large volume of American youth playing the game mean that there is a large pool from which to draw. Consider that there are about 60 million people in soccer-crazed England, which is a mere fraction of the 260 million people in the United States.

Another element, expressed by some youth coaches from other countries, is the open and willing attitude of Amer-

coach's corner

Every joyous moment of my early life comes back when I think of my youth soccer experiences.

In England, soccer is the foundation of our childhoods. Everybody plays, with almost no exceptions. At the end of the professional soccer season in May, I went into a funk until the season began again in August. For the two to three weeks before the season opener, I didn't sleep. Opening day was better than Christmas. As a boy, your first "real" gifts are often a soccer ball, the local team's official jersey, and tickets to a game. Playground talk is about who is the "top of the table."

From the time I was young, soccer has been my special bond with my dad. The majority of English dads are mini experts in soccer, kicking the ball around with their children and instructing them in backyard sessions. We also had thousands of role models on television to emulate.

My mom and dad used to think that they were punishing me by sending me to my room. But I did not consider myself stuck in there; I had an agenda. I would practice my goalkeeping skills by throwing a tennis ball against the wall, or I would do headers or juggle.

My sense of discipline comes from my soccer-playing youth. The preparation of my soccer gear was a sacred ritual. I would check my bag at least 10 times before every outing to make sure that my cleats were not missing. And whether my room needed to be cleaned or I had schoolwork to do, I knew that for 90 minutes, I could completely and blissfully focus on soccer.

Soccer still has powerful bonds for me. In 1994, I telephoned my dad in England to tell him that I was flying him over to the United States to see the World Cup with me. The line went silent. Then he started to cry.

ican children. In their own countries, they say, it is often not so easy to instruct the youth who, with their soccer backgrounds and traditions, feel that they have "already arrived." Because it is new to them, American youth bring a fresh enthusiasm to the sport.

an international, not american, game

Youth soccer in the United States is experiencing growing pains. One criticism of American players in the 1998 World Cup was that they were not as aggressive–in other words, as physical–as the rest of the world's teams. One of the challenges that U.S. youth soccer faces is the recognition that soccer is a sport that has extensive physical contact. American parents praise the game for its finesse and hold it up as a substitute for more dangerous sports such as football. But while the sport is about finesse, it's also about being physically aggressive.

This is part of the overall challenge to define the American game by world standards. International soccer experts argue that Americans should not try to rewrite the rules of a sport that has changed little over the past 100 years, mostly because it will put them out of sync with the rest of the world. Again, an example is the physical, rough-and-tumble nature of the sport. Some U.S. leagues consider kicking a ball by a player who has fallen to the ground to be "dangerous play" and worthy of a penalty. Internationally, this is considered fair play and is actually encouraged.

Some injury risk is inherent in all sports. But that is no reason to shy away from the more physical aspects of soccer. Often, the fear of getting hurt does more damage than the actual risks. Communicating unnecessary fear and worry undermines the confidence of our children.

Brian Davies, the national referee administrator of the American Youth Soccer Organization (AYSO) agrees. "There is a tendency to overprotect the young player (especially the goalkeeper) more so in the United States than in Europe and elsewhere. We talk about soccer as being fair, fun, and safe. In spite of the fact that we try to make it this way, soccer is still a very physical game."

There's an expression in England: You are more likely to get hurt if you pull out of a challenge. Youth players must be taught that it is okay to be physical and to be relaxed about it. Healthy aggression is part of the game. Parents often find that, despite their initial concerns, children do not suffer harm from a regulated amount of physical contact. In fact, they gain inner strength and confidence from being tough. On the other hand, physical recklessness should not be promoted.

Another growing pain in American youth soccer is the divide between recreational and more serious play. Placing an emphasis on one often excludes the other. If a community decides to emphasize the everyone-can-play side of the sport in its program, highly skilled players often go elsewhere in search of more challenging teams and leagues. As a result, these programs lose the chance to develop local talent past a certain level. Many communities are working through the challenges of maintaining recreational programs while continuing to develop more competitive teams.

Another growing problem is practical: having enough soccer fields on which to play. The Soccer Industry Council of

America notes that a rapid increase in participation has created a shortage of fields.

getting involved

If your child does not approach you first with the details, try networking with other parents. Word of mouth is probably the most common way that people find out about organized soccer.

To take a more organized route, call your local recreation department and inquire about youth soccer programs or clubs in your area. You can also call national organizations such as the USYSA or the AYSO or check the *Soccer America Yellow Pages* for local associations (for more information, see the resource list on page 207). Your school district's physical education staff might also know of programs or leagues.

Seeking organized play makes sense, but don't let that keep you from just doing a casual kick-around. Parents tend to throw balls as an introductory way to play with their children. Instead, put the ball on the ground and kick it!

CHOOSE SOCCER

Soccer is an excellent choice for many reasons. Of the many organized sports for youth, the vast network of youth play is unparalleled, and it is easy to plug in to this network. Abundant programs, led by conscientious parent volunteers or professionals, exist nationwide. What's more, soccer offers an opportunity for youth to gain fitness (it is one of the most complete and constant physical activities) and sample athletic competition. Here are some other reasons why soccer is a great choice.

- It's simple. As long as there is a ball and some markers to make goals, the game can be played.
- It can be played year-round, outdoors and indoors.
- It's excellent cardiovascular exercise. You cannot be lazy and play soccer properly; movement is constant.
- It's an excellent activity for developing balance and lower-body strength. If a player is properly trained, the upper body can be strengthened with conditioning exercises.
- It teaches extended mental focus. Unlike other sports that offer breaks, a player is constantly and actively part of the game.
- It introduces children to the experience of winning and losing.
- Numerous leagues for all ages and skill levels ensure a place for everyone.
- It's versatile. Soccer can be recreational or competitive.

CHAPTER 2

they play to have fun

THE BEST WAY TO LEARN THE GAME

Soccer becomes part of your life. You stand around in all kinds of weather, cheering when your child scores a goal, moaning when she loses the ball. Perhaps you've watched your child artfully dribble the ball down the field and wondered how she developed that skill. At some point, you may even be asked to volunteer or coach. Whether or not you decide to help out, it's important to know the best way that children learn soccer skills and tactics. Armed with this knowledge, you'll be able to choose good soccer programs and understand your child's needs as she learns the sport.

"They play to have fun" is the omnipresent motto of Ashley's Soccer Camp in Montclair, New Jersey. It appears on T-shirts and registration forms, and it's painted on the side of the company's vehicles. This simple phrase should be the guiding philosophy of youth soccer.

Belief in this motto is the reason behind the Games Based Approach to teaching soccer. This approach is a decidedly American approach to sports education. While other major youth sports have yet to adopt it on a large scale, youth soccer is the vanguard in adopting this approach. Other youth soccer organizations and coaches may call it by another name, but the Games Based Approach has, for about the last decade, challenged the old school of thought.

Coaches used to believe that control meant having the ability to make children stand around and listen to them. With the Games Based Approach, 20 children can run around simultaneously in controlled chaos. The old style, though, may be a matter of practicality since the Games Based Approach does require more sports equipment.

With the Games Based Approach, all aspects of the sport, from basic skills to more technical moves and strategies, are taught in the context of fun, yet instructive, games. Players practice skills with creative exercises. For example, a commonly used game is Sharks and Fishes, in which players with the ball (fish) try to elude those without the ball (sharks). This fun exercise teaches children dribbling, or maintaining control of the ball while running; turning; and shielding, a skill in which a player keeps the ball away from another player by using the body.

The Games Based Approach differs from the more conventional method of in-

A WINNING FORMULA

The goals and benefits of the Games Based Approach include:

- It creates a sense of fun.
- It enables the coach to isolate and focus on specific skills.
- It allows the coach to teach to the strengths of individual children and improve the weaknesses.
- It enables the coach to better control the group. As a result, discipline is not the focus of the session.
- It allows creative play within the practice.
- It allows for versatility, from beginner to adult. No matter what a player's age or skill level, she can still benefit from games. And often, the games themselves need little adaptation across different levels of skill.
- It fosters a positive learning environment. A significant part of the Games Based Approach allows a player to learn without the intense scrutiny of peers.
- It accommodates children of all skill levels and personality types.

struction, characterized by lining up and standing around, which relies on repetitive drills. Groups of players standing around waiting to take a turn at a skill is a sure sign of this type of instruction.

When you drop your child off at soccer practice, she will invariably sprint to join the action. Children do not come to be talked to or to stand around; they show up to move and to play. That is just what you will see in a good program: active, enthusiastic children. In addition, children learn best in a nonthreatening environment, both physically and emotionally. The games that they play should not expose children to criticism, ridicule, the use of exercise as punishment (such as the loser does 10 pushups or a team that performs poorly runs laps), or unnecessary individual work, which puts them on display to their peers.

If you watch at any random moment during Games Based Approach–style training, you will likely see your child engrossed in a particular task. This is because the system facilitates maximum participation, with time on task at least 80 percent for all players. The beauty of this high activity level is not only that it satisfies the needs and desires of the children for maximum participation but also that the constant movement mimics the fast pace of competition. If players practice constantly and intensely, they will employ this lively, involved style of play and enthusiasm in competition. As a common sports phrase goes, "How you practice is how you play."

You will not find the Games Based Approach in every youth soccer program because it breaks with the traditional system of sports education. Once you realize that children love to move and want most of all to be part of the action, then you'll see why the Games Based Approach makes sense and encourages children to learn.

room for technique

If you watch your child during soccer practice and especially on game days, you will see another part of the soccer equation. The Games Based Approach does not eliminate more conventional instruction. There is also a need for tactical instruction, particularly for those with a higher level of skill. While it may appear as if the more tactical aspects of the game are sacrificed by focusing on games, in fact, there is always a blend of conventional and creative education. A creative coach can imbue the tactical lessons with a sense of fun.

For example, a more conventional lesson for teaching defensive tactics would be to line up about half the team in two opposing lines—attackers facing defenders—while the rest of the team looks on. The coach then gives conventional explanations about where players should move and position themselves, after which the players attempt to carry out the instructions. In the Games Based Approach, the entire team would be divided into three groups to play a variety of keep-away games, which are custom-designed to stress the relevant points, such as proper positioning and when to tackle (take away a ball from an opponent using your feet).

one skill at a time

In addition to the Games Based Approach, there is another crucial element in an ideal youth soccer education: the learning hierarchy. Children learn soccer, and most sports, for that matter, most easily when they are taught in a logical, sequential fashion. It is essential that skills are taught in proper order and at an appropriate age or skill level. For example, a six-year-old should not be taught how to do a complicated move, such as a bicycle

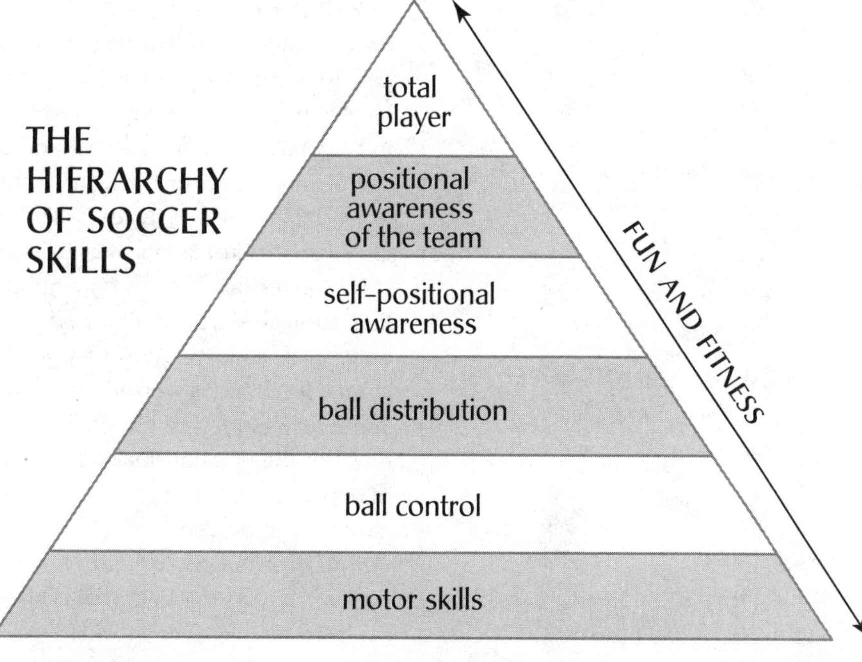

kick. Instead, that youngster needs to concentrate on basic motor skills, such as running, jumping, hopping, and moving around with others on the field. Disrupting this order will result only in frustration and lack of success.

The learning hierarchy consists of six levels and encompasses an entire soccer education. While it is important for a child's overall education to move in a sequential order up, the levels can blur at times. A player moves up and down the triangle, touching on different skills, as all the skills contribute to one another.

SIGNS OF A GOOD PROGRAM

How do you know if your child's soccer education is on the right path? Here are some positive indications.

- She'll want to go to practice. If she has the desire to play and learn, the skills will come much more easily.
- She'll want to demonstrate to you what she has learned.
- At practice, you should not hear the coaches screaming or yelling. The children should be moving a lot and focusing on the session, even if they are not directly involved in an exercise.
- You should see your child's skills improving.
- The coach should be able to provide a verbal and written plan for teaching the game and its skills.

Motor skills. A soccer player, or a player of any dynamic sport, is constantly jumping, hopping, spinning, and running; in short, she incorporates all motor skills into her activity. Fluidity in motor skills is taught simply by moving the body using various equipment (balls, mats, cones) and in every way. This includes jogging in all directions, tumbling, hopping, and jumping. Children must experience all of these movements at different speeds and with different stimuli (for example, with other children moving near them), both with and without equipment.

Balance plays a large part in the game and is emphasized at this level. Balance exercises use all body parts, with and without equipment (for example, standing on one leg while balancing a ball on the other foot or thigh).

Taught with repetition and positive encouragement, mastering this level is not only possible but a clear necessity.

Ball control. At this level, a player concentrates on interacting with the ball. To master this level, a player must be able to use every body part to control the ball as it comes to her and as she moves with it or passes it to another player. A variety of skills are taught so that just kicking the ball away is no longer the player's only option. Ball control starts at the beginning level, is developed more fully at the second level, and is worked on forever. Some players may be physically superior, but the decision-making process of how to control and pass the ball can always be improved.

Ball distribution. Ball distribution is what a player does after the ball is under control. She must decide what type of

coach's corner

Youth soccer in the United States is being deluged with international influence, from professional players to youth coaches. My youth program is one of a number conducted by former players and coaches from England. Our passion allows us to make a unique contribution to American youth soccer.

The English, however, are not unique in their love of soccer. With the notable exception of the United States, the rest of the world shares a passion for the game. This enthusiasm can be found, however, in American youth soccer. The intense interest by soccer parents that I see every day almost replicates the passion in other countries.

Despite their level of enthusiasm, soccer parents cannot duplicate the experience of a lifelong involvement with the game and often aren't the best people to coach youth soccer. There are innumerable benefits to being taught by someone with a strong soccer background. The most important is that children learn best by seeing and doing under the watchful eye of an experienced coach.

An experienced coach also brings the insight of his own soccer education. My fun approach to learning soccer is partly a reaction to the painful way that I was taught the game. Much of the time, I learned through drudgery and the school of hard knocks.

The best times were when we played without teachers or coaches. Casually kicking a ball around with my mates and making up our own games is why I created the Games Based Approach. Despite the difficulties of my formal soccer education, I was able to combine both my love of the game with my knowledge to bring a new system to the United States.

shot, pass, or other movement to make (or not make) and to which player or location. A player cannot succeed at this level without mastery of ball control.

Self-positional awareness. This requires confidence in putting oneself in a position to have an impact on the game. A player will tend not to do this if she does not have the skills from the lower levels. It includes movement away from the ball, talking on the field, and timing of various plays, such as passing. If a player does not actively seek out positions that involve her in the game, it is said that she is "hiding" on the field. She might get the ball by default, but she is not contributing meaningfully to the team effort.

Positional awareness of the team. Self-positional awareness facilitates this skill. The team as a unit will not have a sense of the game if individuals have not mastered all of the preceding levels. The team concept breaks down, and the end result is a lack of fluidity. The best illustration is to watch a team that is knowledgeable in this area. Even to the untrained eye, their game looks decidedly choreographed, without thoughtless, random movement. While it is important that the team as a whole is well-coached to master this level, it is not as essential as having mastered the skills of the preceding levels.

Total player. This is where all of the skills acquired at the lower levels come together. Whether a particular pass, a shot, or a particular decision, the skill is done perfectly. It means making the best decision for the good of the team, choosing the appropriate skill for that particular moment, and executing that skill with the correct body surface, force, and technique. And the chosen skill is the best choice for the good of the team.

While a soccer program may not have this exact learning hierarchy, a good program will at least follow its spirit. A good soccer coach should have a structured training plan for the entire season. With this plan in place, she will recognize that each session should have one, or maybe two, focus points.

how to win graciously and lose honorably

The Games Based Approach to soccer does not eliminate competition. Rather, it stresses noncompetitive skill acquisition, at times, with activities that produce a winner and a loser. Parents know that their children enjoy a challenge. They use this technique of self-competition all the time. ("See how fast you can clean your room.") It is this type of self-competition that sparks children's drive. That is why the Games Based Approach presents competition in a positive format.

But the basic reality of winning and losing must eventually be dealt with directly. Children can gain a sense of winning or losing in practice, particularly if it is used judiciously. An education in winning and losing is important because it is what happens in a soccer game and in life.

As you witness your child's soccer education, you become aware of personal skills that soccer helps her develop, such as cooperation, camaraderie, decision making, leadership, and dealing with criticism. The real test of success is how your child deals with the difficult challenges—trying to master a hard skill or losing a game, for example. A supportive soccer program should provide a secure atmosphere of learning.

CHAPTER 3

soccer gear

DRESS FOR SUCCESS AND COMFORT

In the early days of youth soccer in the United States, players frequently looked like they were playing in a pickup game–dressed in gym shorts, T-shirts, and sneakers–regardless of the level of competition. But as the game has grown more sophisticated, so has the equipment that the players wear.

Today, there's a wide variety of specially designed clothing, shoes, and accessories available. There is so much of a selection that the choices may seem a little overwhelming. Don't let them be. Your goal should be simple: to pick equipment that is durable, comfortable, and designed to protect your child. The biggest challenge will be judging how long the gear will be usable (due both to fit and wear and tear) and balancing that with the price you are willing to pay.

where, when, and what to buy

If you are new to soccer or need specific assistance and advice on selecting equipment, soccer specialty stores are the best places to shop. They usually have knowledgeable staffs and the largest variety of equipment. But the advice and selection may come at a price. Items at specialty stores often cost more.

If you have experience in buying soccer equipment, you can often find what your child needs at standard sporting-goods stores or through one of the many mail-order outlets (see the resource list on page 207). The prices at sporting-goods stores often will be lower than at specialty stores, although the selection may not be as large. Mail-order prices may be cheaper still.

No matter where you shop, you'll find that the heaviest shopping traffic will be two months prior to kickoff in the fall and spring seasons, which generally start in September and May. This is also when stores are likely to have the most equipment on hand. You may want to buy early in these shopping seasons, when the stores are well-stocked and the best merchandise is available. Buying at this time also gives your child time to break in his new gear before competition starts.

Soccer clothing and shoes come in two size categories: youth and adult. The materials in both are the same, but as with other clothing, the youth version is less expensive. There is no gender difference between boys' and girls' soccer clothing, though in adult sizes, there are men's and women's versions that vary in size and cut. Moving from the bottom up, here's a guide for the youth soccer shopper.

Cleats. Because soccer is synonymous with the feet, footwear is the most important item that you'll buy. While sneakers may serve for a very young child's introduction to the sport, a pair of cleats specifically designed for soccer is worth the investment. This is for safety as well as efficiency of play. The rubber studs of cleats, for example, provide better traction and stability than sneakers. Cleats are also the single most important piece of gear that identifies a person as a soccer player.

There are two major types of youth cleats. The first is manufactured only for young children, and the uppers (upper parts) of these shoes are made of synthetic materials that do not stretch. The second type, for the more serious player, is made with leather uppers. While fit is fairly straightforward with the synthetic models—they should basically fit like children's sneakers—leather cleats are a bit trickier because the leather will stretch and mold to the feet once the shoes are broken in. Like all soccer gear, the cost of cleats varies. Synthetic cleats are usually less expensive than leather.

In general, cleats should fit snugly with no more than a thumb's-width of space between the toes and the front of the shoes. Close-fitting cleats actually are a plus in soccer because they facilitate the best touch—the feel for the ball—and touch is everything in this sport. If you're buying cleats for a younger player whose feet are still growing rapidly, go for loose-fitting shoes so that the cleats don't affect the growth of the feet. But, it is not advisable to buy shoes that will last two seasons (fall and spring). The shoes will be too big initially, which is potentially unsafe and uncomfortable and can cause blisters. To ensure a good fit, your child should try on cleats while wearing both soccer socks and shinguards. It's always a good idea to consult an experienced salesperson when trying on cleats, especially when buying them for the first time.

For older, more serious players, there are cleats with replaceable studs. These are more expensive and harder to maintain than the cleats described earlier, which are molded. The studs come in various sizes and are changed to play on different field conditions. Even the most expensive replaceable models come in perfectly functional molded models.

Turf and indoor shoes. When players compete on surfaces other than grass, they often wear special soccer shoes. Multi-studded turf shoes are used on very hard ground (including some hard grass fields) or artificial turf because standard cleats do not provide enough traction. For indoor play, there are shoes that feature a flat outsole (the undersurface of the shoe) and rubber bottom for better traction on wooden floors.

Many children, especially beginners, wear sneakers on both these surfaces since they don't frequently play on them. If you choose this option, use sneakers that provide stability. Those built high off the ground are less stable. With sudden stops and turns, a lack of stability means that the ankle can have a tendency to roll. The foot should stay as close to the ground as possible, and the shoe should be built for lateral movement. Cross-training shoes are best. Running shoes

coach's corner

Cleaning their football boots (soccer cleats) is an important ritual that English players perform from a very young age. It is a measure of respect for their equipment and their game. They clean the entire cleat, top and bottom, stuff it with newspaper to dry, then polish and buff it. Boots must be cleaned before practice and polished for games.

or basketball shoes are not recommended.

Shinguards. Made to protect the front of the lower leg from errant kicks, shinguards are regulation wear in all levels of the sport. There are several basic types, all of which protect the player from right under the knee to the top of the ankle. One is made from a solid piece of plastic with foam backing. Another is made from cotton cloth that surrounds ribs or spines in the shinguard (some of this type have removable ribs to facilitate washing).

A third type is made for the serious player, beginning at about age 11. Made of fiberglass cloth wrapping with a foam pad backing, these guards are designed to mold to fit the shin, and they offer the best fit and strongest protection. Because they mold to the leg, these are virtually unbreakable and should last until your child outgrows them. These types of guards are usually worn without ankle protectors, but protective stirrups are available as accessories. Most other types of shinguards come with or without ankle protection. The only reason to forgo this added protection is if your child is an upper-level player who prefers the least constriction and the lightest weight, or a very young player whose ankles are too small for protectors to fit them.

To properly fit and wear shinguards that come with protective ankle stirrups attached, your child should pull them up as far as he can from the stirrup without causing the guard to hit the knee. He should make sure that the ankle cup fits snugly around the ankle bone above the collar of the cleat. You can measure your child and order shinguards from a catalog; the length in inches is provided in the product description. In general, measure one inch above the anklebone to one inch below the kneecap. For additional help, call in your order and speak to a salesperson.

Socks. Soccer socks serve three major purposes. First, they provide comfort and support for the ankle and, depending on which style, the foot area. Second, they protect against blisters. And finally, they hold shinguards in place. Socks are usually provided as part of the uniform in most leagues, but if you're buying socks for your child, there are a number of choices. Lower-end socks are made of 100 percent acrylic/polyester with perhaps some cotton added for comfort. Higher-end socks contain microfibers that help wick perspiration away from the body. They may also contain elasticized yarns for durability and support. Some soccer socks have padded footbeds (heels and toes) made with durable yarn and elasticized arch support.

Be sure to get socks in a bigger size than normal since they will be worn over your child's shinguards. Also make sure that the socks are long enough—leagues usually require that socks cover the entire shinguard.

If you're unsure how much to spend on socks, keep in mind that children usually wear them out before they outgrow them. Given this, you're better off buying sturdier socks since they last longer and also provide added support. Midpriced socks are usually the best compromise between price and quality.

Shorts. There are two basic types of soccer shorts. One type is knit and the other is woven, and both are made of polyester. Shorts that are woven are much more durable and tear-resistant. Although general fashion dictates baggy shorts, overly baggy shorts can hamper your child's mobility and agility with the ball. A good guide is that the inseam (from the crotch to the bottom of the shorts) should measure five inches for adult sizes and three to four inches for youth sizes.

Constriction shorts. These formfitting shorts are worn under soccer shorts. Their primary purpose is to keep muscles warm, though they do help protect your child's hips and legs from abrasions if he falls or skids, as when making a slide tackle. Some players wear these shorts only in colder weather; some wear them no matter what the conditions.

Constriction shorts come in both unisex models and separate models for men and women. They are usually available only in adult sizes, though you may be able to find an adult extra-small size if you're persistent. Constriction shorts are supposed to fit tightly around the legs and, generally, if your child is younger than 10 or 11, his legs will be too small to get any support from the shorts. Constriction shorts are made of a blend of Spandex and cotton or cotton and Lycra. The more expensive the shorts, the better they'll be able to "breathe" and wick away moisture.

Training jerseys. Children can wear whatever tops they want for practice. From their point of view, shirt colors, logos, and messages (if there are any) are often priorities. But your goal should be to find jerseys that are made of materials that will keep your child comfortable. For example, cotton T-shirts are popular, but in the heat, especially if your child perspires a lot or pours water on himself to cool off, they can be heavy and uncomfortable. It's better to choose polyester-based jerseys that are lighter and wick away moisture. As with other pieces of equipment, the more high-tech the fabric, the better the function—and the higher the cost.

Team, or game, jerseys. Team uniforms are likely to be in traditional colors (red, royal or navy blue, black, maroon). It is especially important with these monogrammed jerseys to pay close attention to the washing instructions because of the custom printing for names, numbers, and logos. Turn the jerseys inside out to help preserve their printing,

MOM'S VIEW

Dirty equipment, lost equipment. It's part of the routine with youth soccer. But there are some steps you can take to improve the chances that your child will reach the game with everything he needs to play successfully.

- To avoid loss or confusion with other children's gear, label soccer gear, including cleats and balls, with permanent marker.
- Tie a piece of colored yarn or put another distinguishing item on your child's bag to make it clearly recognizable and easily retrievable.
- Bring a change of clothing or a towel to use after playing in muddy conditions. Keep an extra towel or two on the seat to protect your car.
- Keep a permanent bag of clean, dry clothing in the car in case your child forgets his gear or gets it dirty and needs a change of clothes. Replace any item that your child ends up using.

and wash them in cold water. It is best not to put these jerseys in the dryer; rather, hang them to dry.

Jackets and pants. When your child practices in cooler weather or stands on the sidelines during a fall or early-spring game, he'll need to dress for warmth. Special soccer warmup suits are one option. If you decide to buy one, think first about how your child will use it. A standard warmup jacket with loose-fitting pants will do if your child is wearing them just to keep warm, but the jacket could trap moisture and the wide cuffs on the pants could cause him to trip if he wears them to play. A better choice is a jacket that can "breathe" and a pair of specially designed training pants that have a tapered leg with an elasticized cuff. For convenience, it is best to buy pants—whether for playing or not—with zippered bottoms so that your child can put them on and take them off without removing his shoes. You can buy the jackets and pants separately, but they are usually less expensive when purchased as a set, provided that your child wears the same size for both the top and bottom.

Goalkeeper gear. Goalkeepers wear the same shoes, socks, and shinguards as field players, but regulations require that they wear a different color top from field players on both their own team and the opposition in order to differentiate themselves. Rules do not require a long-sleeved shirt, but many keepers wear them for added protection. These shirts are available with or without padded elbows, and most experts feel that extra arm protection is especially important in youth soccer, as keepers tend to fall on their elbows until they learn the proper way to dive. Beginning goalkeepers often share a shirt with other players as they rotate through soccer's other positions to learn the game, and the shirt is kept by the coach.

Goalkeepers can wear the same shorts as the field players, or they can take advantage of specialty shorts. These have a longer inseam—6 to 8½ inches—for protection from abrasions. Shorts can be padded on the hips, baggy, or formfitting. Some keepers wear constriction shorts under a baggier pair to provide for extra warmth and support.

Long pants are also available, with or without padding. The maximum protection is long pants with padded hips and knees. A good rule of thumb is, the harder the surface (such as in indoor play), the more padding your child should wear.

Goalkeeper's gloves allow for a better grip on the ball and, to some degree, protect the hands. Good gloves usually have thicker palms for added grip and

SOCCER BALLS

The final piece of equipment that your child will need is the ball itself. Some soccer programs provide balls; others require players to bring them. Regardless, you will likely need to purchase a ball for home practice. There are three sizes of soccer balls, all of which follow standards for size and weight. Age 8 and under use size 3; ages 8 through 12 use size 4; ages 13 and up use size 5 (the official FIFA, or international soccer federation, ball). Novelty size 1 and 2 balls are also made and are sometimes used for close control work.

There are two types of balls: stitched, which are made with a fabric backing, and laminated, which are glued together. Advanced players often prefer a harder ball, which is better for striking, because it "pings" better, meaning that it has the right feel, like a sweet spot on a tennis racket. The softest balls are best for younger players, particularly for those just learning to head a ball (using your head to pass or stop the ball). Another type of ball is a soft-touch PVC plastic ball, geared specifically for youth soccer and made in all sizes. This ball is better for heading and easier to control.

The key to the feel of the ball (hard versus soft) is not only the outer material but also the bladder, or the inner portion, which holds the air. One type of bladder is made of butyl material, somewhat like a car tire. This type holds air better and longer, but butyl makes for a much harder ball, particularly in the cold. While you need not pump up this type so frequently, it is not as soft as those with bladders made of latex.

A good sporting-goods store should have a selection of several brands, with several offerings in each brand. It should have some fully inflated balls to test. Also, you can pick up the display box and press into the ball with your thumb, testing for softness. Judge balls on their reputation—you can ask a coach or an experienced player. You might want to have several balls for various purposes. Teams, for example, often have balls that they use for practice as well as better-quality game balls that are reserved for competition.

For higher-end balls, look for a stamp with the words "FIFA Approved" or "FIFA Inspected."

protection. Beginning players often share equipment belonging to the coach or team, but if you intend to purchase gloves, the lower-end gloves are perfectly acceptable for younger children. At their level of ability, the ball is not usually kicked very hard. A better pair can be purchased around age 11 or 12.

Some gloves are better for wet conditions, and some provide more breathability for hot weather. Usually, the tags on the gloves will tell you the conditions for which they're designed. Or, you can ask an experienced player or salesperson for advice.

For lower-level players, gloves will probably last for one season. At the higher levels, goalkeepers often use different pairs for practice and competition and may go through two or more pairs per season. For these players, the latest technology provides gloves that help prevent hand injuries. For example, one type that's on the market is made with ribbed plastic spines that run the length of the backside of the fingers. This allows the fingers to bend forward, but prevents them from being jammed or bent backward by shots.

To store gloves, inexpensive glove bags are available. Gloves can be cleaned carefully by hand (some players take them right into the shower after playing), but should not be put in the washing machine. Never use soap; it causes the latex to break down, as does machine drying. Keep them out of sunlight and away from artificial heat sources, such as radiators. Although it will not totally prevent perspiration odor, some keepers put baby powder on their hands before using the gloves.

An added item for goalkeepers is a baseball-style cap, which can be worn to shade the eyes against the sun, if necessary.

dressing for extreme weather

It's a fact of life: Children have less body fat and less skin than adults do. That means less insulating fat to protect against cold and less skin surface to carry away excess heat. So it's important that they dress properly for both weather extremes.

In cold or wet weather, the key to staying warm and comfortable is layered clothing. Several thin layers that your child can shed as he warms up are much better than a T-shirt and one bulky sweatshirt. Keep in mind that leagues may require your child to wear color-coordinated clothing. You'll need to check the rules of your league, then buy a plain turtleneck shirt to wear under the uniform jersey, or have your child wear an undershirt. Some leagues allow tights or leggings, but these are usually worn in practice only. Tights come in all thicknesses, but sports tights (made of lightweight performance fabrics) are also available.

An even more comfortable cold-weather option is wearing lightweight, high-tech garments that retain heat and wick away moisture at the same time. These are more expensive, though, so you should consider certain variables before shopping for them. First, does your child tend to perspire heavily? It is usually less critical to have high-tech clothing if he doesn't. Second, can the clothing be handed down to a sibling or friend? If cost is a consideration, you might compromise by buying items made of performance fabrics for the layer that's closest to the skin, such as an undershirt or a short or long-sleeved T-shirt worn under a jacket or sweatshirt.

The majority of the body's heat loss is through the head and, to a lesser extent, through the other extremities. You should consider hats and headbands that cover the ears if your child's coach and the league allow them. (Goalkeepers, however, can wear baseball-style caps) Field players also can wear special gloves. These not only keep hands warm but they also have grips on the fingertips to enable players to better perform throw-ins.

When dressing your child for hot weather, choose breathable, light-colored loose clothing, preferably made from high-tech synthetic fabrics as opposed to heavy cotton. Sleeveless shirts will help keep him cool, but they will also increase sun exposure. A compromise is a lightweight, breathable, polyester-based T-shirt, which protects the shoulders.

for girls only

Girls who wear a bra will be most comfortable with a supportive one like a sports bra when playing soccer. These bras are designed for high-impact activities and are made with high-tech fabrics, which wick moisture away from the body.

When shopping for a bra, you might want to go to a sports specialty store and ask the advice of an experienced female clerk. Have your daughter try on the bra; it should be snug but allow her to breathe comfortably. While trying the bra, she should duplicate her activity as best as possible: running in place or doing a throw-in motion with her arms (arms extended over her head moving back to front). Also, run your fingers over the seams to make sure that they are smooth and that there are no spots that can potentially cause irritation.

programs and coaches

CHOOSING THE RIGHT ONES FOR YOUR CHILD

A soccer program is comprised of many facets, all of which come together to affect every aspect of your child's soccer career. While the program may appear to be merely the backdrop, it is actually the bedrock that ensures safety, player development, and overall success.

The most important feature of a soccer program is one that you should not compromise on: It must ensure your child's safety, both physically and emotionally. This ranges from maintaining safe fields–kept clear of hazards such as rocks or broken glass–to having knowledgeable coaches who do not destructively yell at or insult young players, to having emergency first-aid procedures and providing adequate adult supervision at all times.

Other aspects of a good soccer program include creating a structure of good training and competition and purchasing quality equipment. A good soccer program has a set of bylaws, a clear mission statement, and a board of directors. An official soccer program is insured, and players as well as volunteers should sign legal waivers before participating. These waivers are generally meant to avoid frivolous lawsuits and are also often used to verify that a child is healthy enough to participate.

A good soccer program meshes well with the community. It has a positive working relationship with such entities as the board of education, the schools, and the town recreation department. A good relationship pays off because inquiring parents will be referred to the soccer program. The soccer program should also have a cooperative relationship with other sports programs in the area in order to ensure harmony in the scheduling of fields, particularly since soccer has become a year-round sport.

finding a good program

To find a youth soccer program for your child, call the local parks and recreation department or a youth soccer organization or club (for more information on national organizations, see the resource list on page 207). For a typical nine-week recreational session, you can expect to pay at least $40. Be prepared to pay more if the session is professionally run. Even if the program is run by your town, you will usually have to pay a fee.

Most programs have beginning sessions starting from ages 4 to 6. The oldest players are generally not older than 18. Depending on your area and types of leagues, soccer can by played year-round, with regular seasons in the fall, winter, and spring. Team categories identify what children may participate in them. For example, a U-9 (under age 9) team will have no players over age 9 by a date determined by the program (most use either the calendar year or school year) and will include children who are too old to play on the U-8 team.

Once you have found a program, there are questions that you should ask the staff, who should be willing to answer your inquiries. If they're not, that's a sign that the program might not be of good quality. Here are suggestions.

- How many sessions are in the program? Once a week for 8 to 10 weeks is sufficient for beginners.
- What is the ratio of children to coach? Twelve to 14 children per coach is acceptable for beginners, but no more than that; 8 to 10 is ideal.
- Does the program have a sensible curriculum appropriate for the level of play? For example, a beginner program should emphasize having fun and developing skills, leaving competition for higher levels.
- Do coaches have lesson plans for individual sessions? Ask to see one of the lesson plans.
- What kind of training and background do the coaches have? Have they received specialized training? Do they hold the introductory U.S. Soccer Federation (USSF) F license or youth license modules? After the F license, a coach can earn E, D, C, B, and A (the highest) licenses. Keep in mind, however, that a license does not guarantee a good coach. A growing number of programs are hiring professional trainers and coaches, many of whom grew up playing the game in their home countries.
- Will adults other than the coaches have contact with the children, and if so, who are they?
- Are there other parents you can talk to whose children have been through the program?
- Is there a plan to handle children of different abilities?
- Are there emergency procedures for injuries?
- Does the organization conducting the program have liability and medical insurance to protect the program and the players? This is often a state requirement.
- Is the field safe? There should be no broken glass, embedded rocks or tree roots, or broken fences.
- Are the goals securely anchored so that they don't fall on players?

The best way to evaluate a program is to observe it firsthand. If this is possible, here are some things to look for.

- Observe the levels of activity and participation. How often are the children moving around, sitting, and lis-

THE MARK OF EXCELLENCE

You know that you have an excellent soccer program that is above the norm when it:

- Pays attention to and accommodates the needs of all players. Examples include giving scholarships to those in financial need, making a place for less able children, and guiding exceptionally talented players to achieve their potential.
- Reaches out to all parts of the community, such as schools and disadvantaged neighborhoods, by recruiting players in all areas and providing free soccer demonstrations and lessons.
- Requires tryouts and has its players selected by a group of experienced volunteers and coaches, and selections are made in consultation with professional coaches and trainers.
- Has clearly defined objectives for boys and girls, different age groups, and different playing abilities. For example, do girls play with boys? Or, should U-8 (under age 8) be coached and compete with the same philosophy as U-14? Is the focus on winning or developing skills?
- Has an extensive written training plan for the players and a teaching program for volunteer coaches.
- Is aware of and seeks to create a balance between training and competition. Some experts recommend an ideal ratio of five practices for each game. Although most programs do not come close to achieving this ratio, a good program does not overdo the competitive aspect.
- Has a thorough and continuous evaluation system for both volunteers and professionals. The program is also willing to take appropriate disciplinary action against players and coaches when necessary.
- Has a good working relationship with local high schools' programs and coaches. This is important because serious players usually aspire to play high school soccer.

tening to the coach talk? Ideally, children should be active 80 percent of the time.

- Watch out for the dreaded lines, which, unfortunately, are far too common. If you notice children standing around waiting in line for their turn at a skill, it's a bad sign. Too much waiting means too little time being active.
- There should be no negative screaming or yelling by the coaches.
- There should be at least one ball per child.
- The children should be taken through an adequate warmup and cooldown. Five to 10 minutes of some type of running followed by other exercises and stretching both before and after the session is

important. Stretching exercises as part of the warmup and cooldown are a very good sign. (For more information on specific stretches, see chapter 5.)

- Do the children look like they're having fun?

If your local program does not meet acceptable standards and things look pretty poor, it may be worthwhile to investigate other programs in nearby areas. Adding a few minutes to the trip to practice can be worth it for a superior program. If, however, this is not an option, or if your program is largely positive, take the assertive, creative approach. Try to institute some positive aspects in your local program. Look around until you find the best coach in your system. Even if it means playing up a year in age or considering having a girl play on a boys' team, getting onto a good team can be worthwhile. Help organize a parent-coach training seminar run by an experienced coach. Volunteer to help. These options have worked successfully for families in many communities.

working together

Ideally, a good soccer program has good coaches. This is important because both play vital roles in your child's soccer education. They should both work closely together to provide the best environment and instruction. Volunteers and administrators of a good program manage organizational issues such as scheduling games, training times, and use of fields and ordering equipment like goals, balls, and team uniforms. This allows the coaches to concentrate on instructing the children. With a supportive organization in place, the coach can focus on his crucial relationship to the players.

Educating your child to deal with the coach helps foster a feeling of independence. Encourage your child to express her needs to the coach and teach her the appropriate way in which to do it.

When you want to talk to the coach, it is best to do it in a nonconfrontational manner away from the field. Coaching children is a tough job, and many coaches are defensive from dealing with negative comments from parents. By taking a positive approach, you can create a positive and rewarding working relationship with your child's coach.

men and women coaches

Many soccer parents wonder if a coach's gender really matters. This questions arises mainly for girl players, since the majority of all players are coached by men. Boys have their same-sex role models; shouldn't girls have theirs?

Obviously, quality coaching is not defined by gender. There are, however, the social issues of how both girls and boys are affected—hopefully, motivated and inspired—by adults. There is no denying that potentially, it adds a positive element for girls to be coached by women. The reality is that this rarely happens because the number of women coaching is so small. As current women players move through the system, they offer the hope that after their active playing days are over, they may coach. In the meantime, fewer women coaches

GOOD COACHES

A good coach is absolutely necessary for your child to have a fun and meaningful soccer education. A good coach possesses a variety of qualities that range from experience and formal training as a coach to strong interpersonal skills and patience with children. A coaching license alone does not mean that he is a strong all-around coach. Look for a coach who has these qualities.

- Holds at least the introductory U.S. Soccer Federation F license or youth license modules. This is important not just to teach the game but because the licensing course also stresses safety rules and physical education principles. The higher the license, the more time the coach has spent in special courses of study. After the F license, a coach can earn E, D, C, B, and A (the highest) licenses.
- Has previous youth soccer experience either as a coach or assistant coach or received training from a youth soccer professional.
- Has knowledge of or certification in first-aid, preferably from the Red Cross.
- Has played organized soccer or, at the very least, other organized sports.
- Frequently communicates with parents and players. Provides a verbal or written explanation of goals and expectations of parents and players.
- Always plans the practices and works from written lesson plans.
- Teaches skills one at a time and in a logical order; understands the difference between abstract (tactical awareness) and concrete (specific skills) concepts and knows how to teach both.
- Stays abreast of modern coaching and teaching techniques.
- Understands and accommodates the lives that children lead outside of soccer and how they impact on what happens on the field.
- Has a track record of success, not just with win/loss records but in all aspects of team management, such as retaining players and successful parent-coach relationships.

does not mean that girls cannot get a fulfilling soccer experience.

There are some positive additions that can be made to both girls' and boys' soccer, and to their lives. Parents can make an effort to find women coaches, ask soccer programs to recruit them, or become coaches themselves. Women can learn more about coaching by taking part in a course or a clinic or by playing the sport, on any level, in an adult league. Women, including moms, can be involved in practicing and casually playing with their children.

referees and officials

At some point in every child's career, she will hear disparaging comments from both parents and coaches: "Ref,

MOM'S VIEW

Like many other parents of youth players, there have been times when my children required the advice and opinion of the coach. Eventually, one of those issues became so important that we sought a meeting with a coach. We wanted his advice on our older daughter's goals and direction.

Rather than talking on the field, my husband and I sat over lunch with her coach, who we were just getting to know at the time. We confided to him our uncertainty with how to proceed with our daughter's soccer education. She showed an intense interest in the game, and we didn't want to harm that. He gave us both the good (we were supportive parents) and the bad (we needed to learn when to back off a bit). He gave us some concrete suggestions, such as not staying to observe practices and not discussing certain soccer issues as a family unless our children brought them up first. Most of all, he emphasized that she would continue to love the game if it remained primarily fun.

It soon became clear to us that this was a talented, insightful coach who had our daughter's best interest at heart. In subsequent meetings, we let him know that he had our trust, and we expressed an interest in having him map out our daughter's long-term soccer education and progress. Seeking his guidance and putting our trust in him allowed us to take a more relaxed approach.

This was the first step to understanding and making use of the coach in his larger role—not only on the field but off it as well.

that's a foul!" "Ref, you're blind!" Or, she will see T-shirts marketed to youth players with slogans such as "Ref, would you know a foul if you saw one?" or "Three Blind Refs."

This trend of abuse unfortunately happens on every level of play and sets a poor example for children. An important part of your child's soccer education is learning to understand and relate to referees and assistant referees (formerly known as linesmen).

First, it is important to understand exactly what the mission of a referee and his assistants is. A game is controlled by one referee and two assistants.

The number one task of a referee is to ensure the safety and protection of players, according to Essie Baharmast, director of officials for the USSF. Second, that person seeks to uphold fairness for both teams. And finally, the referee should enhance the enjoyment and education of the game. Says Baharmast, "We are the fourth wheel of the car. If any of the tires are flat, the vehicle will not get to its destination. It takes all of us—players, coaches, administrators, and officials—to work together."

In order to understand the nature of refereeing in American youth soccer, you have to look at its meteoric rise. Because the game has expanded so quickly, many inexperienced volunteers are trained as referees, according to Alfred Kleinaitis, manager of referee development and education for the USSF. The system could not function without them, says Kleinaitis, but officiating is complicated. To make matters tougher, most of these volunteers never played soccer when growing up and have not had the benefit of years of experience with the sport.

Baharmast points out that while young American players are being developed with financial aid and special training programs, there is no equivalent backing for referees. Thus, they have not developed as quickly as the players. Some clubs and the national youth soccer organizations conduct referee training courses. Fees and course lengths vary. In New Jersey, for example, it takes about $40 and nine hours of instruction, including a written exam, to become certified as a referee. Increasingly, parent vounteers are getting certified and are serving as referees.

Baharmast and others promote mutual respect among players, spectators, and officials. It is the "do unto others" principle, he says. "Referees should be treated just as the players are treated. If you put pressure on children or criticize them when they make mistakes, how long do you think they will last? If you think that you can sway an official by negative feedback, think again." The bottom line is that watching your manners is a law of the game. Players, coaches, and even spectators can be given official warnings and ejected from the game for abusing the referee.

On the other hand, it is understandable that for both players and spectators, the game is often very emotional. A referee must be sympathetic to the fact that, like it or not, these emotions exist. He must learn to regard himself as outside the game, not as part of it. He must understand that he controls the flow of the game, and that excessively stopping the game interrupts that flow. A good referee is able to bring both humor and calm to any potentially volatile situation. A good referee not only applies the rules fairly and clearly but he also educates the players and cools off any tempers.

If a problem arises, such as what you perceive to be a missed call or a misapplication of a rule, deal with it after the game. Having that chance to cool off and approach the referee in a calm manner will likely get a more cooperative reaction from him. To complain about an official more formally, speak with your coach or contact the person who assigns officials for your club or league. And if the officials do a good job, offer them thanks and praise. They really appreciate this rare gesture.

To give your child insight, discuss with her what it must feel like to referee a game. Older children can gain understanding by taking a referee course. "It helps to walk in another's shoes," says Baharmast, "to try to understand what it is like to make split-second decisions, one after the other."

CHAPTER 5

getting ready to play

THE IMPORTANCE OF WARMING UP AND COOLING DOWN

Soccer is a game of constant motion. To play it effectively and safely, a player must have muscles that are sufficiently warmed up. In other words, you cannot play "hot" if you are "cold."

Yet, a proper warmup is certainly not universal. In fact, all of its aspects, properly performed, are rarely seen on the fields of youth play. Many pregame warmups involve one player doing some activity, shooting goals perhaps, while the rest of the team looks on and waits their turn. Soccer is not static, and the preparations to play it should not be either.

On many teams that conduct warmups, exercises that are unrelated to soccer's specific movements and rhythm, such as jumping jacks, seem to dominate the routines. These may be unifying drills for the team, but they do not adequately prepare players for an active session of soccer. Ideally, an appropriate warmup should be both fluid and varied. It should duplicate actual game situations and be done by the players, perhaps even led by the team captains, with minimal, if any, assistance from the coach.

A good warmup helps children prepare their bodies to play both physically and mentally. It sets the tone for a good practice or competition, and it helps create a bond and a sense of teamwork among the players. In competitive situations, a well-choreographed warmup will help the team feel sharp, and it may even help psych out the opposition. Simply put, a good warmup sets a positive tone for everything that follows.

In addition to getting children ready to play in practice or competition, good warmups lessen the risk of injury by increasing the range of motion of the joints (the ability of a joint to go through the full range of possible movement). One study revealed that soccer players who performed 20-minute pregame warmup programs that included 10 minutes of stretching were 75 percent less likely to sustain injuries.

A warmup also helps the body perform better: A one-degree increase in muscle temperature makes a muscle 13 percent more efficient. Imagine trying to kick a ball as far as you can with tight muscles, and you'll understand the value of a proper warmup.

a proper warmup

A proper soccer warmup takes about 10 minutes for younger children (ages 4 through 10) and 10 to 15 minutes for older children. The warmup may be shorter during hot weather or on tournament days, which include numerous games. Both are cases when the body warms up more easily and in which fatigue may be a factor.

With the exception of tackling (taking the ball away from another player by using the feet), which is done only in a modified form during warmup, soccer players should incorporate all basic components of the game–sprinting, dribbling, heading the ball (using the head to pass or control the ball), and making short and long passes–into their routines.

A good soccer warmup may include the following:

- Jogging with the ball at the feet, long enough for players to break out in a light sweat
- Stretching exercises
- Running (ideally, this should include sideways and backward running in addition to forward sprinting); running and jumping in the air on one or two feet; grapevine (feet alternate crossing over one another while moving sideways); and sideways shuffles
- Ball work, in which the game is duplicated on a small scale; quick passing in twos or small groups; long and short passing with a partner; ball control with body parts other than the feet; juggling, which is keeping the ball airborne with body parts other than the hands and arms; feints and dummies, which are moves intended to fake out opponents; keep-away games with three or four players; throw-in motion, first without the ball, then with the ball, for short and then long distances
- Goalkeeper's warmup should incorporate all of his skills

There is no set order in which these activities have to take place. It is highly recommended, though, that the stretching occur after several minutes of light activity. This allows the muscles and tendons to warm up so that the stretching can provide maximum benefits.

Many players warm up halfheartedly or not at all because they view it as boring and a waste of time. "Why can't the first few minutes of the game or practice be my warmup?" is a commonly heard plea. Here are some tips to ensure that warmups boost performance and are fun rather than a waste of time.

- A regular warmup routine, used in both practices and games, should be established. Create a sequence that is easy to follow and remember. The sequence should be identical for practice and games so that players prepare properly for both.
- Do a total-body warmup. People think that soccer is played with only the feet and legs, but the entire body should be adequately prepared.
- A warmup should have some flair. Players should attempt turns, spins, headers, and other skills. The object is to practice these moves so as not to do them for the first time in the game.
- Use the warmup to prepare mentally. Players can use focus and visu-

alization and encourage their teammates by talking to one another about the game.

- Wear proper clothing. Players should have layers that they can easily shed or put on. Children can be stubborn about this and many times will only want to wear shorts and a T-shirt.
- Do not skip the warmup. If time is a factor, cut something else short in favor of a light jog and stretching.
- Do not use too much energy during a warmup. It is supposed to prepare players, not exhaust them.
- Do not compete. The warmup, including stretching, is not a contest to see who can go farther or faster.
- Do not let the body go cold after the warmup. Often, there is a lot of standing around between a warmup and a game, during which the officials check the players' equipment, for example. Players should be urged to keep moving—lightly stretching or jogging in place.

What can you do if you sense that your child's team is not using good warmup or cooldown techniques? Try approaching your child's coach in a positive, upbeat manner and do it away from other coaches, parents, and children. Discuss the subject without sounding as if you are telling him what do. First and foremost, praise the coach's efforts, then perhaps suggest that he consider something new that you have read.

If the team does not warm up or stretch thoroughly, you can still teach and assist your child in these exercises. A nice approach is to try "buddy stretching," in which a partner assists in doing the exercises. While helping your child do the stretches in this chapter, use the hands-on approach. Often, a touch is more instructive than words. Touch the areas that need to be stretched to make sure that your child feels the stretch in the proper location. Also, touch the back to reinforce good posture and help steady him.

A parent overseeing proper form can help a player stretch better. Buddy stretching also relies on trust and communication—great qualities to share between parent and child.

active-isolated stretching

As adults, we are told how important it is to stretch as part of an exercise program, and for good reason. Improved flexibility reduces the frequency and severity of injuries, can improve agility and speed, increases the joints' range of motion, and can help ward off arthritis. For these very same reasons, stretching is important for children, especially children who play youth soccer.

"As adults, too many of us experience wear and tear and arthritic symptoms because we weren't taught to stretch correctly as children. Only now are we recognizing that children are small adults who need to supplement exercise with a good warmup and cooldown, including stretching," says Paul Trinkoff, D.C., a chiropractor in Orangeburg, New York, who is a soccer dad, coach, board member in his 2,000-plus member local youth soccer program, and a former All-American soccer player.

"Because children are much more resilient, they warm up more easily and can absorb more shock," says Dr. Trinkoff. Good flexibility can prevent injury during lunging-type movements, especially when playing on a wet surface. It can also cut down on overuse injuries, such as tendinitis, which are caused by repetitive motions such as kicking. One study found that soccer players who had tight groin muscles were susceptible to muscular strains or pulls.

Looser muscles allow a player to change direction more quickly or get a quicker step on chasing down an opponent. Muscles that are warmed up and flexible use less energy to move, and in soccer, endurance is critical.

The state-of-the-art stretching technique is called active-isolated (AI) stretching. It entails isolating the muscles and stretching them for a short period of time (three to eight seconds). This form of stretching has several important aspects. First, the body is put in the safest anatomical position. This is important since stretching incorrectly causes more harm than good. Second, the muscle to be stretched is isolated with precise localized movements, thus enhancing flexibility. Third, holding the stretch for shorter periods and doing repetitions increases blood and oxygen flow to the tissues being stretched. This encourages the muscle to lengthen and provides more flexibility than if the player held the stretch longer. In a longer stretch, the muscle becomes fatigued and, in a protective fashion, fights the stretch. Here are several suggestions to help your child stretch correctly.

- Stretch to the point of feeling a stretch, not to the point of pain.
- Do not overstretch.
- Never bounce when you stretch.
- Be gradual. Increase the stretch with each repetition. Relaxation helps you stretch better (tight muscles are harder to stretch). Think of "breathing out" of your muscles to aid relaxation and increase the stretch.
- Use proper form at all times. This is important because you get maximum benefits from a proper stretch so you look good, feel good, and play well. It psychs out the competition to see a sharp, focused team.

the stretches

Have your child do each stretch at least three times and hold each stretch for three to eight seconds. The order in which he does the stretches does not matter, but if time is limited, he should do at least the lower-body stretches. Between stretches, have him return to the neutral position. He should keep his shoulders down and relaxed, stomach in, and hips slightly forward, without locking the knees.

don't forget the cooldown

Even more egregious than improper warmups is the near total lack of cooldowns after soccer practices and games. Children usually finish playing and walk right off the field. But a cooldown—specifically, a gradual slowing down of activity followed by stretching—is one of the most important aspects of sports and exercise. Since stretching is best performed on warm muscles, post-activity stretching is very efficient. Also, it keeps muscles from tightening, which happens if a player just stops the activity without stretching. Blood circulation is facilitated by stretching, which aids in recovery after exercise. If nothing else, suggest to your child's coach that the players take a few minutes to stretch after practice and games.

The cooldown need not be as elaborate as the warmup; its purpose is to unwind, both physically and mentally, rather than to "get up" for practice or competition. Stretching major muscle groups, however, is a must.

After exercise, a player should walk until his heart rate has slowed. This will also give the coach a chance to review the practice session or game. Parts of the same routine used to warm up can be used for the cooldown. Players should stretch immediately or within 10 minutes of playing.

HAMSTRING STRETCH

This stretches the back of the thigh. Lying flat on your back, pull your right leg gently toward your head, keeping your right knee slightly bent. Both hands should be cupped around the back of your right knee, thigh, or calf. Make sure not to pull so far that the hip of the stretched leg is pulled off the ground. Keep your left leg straight and on the ground. Switch legs and repeat.

Buddy stretch: *Stand in front of your child and gently push her leg toward her head. Push each time she breathes out. Encourage her to relax, and ask for feedback. Make sure that she keeps her knee slightly bent.*

GLUTEAL MUSCLE STRETCH

This stretches the buttocks. To reinforce good, upright form while playing, maintain it during stretching. In this case, keep your back straight and pull your left knee to your chest using the crook of your right elbow. Your left foot should cross over your right thigh and your right leg should be extended. Your left arm should extend back, palm resting on the ground, to maintain balance. For a more extensive stretch, twist the trunk of your body to the left, pulling your left knee even closer to your chest. Switch legs and repeat.

QUADRICEPS STRETCH

This stretches the front of the thigh. Alignment is important. Lying on your left side with your left arm extended above your head and your left ear resting on your left arm, keep your body in a straight line. Both knees should touch each other. Grasp the top of your right foot with your right hand and pull your right foot directly to the center of your hip. For a more extensive stretch, push your left hip forward while focusing on tightening your buttocks. Switch legs and repeat.

LOWER-BACK STRETCH

This stretches the lower back. Lying facedown in a straight line, keep both palms down and at shoulder level. Push straight up as far as is comfortable. Keep your shoulders relaxed, your legs together, and your eyes forward (as opposed to tilting your head back to look up). Most young players are flexible enough to form a right angle with their bodies.

BUTTERFLY STRETCH

This stretches the groin muscles. To encourage better posture, imagine that a rod is running through your back. Keep your heels together. Hold your ankles with your hands. Push down on your thighs with your elbows, remembering to relax your shoulders to keep them from rising. Do not stretch by grabbing your feet.

FROG STRETCH

This stretches the groin muscles. Squat down, keeping your back straight and your hips under your body. Do not stick your buttocks out while squatting down. Place your fingers on the ground in front for balance. Let your heels rise off the ground. Push out on your inner thighs with your elbows with as much pressure as necessary.

CALF STRETCH

This stretches the back of the lower leg. With your body bent at the hips, place your right foot flat on the ground and keep your left leg relaxed. Place your hands flat on the ground in front of your head. Feel free to experiment with the angle. Make sure that your right heel stays on the ground. To stretch your lower calf, remain in the same position, but bend your right knee slightly, making sure that your right heel remains on the ground. Switch legs and repeat.

Standing stretch: *Lean against a wall or tree.*

LATERAL TRUNK STRETCH

This stretches the upper back, chest, hips, and shoulders. While standing, extend both arms over your head. Keep your arms straight, elbows locked, and fingers intertwined with your palms facing up. Lean to the right, but do not tilt to the front or back. Holding form, lean only far enough to feel the stretch. Return to the upright position. To open your chest, clasp your hands behind your back and pull your arms up toward the center of your back. Switch sides and repeat.

NECK STRETCH

This stretches the neck and shoulder muscles. Using your left hand, placed flat on the right side of your head, pull your head gently to the left. Your shoulders should remain level, with your right arm hanging loosely at your side. Continue to emphasize good form—standing straight and facing forward with your feet parallel and slightly spread. Switch sides and repeat.

OPEN–THE–GATE STRETCH

This stretches the entire hip area. Standing on your left leg, open your right hip as if to receive a pass. Do this in two distinct steps: With your right knee raised in front, swing open to the side, then bring your right knee back to the front and then down to the ground. Keep your hips under your body (your buttocks should not stick out), and extend your arms out comfortably to maintain balance. Open your leg only as far as it will go without twisting your body, which should remain facing forward. Switch legs and repeat.

adidas
adidas
adidas

2 SOCCER SKILLS

6. beginner 43
7. novice 49
8. intermediate 58
9. advanced 67
10. expert 78
11. goalkeeping 86

beginner

UP TO ONE YEAR OF EXPERIENCE

You want your child's education to be complete in every way. And for it to be so, it has to go beyond educating the mind. It also has to include a physical education. The beauty of soccer is that it is an ideal vehicle for a young child's versatile, complete, and fun physical education. It is no wonder that soccer is so popular with four- to six-year-olds.

At this stage, children are learning not just to play soccer. They're also learning how to control their bodies. A good beginning program is largely an introduction to basic physical skills, some of which are running (forward, backward, and side to side), balancing (on one foot, for the purpose of striking the ball), and generally understanding how the body moves in space. Soccer is simply the medium through which these basic skills are acquired. And soccer is a great medium to do so, because it uses so many physical skills, such as balance, coordination, and manipulating the body in many different ways.

One of the most difficult messages to convey to parents is what should be taught at this stage. Parents often view a soccer session for beginners with confusion or disbelief. They see children rolling on balls or balancing balls and wonder what's going on. A typical question is, "Can't you teach my child to kick the ball up in the air?"

For most young children, that skill is a couple of years away. They are so consumed with simple tasks like coordinating the feet and body to kick a ball that the ability, for example, to control a ball, make a pass, and score a goal with any degree of intent is too massive an achievement for most of them.

It's also important to realize that practicing basic skills at this level does not mean diving right in to passing, dribbling, shooting, and other soccer skills. Each one of these skills is made up of different parts, and it is these parts that beginners must master. Kicking a ball, for instance, entails a number of basic skills such as the proper positioning of the feet, the transferring of weight, the ability to balance on one foot, and eye-foot coordination. A good beginning program emphasizes the elements that make up soccer skills.

This does not mean, though, that children who have the capability to master more complicated skills cannot be accommodated in a good beginning program.

MOM'S VIEW

Children cherish their soccer gear. A special shirt or ball is tangible evidence of their love of the sport and a sign of their commitment and accomplishment. You can use soccer gear as an introduction to a beginning session and to make your child feel comfortable with a new experience. Have your child try on the clothing that she intends to wear while playing. Have her get used to putting on shinguards. Definitely do not arrive at the field and try to put them on for the first time. Finally, try something that even advanced players do to get a psychological edge: Allow your child to sleep with a soccer ball the night before a practice or game.

If children have a basic skill down pat, they will show signs of boredom if they are not challenged. If this happens, good coaches will partner up advanced players or form small groups to practice more advanced skills. They can also use a more advanced child to demonstrate basic skills to the others, which makes the youngster feel great and inspires other children to excel in order to get the chance to show their stuff. Coaches should emphasize to children that mastering the basics is necessary before moving on to the more advanced skills.

Could a coach skip the introduction to basic physical skills and just teach young children to kick the ball up in the air? Yes, it could be done, but it would probably come back to haunt the coach later. If you view a child's soccer education as a triangle in which skills progress gradually, the basic physical skills form the all-important base. The wider this base of control, knowledge, and experience is, the higher the peak of the triangle can be. In other words, a strong mastery of the basics leads to a potentially better soccer player down the line.

early involvement of parents

In the mid 1990s, the Montclair (New Jersey) United Soccer Club noticed it had a problem. It realized how difficult it was for the majority of its players to make the leap from recreational to more advanced travel teams. It seemed that the problem lay in the lack of education of volunteer coaches at the grassroots level. The best young players on the more advanced teams tended to have both involved parents and good coaches—who are often one and the same.

Soon after this problem was recognized, the club formalized a training program for volunteer coaches at its KinderKicker, or beginner, level. The club decided not to automatically replace parent coaches with professional trainers, as it had done in the past. As a result, the new U-12 (ages 10 to 11) players retained 75 percent of their parent coaches. This policy change came about because parent coaches who started their training when their children

coach's corner

Here is a partial excerpt from one of my beginner lesson plans, along with some notes.

1. Introduce and review rules and safety issues.

2. Have players walk and then jog, with the ball kept close at the feet.

3. Have players balance the ball in one of their palms (teaches coordination in motion), then between their knees (teaches balance and coordination), and then on a foot and between their ankles.

4. Play a game called statues. Players dribble within a marked-off area. If tagged by the coach, a player stands still like a statue, with the ball at her feet and her legs apart. She can only be released by another player passing the ball through her legs and then crawling through and retrieving it. This game teaches dribbling, passing, moving the ball in a set space, and awareness of the ball against opposition (the "frozen" players). Other games in this lesson plan teach dodging, weaving, and running fast while controlling the ball.

Most youth soccer practices end with a scrimmage, where skills are combined with actual game play. This is fine, as long as maximum participation is encouraged, for example, by adding extra balls or extra goals.

were beginners were now qualified to coach at higher levels. Clearly, early coaches' training can pay dividends.

While this positive nurturing does not always begin so early on, it certainly can, and frequently does. It made sense to train parent volunteers to coach properly at the earliest stages. While better training of parent coaches may not completely solve the problem of the gap between recreational and serious levels of play, since the program was formalized, a sign of some progress is the increasing number of parent volunteers who have successfully made the transition to advanced-level coaching.

Experience proves that teaching parents to be good coaches when their children are young not only establishes a good foundation of skills for their children but also enables the adults to go through life as good sports parents. KinderKickers and programs like it exist throughout the country. An ideal way to ensure that programs are well-run is to check if there is a training program for parent coaches that includes active supervision (an experienced coach should be at training sessions). In addition to conducting regular training seminars for parent coaches, it should teach parents how to create and implement effective lesson plans.

BEFORE AND AFTER PLAYING

Before each session, you should have your child:

- Go to the bathroom.
- Eat a good meal, preferably one to two hours before playing.
- Get appropriate equipment, including shinguards, sneakers or soccer cleats, and a full water bottle.
- Wear sports clothing such as shorts, a T-shirt, socks, and cleats. (Jeans, for example, are not recommended, because they have metal buttons and rivets that can cause abrasions.)
- Wear clothing marked with her name and identification and have an emergency ID card inside her sports bag (if she uses one.)
- Dress in layers, if it is cold, that can be removed after she warms up.
- Remove all jewelry.
- Tie up her hair to keep it out of her face.
- Lace up and tie her shoes, with double knots, if necessary.

After the session, you should:

- Provide water and a healthful snack, such as fruit.
- Check for understanding by asking your child to tell you about the fun things she did and the new games she learned.
- Offer praise to reinforce positive behavior. Tell your child you thought it was great when she worked hard to balance the ball, for instance, or when she congratulated her teammate.
- Do not dissect the lesson or take a negative approach such as asking why she could not get the ball more often or score a goal.

coach's corner

When I was seven years old, my parents started me on accordion lessons. I loathed the lessons so much that I had a headache every Thursday an hour before they started. The memory of myself as a little boy with that huge instrument strapped onto my body is still a painful one. And the sight of an accordion still sends shivers down my spine.

Soccer, my lifelong love, was just plain fun (and it still is) long before it became hard work. I grew up in England about 200 yards from a professional stadium, and I spent every free hour there.

Parents have expressed concern to me that all their children want to do is play soccer. I think it is okay to let children follow their instincts. Some naturally will want to take up other activities, while others, like me, will just want to play soccer. Pressuring or forcing a child usually results in negative consequences.

Fortunately for me, after about seven weeks of torturous accordion lessons, my parents allowed me to concentrate solely on soccer.

Even if a child is not serious about soccer or does not wish to continue formal involvement, a good beginning program can be invaluable. After all, its main objective is that children learn to enjoy vigorous physical exercise. If your child comes away from a soccer session saying, "I had fun," she will associate that good time with soccer. When you see her smile often, you have likely found a good program and a valuable sports experience.

the well-prepared child

There is a lot you can do to be involved in and to facilitate your child's early soccer participation. Before signing up for a beginning program, you should consult your child. Explain exactly what the program is, and then specifically ask your child if she wants to play. In fact, you can show her what a beginning soccer program will be like. Take her out in the backyard and pass a ball together. Explain what you are doing and tell her that she can expect such activities in soccer sessions.

Some children need a lot of information. They feel most comfortable if they know exactly what is going to happen. Give them that knowledge, using soccer language when appropriate. You can demonstrate expected activities and also explain that there will be a lot of children at the sessions and that your child may have to share a ball or that other children may try to take her ball away as part of a game.

remember to keep it fun

It may seem obvious that parents should never make negative statements or judgments, but you would be surprised how often it happens. In fact, there are several common inappropriate acts and beliefs regarding soccer education at this age. Parents may acknowledge, for example, that mastering basic physical skills is the main objective in the early years, but many of them merely pay lip service to accepting this principle. They still expect their children to have put all the skills together and be playing good soccer at a young age. Even while agreeing that basic skills and fun are the goals, there is often a "but. . . ." A common impatient question from parents is, "But why can't my child dribble and shoot the ball?"

Parents also often push the work ethic too hard at this age. Another comment is, "To get to the top, you have to work hard." The only hard work that young children need to do is to work hard at having fun.

Trying to master advanced skills too early may only frustrate children and rob them of a good time. There should be an element of fun at every level of the game, but especially for beginners. If fun does not exist, it's likely that your child will not be interested in continuing to play.

CHAPTER 7

novice

ONE TO TWO YEARS OF EXPERIENCE

Young children have such a zest for life. Along with this joy for life is a willingness to experiment, primarily because they are less intimidated and have less of a fear of making mistakes than older children. There is also usually less pressure from parents and peers to perform well at this age (approximately seven to eight years old). With sound coaching and positive experiences, this is the stage at which both the willingness and ability to absorb soccer is established. The dominant feature of this stage, just as in the beginner stage, though, is having fun.

The novice stage is when the most basic soccer skills are introduced. This is where the foundation of a child's soccer education is built. The beginner stage defines the general physical skills of soccer, such as running, jumping, kicking, turning, and sliding. At the novice stage, children are taught specific skills, such as dribbling, passing, ball control, and shooting. These skills are not taught in any particular order. And because the foundation of skills laid down is so extensive, it is important to understand that perfection is not expected.

At this stage, players can make some marked advances—if they are properly nurtured. Young children are like sponges and soak up most all that is offered. Filled with this new knowledge, they flourish.

It is important to remember that your child's education at the novice level is also a learning opportunity for you. Once you understand what should be taught, you can encourage and build upon his learning. Working at home with your child on these skills not only helps develop his abilities but it also provides you with the pleasure of sharing the sports experience.

the skills

Depending on your child's soccer program and coaches, the skills described in this chapter may or may not be taught, while others not listed may be included. At this stage, however, more time should be spent on skills like dribbling, passing, and shooting, with less time spent on skills like heading.

coach's corner

I have coached Leroy Watkins since he was a young boy. Leroy was a fun-loving child who always enjoyed the game of soccer.

At age 17, he became the captain of his high school's highly competitive and successful soccer team. Yet even now, his smile is as big as ever. It has stayed that way because he has had a series of good coaches and positive learning experiences.

Despite the intense pressure of high school soccer, Leroy has displayed the same enjoyment of the game that he did as a child. But having fun should never mean sacrificing high standards. Quality is always required and high standards should be set, even at the novice level. This will ensure that, although the meaning of high standards is different at every level, the concept of striving for excellence is instilled and, hopefully, will always be maintained.

Leroy balances fun and striving for excellence by having variety in his life. He plays other sports throughout the year, like basketball. He also loves to socialize. Yet when he is on the soccer field, he is 100 percent focused on the task at hand.

Note: Leroy is pictured demonstrating a side volley, swerve pass, scissors kick, and bicycle kick in chapters 9 and 10.

Dribbling and passing. Two of the first soccer skills taught at the novice level are dribbling–maintaining control of the ball while running–and passing. While dribbling is a skill initially taught to beginners, they will not have mastered it, nor will they have connected it with passing. Passing learned by players on the novice level (the inside-of-the-foot pass) is an essential skill used extensively at even the highest levels of the game. This pass is hard for many children because of the unnatural motion of turning the foot out at a right angle.

While those at the beginner level are encouraged to kick the ball any way and anywhere they wish, their efforts should now be targeted toward more deliberate passing and shooting at the goal.

It's important not to have expectations that are too high at this level with regard to passing. Many children are still blasting away at the ball any way they can.

Passing is a good example of how complex soccer skills are. It is a skill that requires learning a series of new movements. From the first day we walk, we know that one foot moves in front of the other, with the body balanced and feet firmly planted. But in order to pass, you must balance on the nonkicking leg, bend the knee of the kicking leg, turn out from the hip of the kicking leg, look down at the ball, and then swing the kicking leg.

The inside-of-the-foot pass is a good example of how you know if your child is performing a skill properly. Even with an untrained eye, you can tell if a pass looks smooth and natural. Achieving balance, the flow of the movement, and the desired direction of the ball are good clues. From the beginning, it is essential to praise and emphasize good form in your child, not only to ensure the desired result (that the ball will be well-played) but also because good form reduces muscle strains and other injuries.

Shielding (guarding) the ball. Like a chain of events, dribbling and passing are connected to several other fundamental skills, all of which should permeate every practice session at the novice level. One is shielding, or guarding, the ball with the body. This means keeping the body between the ball and the opponent.

Learning how to shield is a good example of learning by mastering a progression of skills. Shielding is taught by first having a player practice moving the ball without the presence of an attacker. Then, light pressure is added by having an attacker move closely around the defender as he shields the ball. Once the defender is comfortable with shielding, high pressure is added by having an attacker attempt to take the ball away from the defender.

INSIDE-OF-THE-FOOT PASS

Push through the center of the ball with the inside of the foot. Striking on the lower part of the ball gives it height; striking on top of the ball results in less power and control. Young children commonly twist the striking leg after passing, which is incorrect. The striking leg should not cross the midline of the body on the follow-through. Weight should be placed on the planted leg, and the knee of the planted leg should be bent for stability. Arms should be out at the sides for balance. The plant foot must be pointing at the target. Look at the ball at the moment of striking and alternately at the target and ball before that.

It is crucial for a coach in a high-pressure situation such as shielding to allow a child to fail properly. In other words, a player may lose the ball to an attacker because he didn't shield correctly. In any skill taught at this level, artificial failure—forcing errors through excessive or illegal force—should not be conducted. (This method can be used on higher-level players in the belief that if they can withstand extraordinary pressure, then they will be able to tolerate an opponent's pressure.) The adult should win the ball only if a player makes an actual shielding mistake. The player then learns that poor shielding results in losing possession of the ball. This is not to say, however, that a coach cannot challenge a higher-skilled player by adding a greater element of pressure.

Shielding and other skills are often taught through games in which players are eliminated for making mistakes (if the player loses possession of the ball, he is out of the game). These games obviously favor the better players and don't do much good for the weaker players, who are usually eliminated quickly. Elimination games should be used sparingly at all levels, with children being recycled back into the game as soon as possible.

Turns. Soccer is like a dance. And like any dance, it has multiple turning movements. The number of possible turns is limited only by a player's creativity. At the novice level, basic turns are taught as part of dribbling. Basic turns are ones made in any direction while moving the ball and are executed with either the outside, inside, or sole of the foot. More complex turns are introduced to more experienced players and are made by different parts of the foot and involve more difficult body movements.

Two basic turns are the outside- and inside-of-the-foot turns. The inside turn is often referred to as a hook turn. With both turns, the two biggest challenges are learning to shift the weight as the player turns and turning the correct way. Especially with the outside turn, players often keep kicking the ball straight as they attempt to turn. Parents can help teach these basic turns by slowing down the motion and walking the child through the turn.

Ball control. Another skill that is taught concurrently with dribbling, passing, shielding, and turning is ball control. Ball control is the crux of soccer. Having complete ball control means that a player is 100 percent in charge of what happens next to the ball. It's the ability to keep the ball close if an opponent is near, to stop a ball coming his way, to make a pass, or to take a shot on goal. This is a difficult skill. At this level, many players simply stop the ball by allowing it to hit

SHIELDING

The defender should keep the ball at maximum distance from the attacker. He senses the opponent with his body. His eyes are on the ball, with the nontouching arm (the one not touching the attacker) used for balance. The defender uses not only his arm but also his knee as a barrier.

their bodies. They have not yet developed the requisite fine-motor skills to optimally trap (receive) the ball and then control it using a variety of body parts. This is a crucial time for coaches to encourage the use of appropriate body parts to control the ball. For example, a ball that is at shin height is always controlled by the foot, not the shin, even if it requires lifting the foot fairly high off the ground.

BALL CONTROL

The most important aspect of ball control is what precedes ball contact. The player should align her body so that maximum body space is presented to stop the ball. Selecting the correct body part to control the ball depends on the ball's trajectory and height. Try to control it on a flat surface (foot or thigh) as opposed to the knee or shin. Also try to absorb and cushion the ball as opposed to striking it. Eyes should be kept on the ball when controlling it. Arms should be out at the sides to maintain balance at the moment of contact.

Juggling. Juggling is tapping the ball and keeping it in the air with any body part except the hands and arms. It is an individual skill that teaches ball and body control. It can also be used in games. For example, the ball could be flicked (kicked up), juggled on the thigh, then kicked over an attacker's head to clear the ball.

It is also an ideal fun activity that requires only one player and a ball, with so many variations and challenges that boredom is seldom a problem. Children love the possibilities. Juggles can be counted (in total or by body part), and

JUGGLING

When using the thigh to juggle, the thigh should be parallel to the ground, like a shelf, so that the ball will rise straight into the air. Children tend not to raise the leg high enough, which causes the ball to be shot forward. The ball should be tapped so that it goes no higher than pictured. The planted leg is bent for stability, and the arms are used for balance.

SOCCER IS A TWO-FOOTED GAME

Children will naturally gravitate toward using one foot to kick a soccer ball. It is extremely important that parents and coaches actively encourage the use of both feet, which is a major asset to good players. The sooner this begins, the greater the chances of success. This can be achieved by fostering games and exercises that narrow in on the task, such as playing with the nondominant foot only.

As your child becomes more confident using both feet, alternate sides on which you defend him, thus forcing him to use both feet. When you play with your child in the park or in your backyard, encourage him to spend equal time using both feet.

One of the ways a coach can help a player develop is to play a right-footed player on the left side of the field or vice versa, where he will be forced to use the less dominant foot. A coach who plays a child only in positions in which the dominant foot is likely to be used may be interested in winning the game, but he is not helping the development of the player.

Many parents and coaches refer to a right-footed child's left foot as the "weaker" or "bad" foot. Always refer to the nonpreferred foot as the "other" foot.

personal records can always be bettered. Juggling is often part of a warmup or used as a filler when the coach is setting up another activity or working with a limited group of players.

Shooting. Shooting is the skill that every team works hard to master. Shooting means taking a shot at scoring a goal. It's a complicated task that requires a player to make a split-second decision about how to strike the ball and what direction he is going to send it.

At this level, the focus is not on the style of the shot itself (types of shots will be introduced at a more advanced level) but on its direction. The most common shooting weakness of novice players is to shoot the ball directly at the goalkeeper. This is usually near the center of the goal since that is where young goalkeepers tend to gravitate.

Now is the time to begin training in shooting the ball low and to the corners of the goal and to instill in a player that shooting the ball away from the goalkeeper greatly increases the chance of scoring.

Hitting the midpoint of the ball and higher will ensure that the ball stays low. Keeping the head steady helps the body stay in position and helps the eyes stay focused on the ball. It is key to focus on the ball at the moment of striking it. Before striking, your child should alternately look at the target and the ball.

It is important to hone shooting to the corners of the goal in practice rather than trying to learn it in a game. One technique to try at home is to set up goals that enable players to score only by hitting markers on the right or left sides of the goal, not in the middle.

Heading. A brief introduction to heading the ball (using your head to pass or control the ball) is taught at this level. Using soft balls (playground balls or beach balls) encourages a player to feel comfortable with this new skill. A common problem with introductory heading is hitting the ball in the wrong spots, such as on parts of the face, the top of the head, or the ears. It is crucial that good technique be established early to avoid heading the ball in these painful areas and to prevent a subsequent fear of heading. This can be done by directed, step-by-step practice. For example, initially it is better for a player to head a stationary ball, which can be held out for him, or he can regulate his own heading by self-serving the ball. These methods are easier than trying to initially learn with a moving head and a moving ball.

The forehead is the proper part of the body to head the ball. Make sure that your child doesn't stick his tongue out so that he doesn't bite it (clenching the teeth can help with this). Although the eyes naturally close when the ball makes contact with the forehead, encourage him to keep them open so he can focus on the ball.

HEADING

A confident posture, with eyes focused on the ball, allows a player to meet the ball, not be met by the ball. Feet that are wide apart allow for better balance. The arms should be spread out to maintain balance and leverage. The eyes should be locked on the ball and should remain open. The mouth should be closed to prevent tongue and teeth injuries. The final lunge to head the ball is done with a snap of the neck. Leading up to that, though, the whole body is used.

positional awareness

Positional awareness is an abstract concept that refers to being in the right place at the right time and having an idea of where the other players on both teams are in relation to you.

A familiar scene in young children's soccer games is "swarm ball," where a cluster of players kick aimlessly at the ball in the middle of the mass. Encouraging children to move into an open space away from fellow players and the ball is one of the hardest concepts to teach. They find it very difficult to believe that sometimes being away from the ball can help the team.

Once you realize how difficult it is for young children to grasp the concept of positional awareness, you can appreciate the futility of the common cry, "Spread out!" A child hears this vague and nondirectional cry as an order to run away from the ball. While that is certainly part of the coach's intention, the

MOM'S VIEW

All sports have their rituals—little things that add to the feeling of being psyched. The look and feel of proper soccer gear gives a player the mental edge and sends an important message to the opposition to take this player seriously. It is also a part of game readiness and feeling good about yourself, and it should begin at a very early age. After all, a player with his shirt out, his socks down, and his cleats dirty doesn't make much of an impression. In short, looking sharp can translate into playing sharp.

This was first made clear to me when my daughter's English coaches insisted that players come to games and practices with their soccer cleats cleaned and polished, a habit that they had developed in their childhood playing days. "What for?" I wondered. "They'll just get muddy within seconds." It was explained to me that cleaning and treating soccer cleats not only preserves their leather but is also a sign of respect for the sport and shows the seriousness with which a player takes the game. This ritual is now a sacred part of our household. As an adult athlete, I would never run a road race in dirty or second-class gear, and I now understand why athletes of all ages and levels benefit from looking clean and tidy.

child doesn't gain an appreciation for why he is doing it.

A better approach to teaching positional awareness is to use the phrase "and stop" during scrimmages. These words freeze the players in place and allow the coach to move children around to appropriate positions while explaining the importance of movements.

Positional awareness takes a great deal of experience to acquire. It often takes a year or two before players put its principles into practice. It's important for both players and parents to be patient in learning this critical element of soccer.

concepts and rules

At this stage, players should be introduced to the general concepts of the game, such as defending and attacking. They should also be introduced to positions (midfielder, forward, winger, striker, sweeper/stopper, to name a few), but specific roles should not be assigned. Players are "defenders" or "attackers," not "sweepers" or "wingers."

At this stage, players should also be taught the basic rules of soccer. This is best done informally in short bursts, with fun and creativity. Games can be used to teach such plays as kickoffs, free kicks, goal kicks, penalty shots, drop balls and throw-ins. One example of a game is Exploring the Field, where the coach and team take a trip around the field and talk about the different areas and special kicks.

goalkeeping

Basic goalkeeping should be introduced at this level, although it has no particular

coach's corner

Children intuitively know that having fun is important. One hot day after a fun round of games at my soccer camp, an eight-year-old on one of the teams asked, "Did we win? Did we win?" After adding up the points, I answered truthfully, "No, you didn't." Immediately after this exchange, another player asked aloud, "Why can't we all win?" And why not?

It was not important to the second child that one or the other team won. What was important was that everyone had fun. The fun was not in winning or losing, but in running around on the field for an hour with a bunch of his friends.

order in the teaching of skills. It should be a focus in training in at least two of the nine sessions in a nine-week novice program. Goalkeeping has its own important guidelines and skills, and all children—if they feel comfortable—should be exposed to them.

Goalkeeping is the most volatile emotional experience for a player for various reasons. First, it is often a one-on-one situation with riskier stakes. A mistake by this single player can lead to a goal scored by the opposition. What's more, the prospect of a short, blistering shot coming straight at a player is daunting, as is the potential pain of catching one.

On the plus side, children love the tasks of goalkeeping—jumping, diving, and falling. And a good keeper is probably the most versatile athlete on the soccer field. He needs agility, good hand-eye coordination, explosive power to jump and dive, foot skills, and the ability to perform under pressure. The coach must guard against teammates blaming or harassing the keeper by emphasizing that it is a team game, and if a ball goes into the net, it had to get through 10 other players before it passed the goalkeeper.

A low-key introduction to goalkeeping emphasizes moving the feet, which is the most crucial element of beginning goalkeeping, and the fun of diving and jumping for the ball. In addition to kicking or throwing the ball to your child in the goal, you can focus on general goalkeeping skills at home by throwing and catching a soccer ball (the keeper is the only player allowed to use his hands) and having him shuffle from side to side and sprint from a standstill to collect the ball. For more information on goalkeeping, see chapter 11.

CHAPTER 8

intermediate

TWO TO FOUR YEARS OF EXPERIENCE

The intermediate level is usually when children make significant leaps ahead in mastering the game of soccer. Up to this point in their training, they've received the game's fundamentals, from rules to basic skills. Now, it is important to reinforce those fundamentals and have children master them before moving on to more difficult skills and tactics.

The relatively rapid progress of children at this level affords both coaches and parents the opportunity to positively encourage them to continue their diligent mastering of skills. Some new skills are added at this level, but from this time on, perfecting existing skills is a constant goal.

Other facets of the game, such as tactics, are also introduced at this level. Also, as children get older, competitive leagues start to come into the picture, adding a new element of pressure.

finesse and fitness

At this level, the heaviest emphasis should be placed on developing touch, that is, developing a refined sense of controlling the ball. In addition, physical fitness should be a strong focus.

A strong cardiovascular system is crucial for a game that has lots of nonstop action, much of it running. Getting children used to running a lot early on in their soccer education means that they will be more comfortable with a lot of running when they get older. At the end of practice or a competition, children should leave the field feeling tired but happy.

Unfortunately, many youth soccer practices feature drills with minimal running or with only one player engaged in a skill at a time. A better-coached team will have lots of exercises and games that involve all players running and passing. This positively impacts both skills and fitness. Running should also be done in the context of honing a skill and not be used as punishment (for example, laps around the field for making mistakes).

the skills

Demonstration by an experienced coach or player is the quickest and best way to teach your child the skills in this chapter and all subsequent skills. In addition, there is a lot you can do at home to foster soccer improvement at this level.

Dribbling. As beginners, children are introduced to dribbling, which is maneuvering the ball on the ground with the feet, by moving the ball in different directions, such as toward the goal, away from opponents, or toward a teammate. The emphasis is more on becoming familiar with the ball's feel than on maintaining control when pressured from opponents. At the intermediate level, players should become more comfortable fending off pressure from opponents.

You should see players actively attempting to lose their markers (opponents who are guarding them) by using feints (fake moves), also called dummies. Other dribbling skills to look for are tactical, such as dribbling the ball at the farthest point from a defender. For example, if a player has a defender on his left, he should keep the ball on his right.

Sound dribbling skills allow a player to beat his opponent both offensively and defensively. Offensively, creativity and flair often make the difference between maintaining possession and possibly scoring, or losing the ball. After a defender gets possession of the ball, her mastery of dribbling allows her to move up the field or choose another option, such as passing to a teammate or clearing the ball out of the defensive zone. No matter what the situation, good dribbling skills make a player better.

Trapping. Though a soccer ball spends a lot of time in the air, it is easier to control it when it's on the ground. The skill of bringing a moving ball under control is known as trapping. Common traps are done with the thighs or the insides and outsides of the feet. More difficult traps, which are introduced at a more advanced level, are done with the chest and the head.

You can help your child learn this skill by encouraging her to use various body parts to get the ball under control. Play the ball at various heights to facilitate this skill, while understanding that often, the higher the ball, the more difficult it is to control.

Shooting. To understand intermediate shooting, it helps to understand the erroneous cheers of most youth soccer spectators as a player heads toward the goal. "Boot the ball!" they shout. And most children at this level try to shoot the ball as hard as they can. An important lesson to impart at this stage is that if it comes down to a one-on-one with the goalkeeper, which is frequent at all levels of play, strategy (a well-timed, well-placed shot) will more often prevail over power.

Another common problem at this level is relying on the dominant foot for shooting. Players will often waste time moving the ball from the nondominant foot to the dominant foot, taking valuable time that allows a defender to make a tackle.

It is important to practice shooting with any part of the foot and with both feet. Very often, players who have been running hard are in a high state of fatigue just prior to shooting. Mastering the ability to shoot with both feet will reduce the time and energy needed to take the shot and will enhance a player's composure when shooting while fatigued.

A shot introduced at this level is the laces drive, which can be used as a pass but is generally used to take a powerful shot on goal. With power, however, often comes inaccuracy, which is why the initial emphasis should be on kicking technique and not on hitting a specific target. Pointing the toe, keeping the eye on the ball at all times, and swinging the leg so that the laces meet the ball is a difficult, but possible, move to master at this level. Initially, it should be practiced very slowly, thus reducing the risk of a stubbed toe or of kicking the ball with the toe. Another way to avoid a stubbed toe is to practice kicking on the laces when the ball is airborne.

LACES DRIVE

The kicking knee should be bent and over the ball when the player strikes the ball. This will keep the ball low and under greater control. The kicking toe is pointed down, with the ankle locked. Both feet should be pointed toward the target, with the planted foot about a foot's width from the ball. The hip and knee should be extended to their fullest on the follow-through. Keep arms out for balance and to ward off other players. Keep the head down, with the eyes on the ball.

Acquiring sound shooting skills is very simple: practice, practice, practice. A good game with which to familiarize players with the confusion and excitement of scoring opportunities is goal-mouth scramble. In this game, both defenders and attackers battle in front of a goal.

A tendency that some players pick up at this level is the reluctance to shoot. They give up the opportunity in favor of dribbling or making a pass. This happens primarily because they have difficulty deciding where and when to shoot. A good coach should encourage players to shoot at every realistic opportunity and should praise players who shoot on a regular basis.

More technical shooting training can focus on shooting from more difficult distances and angles and shooting under pressure. Children should have many opportunities to practice these skills.

Heading. Heading skills at this level should focus on using heading to pass or to send the ball over a long distance, such as when clearing a defensive area. These separate skills require using slightly different parts of the forehead and different techniques. Other elements of heading that can be introduced at this stage include jumping to head the ball and jumping to head the ball with other players nearby.

It is crucial for coaches not to pressure players into heading before they are ready. It is likely that fear of heading the ball will be present. This anxiety can stay with some players throughout their careers. An excellent method of overcoming some of the fear is to allow a child to work at her own pace and, if possible, by herself. Independent work allows her to make her own mistakes without fear of ridicule from teammates.

Turns. Players use turns for a variety of reasons: to change direction, to evade the opposition through deception and create space, to move into open space, or to open the opportunity to take a shot on goal.

Children find turns fun to learn because they add variety to the game, build confidence when done right, and allow children to be creative in their execution. After learning basic turns such as the inside- and outside-of-the-foot hooks, players move on to more complex moves, many of which are meant to deceive oncoming opponents.

CRUYFF TURN

This move is best executed with an exaggerated fake kick, followed by quickly hooking the ball backward, behind the plant foot. The knees are deeply bent for balance, the arms are out for balance, and the standing foot is parallel with the ball. A beginner can practice by standing straight and isolating the move, simply hooking the ball behind with one foot. Once the technique is mastered, players can work on quickening the speed of the turn.

The Cruyff turn, named for the legendary Dutch player Johan Cruyff, is one such move. A player with possession dribbles forward with the ball when suddenly, in the middle of a kick, she hooks the kicking leg around the ball, sending it behind her other leg and in a direction away from an oncoming opponent. The player with the ball turns around and continues play, hopefully leaving the opponent behind.

Juggling. Although juggling is usually first perfected on the thighs, which is the easiest place to control the ball, players should now be encouraged to juggle with other parts of their bodies. These other parts include the feet (both the tops and the sides), the head, the shoulders, and even the chest.

It is important for children to be allowed to use their hands to help them get started, as this will allow them to experiment. Just be careful not to make this a habit. It is also important to acquire the skill of flicking the ball up from the ground in order to begin juggling, without using the hands.

Many children ask, "How does juggling help in a soccer game?" While it is true that juggling is not a game skill, the constant touching increases a player's ball-control skills and confidence. Many of the world's best soccer players reached that height through mastering ball control, not through pure athleticism.

Tackling. This skill entails gaining possession of the ball or denying an opponent possession by direct physical confrontation. While tackling, both players simultaneously try to get possession of the ball with their feet. Tackling is a defensive skill that is used as a last resort because a player either failed to evade an opponent through dribbling or passing or failed to take the ball away using other, less physical, methods such as intercepting passes. It requires strength, balance, courage, and good technique.

Block tackling is a basic tackle in which both players lock their ankles and use the insides of their feet as barriers. The player who enters the tackle in the most balanced position and with the most strength almost always wins possession of the ball. Balance, though, is often more important than strength.

It is crucial to emphasize leaning the body over the ball and not shying away or leaning back. Quick foot speed is also important to become proficient at winning block tackles when the ball is not won immediately.

BLOCK TACKLE

A block tackle is made with the inside of the foot and is won by the player with the most balanced position. As the tackle is made, both players move forward over the ball, using the momentum and weight of their bodies to win the ball. Bending the knees gives greater stability. Eyes should remain focused on the ball. After the tackle, it is crucial to use quick foot movement to gain possession of the ball.

tactics

The instinctive reaction of a beginner is, "I see the ball. I go for the ball." Her intent when she kicks the ball is simple: Send it in the direction of the opponent's goal. She doesn't envision the resulting consequences or play out the scenario of anything beyond immediately racing to and kicking the ball.

With tactics at the intermediate level, players are taught to combine skills with deliberate actions to outsmart and outmaneuver the opposition and ultimately score goals. They should also be taught how to make good decisions and think about the consequences of actions.

In order to accomplish this, players must be able to do basic skills. Secondly, as children continue to develop a wider repertoire of skills, they need a better understanding of soccer rules. Some of the finer points can be left to a later time, but the mechanics of the game should be covered in greater detail at this level. Children should know when and how to do a throw-in and understand the offside rule in their league. They should have an understanding of kickoffs, free kicks, penalty kicks, goal kicks, and corner kicks, and why they are awarded. The goal is not to reveal every tactical possibility associated with a skill or action, but to introduce the concept of tactics and the basic ones for each skill or situation.

Following is an example of how to teach the tactical use of a throw-in at this level. A throw-in is used to continue the game after the ball has crossed either sideline. An opponent of the team who

coach's corner

When I was about 10 years old, I spent every spare minute hanging out with the Colchester United Football Club, the professional soccer team in my hometown in England. I was the official cleat-cleaner, laundry boy, ball boy, and tea-and-sandwich-maker of the team—tasks that I performed with the utmost enthusiasm.

My heart raced as the young professionals finished their formal practice session, and I waited in anticipation for an invitation to join them for a game of juggling tennis. In this game, played with singles or doubles, the players juggled back and forth across a net or bench.

At first, the players selected me only if they needed a fourth to round out the teams. Eventually, after two or three years, I was chosen to play because of my skills. Just as I was in awe of the juggling skills of those players, children today are impressed and spurred when they watch good jugglers.

Juggling is used to hone close control and to fine-tune touch. It can also be very intimidating for the opposition to see a team confidently warming up by juggling well. Juggling gives a player the confidence to deal with the ball in any situation.

touched the ball last takes the throw-in. The object is to maximize territorial gain while ensuring that a teammate can gain possession from the throw.

A player should collect the ball and get into position as quickly as possible after the ball goes out of bounds in order to take advantage of teammates who might be breaking away toward the goal. The ball must be thrown from over the head with both hands on it, and it must be released immediately after passing the front of the head. Both feet must always be in contact with the ground, although either or both feet may be dragged as long as one toe remains on the ground. Both feet must remain on or behind the sideline, and no twisting of the body is allowed to propel the ball farther.

While a throw-in has a large number of tactical possibilities, for the elementary tactics taught at this level, a player should be encouraged to:

- Scan the field while collecting the ball.
- Look for an open teammate.
- Throw the ball quickly, to keep the opposition off balance.
- Throw the ball down the line (parallel to and close to the sideline). This results in the greatest territorial gain.
- Throw the ball so that it is easy for a teammate to control.

THROW-IN

Place the ball as far as possible behind the head. Most children tend to hold it above the head, causing a late release. Fingers should be spread to maintain control of the ball. Players can either place the feet as shown, or stand with them parallel, shoulder-width apart. Parts of both feet must remain on the ground at all times.

- Fake throwing the ball to one player before throwing to another to confuse the opposition.

Decision making. In soccer, a player should always make a decision with one of two goals in mind: Either gain or retain possession of the ball and move it to the player who has the best chance to score, or prevent the other team from scoring. Decision making means deliberately controlling and moving the ball with a view to reaching one of these two ends. Good decision making comes from confidence acquired through possessing a range of skills.

After a child has been playing for a couple of years, it is reasonable to expect her to be comfortable controlling a ball that comes her way. Once this is accomplished, the next big step is for her to learn what to do with the ball. The tendency for a newcomer at this level is to lower her head and run at full steam while dribbling the ball, resulting in what can be described as the battering ram approach. The dribbling, and possession, usually ends when an opponent merely stands in the way.

Using a variety of skills that are honed at this level, a child should be able to make short passes to open players to avoid tackles. Parents and coaches tend to cheer players who can kick long distances; many times, the more constructive approach is for players to move the ball up the field with a series of short passes.

It is crucial to stress and compliment good close ball control and subsequent distribution of the ball. A common phrase used by knowledgeable parents and coaches is, "Let the ball do the work." This means that a well-passed ball will get to its destination far quicker than a ball would with a player dribbling it there.

MOM'S VIEW

Parents sometimes mistakenly assume that a point they're trying to get across to their child is always understood by the child. My mistaken assumption came when my older daughter was 11. On and off, for nearly a year, her coaches had gently tried to break her of the habit of occasionally flinching when the ball came to her. She was continually encouraged to be "more aggressive." Here and there, she would mix it up with the opposition, but basically, the habit remained.

One day, I decided to bring it up to her, which, as a parent and not her coach or teammate, I had always been reluctant to do. "Did you understand what the coach was saying to you about flinching from the ball?" We had all assumed she understood what was so clear to us.

In airing the matter, two issues became apparent. First of all, my daughter was able to admit, and thus face, a fear. It turns out that she had been hit hard in the stomach by the ball in her first year of play. Second, to my surprise, she had no idea what was being asked of her. "What do 'flinch,' 'aggressive,' and 'timid' mean?" she asked. "I would do anything the coach asked of me," she said loyally, but in understandable frustration over the abstract concepts.

After our talk, I went directly to the coach and explained the problem. I requested that he guide her and show her what was required. He gladly complied. Her habit of flinching immediately disappeared. A new chapter opened in my daughter's soccer career, and I had an invaluable lesson in parent-child communication.

For the most part, though, a child's focus is heavily consumed by whether or not she can control the ball. Suffice it to say, subsequent passing will be difficult, and patience is of the utmost importance.

Ideally, players should look around before they receive the ball, in order to assess their situation. While field awareness should be introduced at the intermediate level, it will more likely be developed at a higher level.

To foster decision making, have your child practice the important habit of looking up while in possession of the ball. You can challenge your child by asking her to tell you how many fingers you are holding up while she is dribbling.

Fluidity of position. No matter what position a player starts at in a game, she can play any other position as the situation dictates. Fluidity of position means that players can find themselves on any area of the field at any given moment. A well-organized team knows how to have players cover one another in various situations. For example, every player can try to score a goal and every player can and should help defend. On the professional level, positions, and the tasks associated with them, often blend and change, depending on the situation. The development of this fluidity should start at the intermediate level, with players being encouraged to move about the field.

To enhance your child's grasp of this concept, make sure that the coach plays her in a variety of positions, including goalkeeper. This allows her to develop the experience and confidence to be an integral part of the game. If a player can select the appropriate skill or action for each position and execute each efficiently and effectively, then she will be comfortable in both offensive and defensive situations.

Players who lack this knowledge and confidence will typically stay away from the action. This behavior is referred to as hiding on the field.

Jockeying (or shadowing). Jockeying requires a player to pressure the ball carrier in an attempt to force her into making a mistake. This is done by staying close to the opponent without tackling her, and simply watching the ball and waiting until it moves out away from the player in possession, and moves within easy striking distance.

A frequent action of inexperienced players is to rush at an opponent who has the ball, in an attempt to take possession of it. This is not always the prudent approach, as the opponent will likely pass or move in the opposite direction, leaving the pursuer flat-footed (at a standstill). In a situation like this, it is important to emphasize patience. Players should only attempt to get the ball or tackle a player when the opponent makes a dribbling mistake or a poor pass.

Holding up the ball. As a player develops, she should acquire better decision-making skills, which are used when receiving the ball, protecting it from defenders, and making wise decisions regarding its subsequent use ("Do I pass, shoot, dribble, or continue to hold up the ball?"). Holding up the ball means to control it by keeping it close to the feet, and it is part of the entire decision-making process. It is the next stage of development after shielding, which is physically keeping an opponent away from the ball. The decision now becomes one of what to do once the opponent has been held off. Holding up the ball is a difficult, but essential, skill to acquire at this level.

Holding up the ball can be done with the player's back or front to the defender. It is more likely, however, that her back will be to the defender because once she is facing her, she is more likely to be tackled. A crucial element of holding up the ball is learning to sense the whereabouts of teammates and opponents by looking around and keeping her hands out to feel who is around her.

competition

With the introduction of competition at this level, the emotional stakes get raised. This is the time when all the niceties of playing to have fun can get replaced by the fierce desire to improve and to win. Ideally, at this level, fierce competitiveness should be minimized. Your child, however, will experience competition in organized games. In this case, the tone and model set by the coaches and parents is of the utmost importance.

It is likely that at the intermediate level, your child will encounter her first selection process. That is, she will try out to make a team. Explain what this means, and then ask her if she wants to try out. Children should be prepared emotionally for the possibility of failure by recognizing that no matter how they do, they will have a team to play on and they can have fun. Make sure that you understand what this commitment means in terms of time and money, and whether you, too, are able and willing to make it.

CHAPTER 9

advanced

FOUR TO SIX YEARS OF EXPERIENCE

If your child is at this level, you have surely been watching—and living with—a lot of youth soccer. You've probably experienced every weather condition, your child's "need" to have the "hottest" pair of cleats, the tears of a loss, and the joy of a win. But for everything that parents have experienced and understood, few of them are able to keep pace with the intricacies of the game, which are quite extensive at this level of play. Whether or not you realize it, your child has probably evolved into a well-skilled player of a fast-paced, complicated game of youth soccer.

At the advanced level, some basics are a given. A player should be well-schooled in all aspects of practice and game preparation. He will know how to dress and prepare, how to conduct himself on the field, and how to warm up and cool down. Most important, he will be capable of at least attempting, if not properly executing, all of the basic skills and tactics learned at lower levels.

After this many years of play, ability can vary significantly. The ability and motivation gap between recreational play and play that is based on tryouts is often very noticeable at this level. This occurs for a variety of reasons, including self-discipline, commitment, and innate talent. No matter what the level, some children are just more interested in soccer than others.

A major contributing factor to the level of youth interest and ability is coaching. By this time, players have likely been exposed to a variety of coaching styles and levels of quality, from the novice parent volunteer to the highly qualified professional (most likely at a soccer camp). Clearly, good experiences with coaches are an important stepping stone in getting a young person to the advanced level.

It is important to recognize that a player of this level needs to be self-motivated. For the commitment required at this point, he has to be. Soccer often means twice-weekly practices and one or more games on the weekend. Here are some indicators of self-motivation in a player.

- Takes unstructured time to focus on developing individual soccer skills
- Prepares his soccer equipment for practices and games
- Is conscious of practice and game schedules and is concerned about arriving on time

- Can appreciate that in both practices and games he will have to, and want to, push himself both mentally and physically
- Can bounce back and motivate himself after a loss or when faced with a challenge such as developing a difficult skill
- Speaks with enthusiasm and displays other signs of interest and excitement in the sport

the skills

Because of their experience from extensive practice and play, advanced players are able to select from a wide variety of skills and, for the most part, execute them successfully. Just as on other levels, however, not every skill can be acquired at once. In a good system, there is a learning hierarchy. That is, new, increasingly difficult skills are added after more basic skills have been mastered, with the understanding that performing these new skills will take time and practice.

Passing. Advanced passing skills, such as a back-heel pass, chest pass, or outside-of-the-foot pass, are regarded by many as the more "glamorous" skills in soccer. In order to do these skills, a player has to learn them by breaking them down. In every step, the ultimate goal is to gain control. For example, in order to do a chest pass, a player has to master chest control. Children steer away from this skill for fear of pain of catching the ball in the wrong place. Chest control should be introduced gradually and gently. Allow your child to control the ball by serving it to himself–gently tossing the ball in the air. A player progresses from control to passing by learning which angles the ball moves off the chest as he twists and turns his trunk.

The beauty of these "trick" passes is that when used at the appropriate time, they can be devastating to the opposition, largely because they are unexpected.

As children become more advanced, their passing is executed less by luck and more by deliberate judgment. Coinciding with this development, players also have

CHEST CONTROL

The object of this move is to stop and control an incoming ball. It is crucial to offer the maximum surface of the chest. Arms should be out for balance and the eyes kept open. The angle pictured here will cause the ball to pop up and fall at the feet. This angle is used when there is minimal pressure from an opponent. Changing the angle of the upper body will bring the ball down at different points.

a wider variety of skills, such as being able to to execute more turns, passes, and shots. All of these skills together enable players to pass the ball at various angles, distances, and speeds and to teammates closely guarded by opponents. In almost any place on the field, in any position, advanced players are able to select some form of pass, enabling them to dig themselves out of more difficult situations.

Players recognize that the ball can be passed not only forward but also sideways and backward, and with various parts of the feet. Players are also taught to pass with parts of the body other than the feet, such as the head or chest. While passing with body parts was introduced at an earlier level, it is at this stage that players actually use the passing effectively.

Dribbling. Advanced players dribble with intent, as opposed to the novice or intermediate player, who may use dribbling because there seems to be no other option. Players at this level dribble naturally, with the ball under control and without looking at their feet in order to perform.

The secret of good dribbling is knowing when and when not to do it. Less-skilled players may be able to dribble but often are uncertain about when to pass the ball. Instead, they typically dribble until they lose possession because of a mistake or from an opponent's pressure.

Advanced players can dribble in ways that are extremely elusive to defenders by keeping the ball on either foot, whichever is the furthest distance from the defenders. And they can do this under pressure.

Feints, or deceptive moves meant to fake out an opponent, are honed at this level now that players can dribble effectively. One such feint is the stutter step, where the player who is dribbling puts his foot on top of the ball as if he is going to stop it and then flicks his foot over the top of the ball, causing the defender to hesitate. The player then kicks the ball forward with the laces and sprints past the opponent.

Ball distribution and frequent passing are essential concepts that need to be emphasized and employed at the advanced level. Younger players typically overdribble because they get caught up in their footwork and believe that they're contributing the most when they're moving with the ball. Advanced players should realize that they can contribute to the team effort even when they don't have the ball.

Turns. Skilled dribblers have a unique advantage when they are able to add turns, feints (deceptive moves meant to fake out an opponent), or dummies (a run by a person without the ball to draw defenders away from the ball handler) to their dribbling. Often, this allows them to create an extra yard of space or an extra moment of time. With this extra space or time, they can draw upon turns learned at earlier levels. They should now be able to quickly and effectively draw upon these as needed as well as develop more technical and difficult turns at this level.

One turn learned by an advanced player is the stepover, a feint in which a player kicks one way, then moves his other leg over the ball to kick it back the other way and turn in a new direction. The Maradonna turn, named after Diego Maradonna, the famous player from Argentina, is another one.

Shooting. Across the soccer fields of the world, the big kid who is able to put

coach's corner

Fancy footwork is one of the beauties of the game. Just as in dance, soccer has its famous "choreographers." At least two of them created popular turns, which now bear their names. One of these is the Dutch master Johan Cruyff, who brought his trademark footwork, and his now-famous turn, to light in the 1974 World Cup final.

Cruyff's performance was without a doubt the defining moment of the day, as commentators, players, and spectators were stunned by his new move, which involved redirecting the ball so fast that it faked out oncoming opponents. On the days following his game, my mates and I couldn't stop talking about Cruyff's amazing turns.

Another player famous for his now-standard move is Diego Maradonna of Argentina, known simply as the Maradonna. In the 1986 World Cup, he wreaked havoc on the English team with his talents and his acrobatic turn that combines stepping backward on the ball and spinning. His move, and Cruyff's, are now taught to youth soccer players around the world.

Like Michael Jordan in basketball, these two players have added a new dimension to the game of soccer. The "Cruyff" and the "Maradonna" are now part of soccer's vocabulary.

A move seen in the 1998 World Cup is the Blanco, performed by Cuauhtemoc Blanco, a player from Mexico. He baffled the opposition by picking up the ball between both of his feet and moving it forward by jumping into the air with it.

the ball over a tiny goalkeeper's head is cheered and idolized. But the player who places the ball into the corner of the goal, away from the keeper, is the true hero. One day, that tiny goalkeeper will no longer be tiny, and blasting the ball over his head will not be an option.

Advanced players usually encounter goalkeepers of significant size, so the simple strategy of overpowering the keeper is not an option. At this level, players should be making deliberate shooting decisions requiring both skill and choice of strategic location instead of just booting the ball toward the goal. The rule of thumb for advanced shooting is simple: Shoot wherever the goalkeeper isn't. This usually is low and close to the goalposts.

When advanced players find themselves in one-on-one situations with the goalkeeper, they should calmly be able to make the appropriate decision about where to shoot and not panic as lesser-skilled players often do.

Surprise is often a good technique at this level to find the gap that is necessary to score. For example, taking the ball out of the air with a side volley is preferable to letting the ball go to the ground before striking it. A side volley increases the speed of executing the shot and thus decreases the goalkeeper's reaction time.

SIDE VOLLEY

This is a one-touch shot that is very powerful. The ball is struck with the laces of the shoe. The ball should be hit in the middle to upper area to keep it down, and it should be struck lower to get it up high. The upper body acts as a spinning top. The right arm is pulled back as far as possible, and then it swings forward as the right foot kicks the ball. The head is kept still, with eyes on the ball. This also prevents overrotation. The non-kicking foot can remain on the ground or can be airborne.

Heading. Advanced players consciously move one of the most fragile parts of the body toward a moving object. At earlier levels, when players make a rare attempt at heading, they allow the ball to hit their heads and hope for the best. Advanced players break up opponents' plays, make planned passes, and even shoot on goal with headers.

There are usually other players vying for the ball at the same time, and there is jumping, twisting, turning, and scraping occurring at the same time. When all of this is considered, you can appreciate why players even at the highest levels sometimes choose not to head the ball.

At this level, players should be able to divert the ball with their heads, head it sideways and backward, jump and head, deliberately pass with the head, and score a goal by heading.

Players should be introduced to the diving header at this level. It's important with this move to do it wholeheartedly. This is for the players' safety. If done half-heartedly, players could fall on their faces or shoulders as opposed to being cushioned by their hands and arms.

Tackling. Along with learning when to dribble and when to pass, advanced players learn when to tackle (a defensive technique using the feet to take the ball away from an opponent). Players begin to make decisions about whether or not to tackle rather than simply going for the ball at every opportunity.

Players should now be less reactionary and more proactive in their tackling. Whereas at the previous levels, the result of a tackle was usually not thought through, advanced players tackle with a view to achieving a specific result, such as winning possession or clearing the ball out of bounds. For example, if a player has lost the ball, a last-ditch method of getting the ball away or regaining possession is the slide tackle. (It isn't just used to gain possession; it can also be used just to kick the ball away.) It takes incredible timing and bravery. If he misses, he not only looks foolish but he also takes himself out of the play. However, a well-executed slide tackle is akin to a well-executed pickpocketing job. It's clean, and you're gone before the player even knows you were there.

Shadowing. The art of dealing with an opposing player when he has the ball by containing him is known as shadowing, jockeying, holding him up, or standing him up. Often, this looks like two players at a standstill—one with the ball and one without, simply waiting or moving together. In either case, the player is either waiting for the ball carrier to make a mistake or attempting to force him to do so.

An advanced player should know which is the preferred side of the player he is marking (defending). He figures this out by watching the opponent in the first few minutes of the game. Armed with this knowledge, he can force the adversary into using his weaker foot. This invariably means approaching the opponent, or de-

DIVING HEADER

Although this move is rarely used in youth soccer, it is highly effective because it is so unexpected. The arms should be extended, with fingers splayed, so that the impact on the ground is spread out. The eyes on the ball automatically bring the head up. The ball should always be hit on the forehead, and the mouth should be closed upon impact.

SLIDE TACKLE

A slide tackle should be done as a last resort by a player. It can be used to poke the ball away or gain possession, which is what the photo is demonstrating. Here, the left arm and left leg are the springs to push the player up after the tackle. The object of this tackle is to use the outstretched foot to hook the ball behind and out of the path of the opponent, spring up, and gain possession of the ball.

fending him, on the side of his stronger foot. This is an advanced skill because a player has to worry about himself and also dictate what the other player does.

In advanced defending, a player rarely defends as an individual. He is hopefully on an advanced team, which defends as a team instead of as 11 individuals, and is part of a defensive strategy such as low or high pressure or doubling up on certain players.

tactics

The most important realization that an advanced player makes is seeing that space and time become increasingly compressed. With more highly skilled, more physically fit players on the field, the game is much faster. Even a casual spectator can see this. Decision making occurs faster. Players have to know what is going to happen after they get the ball, and they must have assessed their surroundings before the ball arrives. A player's close control and passing has to be much better because he has less time to execute his skills.

With a better understanding of the game's skills and rules comes the ability to grasp more advanced tactics. The difference between advanced players and intermediate ones is that while the latter may understand basic tactics, the advanced players attempt and often succeed in using them. What's more, although they may often be given instructions by a coach, advanced players can develop and alter some of these tactics on their own.

On the advanced level, players start thinking two or three moves ahead. For example, while a less-skilled player makes a corner kick with the hope of just kicking the ball, an advanced player can often place that corner kick in a tactical position, with a view toward how both his team and the opposition will respond.

Making a drop, or back, pass is a common tactic at the advanced level. A player passes to an open teammate, but in the direction of his own goal. Although the direction of the ball is away from the opposition's goal, the player knows that to avoid losing possession, he must both get rid of the ball and find an open teammate. Often, the ball is best moved backward in order to eventually move it forward again.

Rules of the game. Advanced players

should know the majority of the rules of the game. However, the rarely used plays or rules may be blurred or unfamiliar. These are learned as they occur, often after more years of experience. A very serious player should consider taking a referee training course (usually offered to those age 12 or over; call your local soccer club for more information). Not only will he have an even better grasp of the game's rules but a licensed referee is able to get a job working games and earn some money.

Systems of play. It is likely at this level that players will be introduced to systems of play, in which they are aligned around the field for various reasons. A defensive system of play, for example, might mean that a team has only one or two attackers. A more offensive approach might have three or more attackers stay in the opponent's half of the field. Systems of play are very much a part of a soccer player's lingo.

There are essentially three areas of the soccer field: defense, midfield, and offense, within which a coach can play any of his on-field players at any time for any purpose. The way players are aligned in these areas is referred to by a set of numbers, such as 4, 4, 2 or 4, 3, 3. The first number is the number of defenders, the second is the number of midfielders, and the third is the number of forwards. Different alignments are set up to counter an opponent's style of play, to allow a team to play to its own strengths, to cover absences caused by injuries, or even because a coach favors a certain philosophy of play.

In addition to players knowing their tasks, positions, and responsibilities, a system of play is when an entire team understands what will happen at certain stages of the game, and all act to ensure that the system is carried out. The number of players that can be committed to an attack, for example, or how a team will defend (high pressure, low pressure) are elements of systems of play. The most elementary part of system of play is the alignment (4, 4, 2, for example). System of play is how you use that alignment.

Some coaches and aficionados of the game put a great deal of emphasis on alignments. These strategies are discussed as if they are secret formulas to success. But a good program should not get too hung up on alignment because it is too rigid. A good program is based on complete fluidity, with players un-

WHY BASICS ARE SO IMPORTANT

Adults often wonder how their children acquire such complicated skills as the Cruyff or Maradonna turns. To understand, you have to go back to the beginner level and consider the games that concentrated on mastering simple spins, turns, and ball control. At that stage, learning a simple spin of the body or jump seems like a mystery to many parents. "What on earth does that have to do with soccer?" is a common question. But dissect the Maradonna, for example, and it becomes clear. It is nothing more than a sequence of simple spins and turns. Put the spin, the turn, and the feet on the ball all together, and they become the Maradonna.

coach's corner

As players advance, it is likely that their skills and knowledge will outstrip that of most coaches. When this happens, the ability of a coach to recognize his own limitations and his changing role is crucial. At the advanced level, the coach should be working together with the players, not above them. The futile attempts of a coach to try to outdo or excessively control experienced players will ultimately be counterproductive. You'll know that this is happening if the coach becomes highly authoritative, controlling, or defensive.

The best coach at this level is someone who is aware of his limitations yet continues to be supportive at every juncture and allows better-skilled players and those with mature attitudes to become more influential among their peers.

derstanding that they can move all around the field. Besides, it is the basic skills—passing, ball control, shooting—that determine success, and those should not be underestimated in favor of where the players are aligned on the field.

This does not mean that systems of play have no function. Putting a team in basic alignment allows the players to understand their primary responsibilities on the field. But advanced players understand that while they are defined by a position, they are not limited to it. They are, in fact, responsible for everything.

The same holds true for styles of play, such as Brazilian (known for intricate passing and a more deliberate approach) or English (fast-paced and furious). Many people quote these styles as part of a team's character of play. But in youth soccer, these are rigid designations that are inappropriate for the versatility that young players require. Children who are pigeonholed into a certain style of play will become too focused on staying true to the style and will lose the versatility required of a fast-changing game. The education of a young player should include exposure to all styles of play.

Set plays. A tactical aspect of soccer that usually is not practiced enough is set plays. A set play is when a stoppage in play—which results in a penalty kick, free kick, corner kick, kickoff, goal kick, or a throw-in—results in one team having 100 percent control over what happens next. This enables a team to use deception in

MOM'S VIEW

Your child eats, breathes, and sleeps soccer. Sometimes you wonder how there are enough hours in the day for him to do his homework, have other interests, and just plain relax and be a kid.

This scenario is not uncommon at the higher levels. While we respect our daughters' love and devotion to soccer (particularly our older daughter, who is very serious), we have come up with the following steps to try to take the edge off the intensity in our household.

Move on to other things. Whether it is games, practices, or tryouts, from the moment we get into the car, we purposely do not talk about the soccer session unless our girls specifically want to talk about it. Usually, they do not.

Do activities outside of soccer. While on lower levels of play, family participation is encouraged (developing skills with "homework"), on the advanced level, there are often more than enough family soccer activities, such as traveling to tournaments and games and trying out for teams. We deliberately try to devote some family time outside of soccer. This may include walks, playing basketball, going to the movies, or doing art projects. We also encourage our children to build a social network with teammates outside of playing soccer.

Find a mentor or peers. From the moment we realized that our older daughter had talent and strong interest, we sought out the experts to guide her. This was not done casually or randomly. We had several conferences with one coach in particular we felt was knowledgeable and supportive, and we stated our request that he actively guide her—and us.

Keep soccer in perspective. After every high and low moment, win, or loss, we remind ourselves and our children that this is only part of our lives. Every moment has its meaning, yet it is only one of a long line of soccer—and life—experiences, all of which challenge our children and help them prosper and grow.

Believe in the statement, "I love you for who you are, not what you do." This is the phrase that I often repeat to my children. While their soccer accomplishments are wonderful, who each of them is as a total person is why I love them.

addition to skills to gain an advantage on the defensive team. One example is with corner kicks, where a ball may be played to a specific area of the goal. A set play is not just the play itself; it is the strategy you use with it.

Although soccer strategy, or focus, often does not seem to center on set plays, they are crucial aspects of the game. According to Charles Hughes, author of *Soccer Tactics and Teamwork*, at every level of the game, almost 50 percent of goals originate from set plays.

Although the sideline talk, or coach's comments, may turn to mention of "4, 4, 2 versus 4, 3, 3" or styles of play, the experienced spectator knows to look for a team's coordinated, fluid movement, with a lot of communication between the players and well-choreographed set plays.

commitment

This is the stage at which many children are caught in a quandary: whether to participate in other sports or activities or focus solely on soccer. If a child is a gifted athlete, there is often pressure from coaches of other sports for them to play. This does not even take into account the various social and academic pressures that can add to the mix.

Parents should talk with their children about this dilemma as well as watch for and listen to the many less obvious signs of unhappiness such as less smiling and a drop in the level of excitement about soccer. Children will usually try to please their parents, whether or not parents encourage it. After all, children get attention when they do well. What's more, parents of advanced players are often very intense, understandably caught up in the activity that occupies such a large part of their children's lives.

A good advanced-level soccer program is run by coaches and administrators who understand the diversity in children's lives. Beware of the coach who insists on sport specificity. Children need diversity. For some, this may be another sport or reading or music or many other things. Besides, focusing just on soccer could be a recipe for disappointment. Only a small number of players make it to college-level play or beyond. On the other hand, if your child shows interest only in soccer, nurture it. It is better to do one activity than none.

Keep in mind that advanced-level play is a serious commitment. Parents must understand that issues such as failure to attend practices and games have ramifications on an entire team. Parents and their children should use time management to ensure that there are no conflicts.

CHAPTER 10

expert

SIX-PLUS YEARS OF EXPERIENCE

Though the title of this chapter is "Expert," that word can be deceiving when used with youth soccer. While expert youth players are highly skilled, they are not as skilled as professional or college players. For our purposes, a soccer expert is best defined as a high school player. While she may be better than most of her opponents, she still has a lot to learn.

Progress at this level is different than at other levels. An expert player has been practicing the majority of soccer skills for several years, and at this level, she is honing those skills. The new skills that she learns now, however, are learned quickly because she already possesses a wide repertoire of skills. Many of the new skills are variations of ones that she already knows.

At the expert level, there is also an increased need for a high level of physical fitness. The difference between a good and a great expert player is conditioning. These players are all technically proficient, but the ones who stand out as the best are those who make the fewest mistakes. Since mistakes often occur because of fatigue, it stands to reason that the player who is best conditioned has an important advantage.

The greatest expert players have the best "inner workings." That is, they are mentally and emotionally tough and supremely confident. In turn, these players' effectiveness is expressed in the context of a good team. A great player is a team player. She may become the play maker or she may be a leader on the field. In short, all of her abilities contribute to the good of the team.

This is the level at which the impact of a team plays a great part in superior play. The sum of the parts is greater than the individual pieces. While a young player may have desire, it is a good team that helps her get the most out of herself. When coupled with good skills, the "heart" of the team (desire and drive) is what can make the crucial difference.

It's beyond the ability of most parents to teach skills at this stage, but you can still ensure that your child's soccer experience is positive and the best possible one for developing her as a player. Vigilance is especially important at this level, when the competition has higher stakes, and peer pressure can be particularly hard on an adolescent. A good program is run by a coach who incorporates solid teaching

MORE THAN JUST SKILLS

An expert-level player has spent years developing and perfecting her skills. Here is what makes an expert-level player so much better than less-experienced players.

An expert-level player:

- Has a willingness to attempt any and all skills, with successful execution at a significantly high rate
- Creates adequate time to execute skills by virtue of having excellent ball control and experience
- Is able to deal with the ball in any and all situations while remaining calm and composed
- Is able to create situations prior to receiving the ball that will make dealing with the ball a relatively easier task
- Uses both feet adeptly
- Uses fewer touches, makes more accurate passes, and strikes the ball harder and with more control than players on previous levels
- Controls all balls with appropriate body parts
- Is much faster and more physical than players on previous levels
- Has significant knowledge of the game to include rules, tactics, and strategy
- Knows how to train and prepare for competition for maximum effort and results
- Is more likely to play soccer as her only sport
- Is probably looking to continue playing in college

An expert-level team:

- Uses preorganized and practiced tactics and set plays
- Can draw upon a variety of options in terms of styles and strategies
- Can self-adjust by swapping positions in midplay to confuse, or to adapt to, the opposition
- Understands the concept of defending a lead by either stalling to run down the clock or strengthening the defense to prevent a score
- Has an athletic goalkeeper who uses a variety of distribution techniques instead of just punting the ball away every time; an expert-level goalkeeper is often in a leadership role, using her ability to view the game to shout encouragement and instructions to her teammates
- Understands the difference between rigidity and flexibility of positions and puts the concept of flexibility into practice

and coaching concepts and keeps the game fun. It is also essential that the coach is knowledgeable and experienced enough to guide serious players. A good coach at this level keeps track of the latest schools of thought on high-level play. Coaches of expert players should have higher-level licenses, such as the U.S. Soccer Federation A, B, or C licenses.

coach's corner

Players reach the expert level in the United States through a much different route than their European counterparts. But it is likely just a matter of time before they head down parallel paths.

There is no substitute for watching and emulating the game. Where I grew up, it was natural that young players would attempt to do what they had seen on television or in stadiums. And everybody did that, with very few exceptions. For young people all over Europe, this experience is the same.

There is an extensive structured youth system in England. It is set up systematically, from best to worst. You know exactly where you stand. You are either on the top of the ladder or working to move up. But the point is, there is always somewhere for you to go. There are more than 90 professional teams and thousands of semiprofessional teams, all of which sponsor youth soccer teams. Then there are the scores of club teams, with no professional or semiprofessional affiliation, that provide playing opportunities for youth.

In the United States, the delineation is not so clear, and casual play is far rarer. There are national, state, and regional teams and recreational programs. Their numbers are growing every year. But American culture is not saturated with the game as it is in England. There are relatively few top role models in the United States for young people to emulate, and the percentage of participating youth in America is not as high as in England. But in time, it surely will be. England at roughly 60 million people cannot compare with the potential of 260 million Americans. Slowly but surely, young Americans are watching soccer on television and honing their skills on playgrounds and fields across the country.

the skills

At this level, players have been taught, and should have mastered, all basic skills. You will not see many new skills being introduced, and most of these are high-level additions to previously taught skills. You will see an awareness of conditions that affect play. From the effects of foul weather to a wet ball to the height of grass and the field's inclines, an expert player will know how to adjust her play to these conditions.

The primary focus of training for an expert is on mastering the ability to choose and execute the most appropriate skill for every situation. Choosing which of her many skills to use does not come automatically. She now has the ability to select more dynamic skills, such as a scissors kick, nutmeg (passing the ball between an opposing player's legs), diving header, volley, and a variety of other moves. The best players at this level quickly become adept at choosing the best skill to handle every situation.

Passing. Pinpoint accuracy can be expected the majority of the time. Players will have numerous skills to draw on for every situation. One such skill is the swerve pass, which is commonly known as the banana. This is a common pass, or shot, at this level, and is used as a method of bending the ball into the path of a teammate, or to avoid an opponent. Off the foot, all balls look the same. But with a swerve, what looks like a ball that will go straight turns into a ball that curves.

The swerve can be hit with both the inside and the outside of the foot. The more difficult pass is the outside-of-the-foot. The outside-of-right- and inside-of-left-foot swerve passes give the ball the same curving motion. The swerve pass can be used for short distances. As a result, minimal approach needs to be taken and, therefore, deception is maximized.

Shooting. Goalkeepers improve steadily over the years just like their field teammates. With that, the window of scoring success is much smaller than at lower levels. Therefore, accuracy, shot selection, and execution must all be improved upon and given quick but thorough consideration when shooting.

Volleys. A volley is the act of striking (kicking) a ball while it is in the air. Any time the ball is struck after a quick bounce, it is called a half-volley. Both of these moves require good control, but

SWERVE PASS

This is a deception move. Although the ball is struck in a way that it appears to go forward, it is actually being hit by the outside of the foot on the inside of the ball. This causes it to swerve, or curve. The shot pictured shows the pass that will send the ball heading to the right. After kicking, the kicking leg then follows through and crosses the front of the body.

the half-volley is especially difficult. When hit properly, though, a half-volley is one of the most powerful shots in soccer. You can see goalkeepers use this skill to punt, in which they kick the ball using the laces, in order to send it low and long to clear the goal area.

The bicycle and scissors kicks are two extraordinary moves, in which the legs make the motions of the objects that their names describe while kicking the ball in midair. The bicycle is performed heels over head with a player finishing rolling on her back. The scissors is performed with the body parallel to the ground, with the player finishing by landing on her side. They are chosen because the ball arrives at the player at a height and speed that prevent the selection of any other type of shot. On the ground, she can chip it (loft it high into the air) or kick it, but when a ball arrives at certain portions of the upper body, this is not possible. This still leaves the option of the head or the chest, but these passes often don't generate enough required power.

Anytime you're throwing your body around, there is an element of danger. Players should avoid these moves in overly crowded situations (for fear of landing on others) and should never attempt them without first experiencing these moves with extensive practice. The best way to practice is on a crash mat. In order to avoid danger, each element of the move should be broken down in practice.

SCISSORS KICK

The nonkicking leg gives power to the kicking leg by whipping forward and then back, as the kicking leg moves back and then forward (scissoring). The ball must be struck with the shoe's laces, in the center to the top, to keep it down if shooting. If clearing the ball out of your defensive zone, and thus wanting it to go high, the ball is struck below midline. The player uses his arms for balance and to cushion his landing. (The lower arm braces the landing.)

BICYCLE KICK

The player powers off the ground with the kicking leg. The legs spin like the motion of legs on a bicycle. The kicking leg (right leg in the photo) will send the ball over the head. The arms should be held out for balance. They also propel the player up and cushion the landing (on his back).

Sliding. On the expert level, you will see more sliding along the ground. This is done to extend a player's reach, often in a last-ditch move on the ball. A player can slide to poke a ball into the goal if she's close enough, to keep the ball in bounds, or to tackle another player when outrunning her is no longer possible. The latter requires expert timing and runs the risk of committing a foul if she takes out the player and not the ball.

Trickery and one-touch play. Skills are now done more quickly, with more control and a higher success rate than before. You will see a profusion of feints, dummies, and general "trickery." Another feature at this level is one-touch play. Because a player knows where she will send the ball even before it arrives, she is ready to pass with one touch, as opposed to stopping the ball, controlling it, then passing it on. She is better able to ensure that her passes arrive at a teammate at the appropriate speed and time so that the ball can be dealt with appropriately. She is also better at judging an incoming ball's velocity, spin, and bounce so that she can play it successfully.

On-field communication. Youth soccer fields in this country are characterized by their silence. But soccer is not meant to be a quiet game. A boisterous field of play is a sign of a well-trained team. Teammates yelling to each other is an integral part of the entire package needed to be successful.

Expert players talk often and loudly, calling for the ball, instructing as well as encouraging their teammates. They use praise as part of the team effort. An expert delivers specific information to a teammate who might be unaware of an oncoming opponent ("Man on!") or a developing play ("Drop back!"). The emphasis for talking on the field should be on volume. This is not the place or time for whispering. Hand signals are also an important method of communicating.

tactics

At the expert level, coaches and players are not only conscious of their own skills but of the skills of the opposition, which eventually define a team's tactics. For example, a team with less speed will need to ensure that their close-control skills are strong, and they will need to choose passes and methods of attack that do not expose them to situations where footraces are required. Another example is a team with a tall center forward. This team is far more likely to employ a high- or long-ball tactic (using her height by playing the ball to her head rather than her feet) and must ensure that her attacking teammates are close to this player to receive her passes.

Expert play includes some new tactics and also further refinement of ones seen at lower levels.

Offside trap. The offside trap is a tactic in which defenders position themselves to cause attacking opponents to be caught in an offside position when the ball is struck. Any attacker, when in the opponent's half of the field, must have at least two opponents (one of whom can be the goalkeeper) between herself and the goal line when the ball is struck forward. Offside results when this is violated. The offside trap is when defenders anticipate when the attackers will strike the ball forward, and move forward before the ball is struck, thus leaving the attacker standing in an offside position. This tactic relies heavily on timing and coordination by the defense

coach's corner

Some youth soccer teams believe in rotating team captains, thereby giving every player a chance to experience this role. But I have always felt strongly that a team captain is an honorable position; you have to earn it. As captain of six high school varsity teams (field hockey, badminton, cricket, soccer, track, and rugby) myself, I know that this role is a privilege, not a right.

At the expert level, a captain takes on a more significant role, as opposed to a ceremonial one. Whereas coaches generally rotate younger players through the position, older players earn the right through prowess on the field, strong communication skills, and a good work ethic. A captain is a leader in every sense of the word.

Patrick Saunders and Duncan Currie were two team captains on my Select team, the Bombers. (I always choose two because it can be lonely at the top.) From the age of 12, Patrick had tremendous qualities. At this young age, he approached me and introduced himself, saying, "I'm looking forward to working with you."

Both Patrick and Duncan learned very quickly what I wanted, did that, and more. They always organized the players if I was not around and coordinated warmups and cooldowns. They were hardworking and polite young men.

A good expert-level captain will have an opinion and should be allowed to express it to the coach. The captain will act as a mouthpiece for the concerns of the other players, both on and off the field, and be a tireless worker on the field. Maybe he is not the best player, but he is likely the hardest worker.

and the competence of the referee to see it and call it.

Man-to-man marking. Another tactic is man-to-man marking, in which an individual on the opposition is identified and one player is assigned the task of staying with her at all times. Invariably, it is used in an attempt to shut down a key player. This requires that a highly fit player be given the assignment and that a team know how to adapt to the fact that that person must often be out of position to follow her mark.

Set plays. Set plays (also known as set pieces), such as corner kicks, goal kicks, and free kicks are much more complex on this level. This is primarily because they involve players running to specific points to execute plays as well as movement occurring prior to, and as, the ball is struck, which is designed to confuse the opposition. Set plays involving free kicks can have a higher percentage of scoring on this level.

Ultimate flexibility of positioning. Soccer is not a rigid game, nor should the players or their positions be. An expert player should be capable of accomplishing both defending and attacking tasks. If you discount the goalkeeper, every player represents 10 percent of the offense and 10 percent of the defense. Sometimes, offensive and defensive play requires 100 percent effort. In other words, the entire team except for the goalkeeper is attacking on offense or can be back on defense.

working-class players

A good expert player is a working-class player. This means that she is a practitioner of ultimate flexibility. She is the player who will get the job done by going wherever she has to on the field.

It takes confidence, conditioning, experience, and team commitment to do the job well and be a good expert-level player. Often, it is the more glamorous positions (those that result in goals scored) that gain adulation, but if the forward goes back to the defense to do the "grunt work," she provides valuable help toward the team effort.

A working-class midfielder is the hardest-working player on the field, and she is the vital bridge between the offense and defense. Hers is often a thankless task, as this player is not as noticeable—always moving, running up and back in the congested middle of the field. But the true strokes of brilliance in a game are often the passes made by the midfielder, which facilitate goal-scoring opportunities.

An expert defender challenges in all areas of the field. She is an aggressive player who often does aerial combat—playing high balls such as headers. She is a hard tackler with a high rate of success at winning those tackles. She is proactive, as opposed to reactive, as on other levels of play. That is, she anticipates an opponent receiving the ball and steps in front to intercept the ball. The two central defenders are usually two of the bigger players on the team, with at least one having good speed.

A working-class forward has an equally tireless job. Good forwards constantly readjust their positions along the front line according to the ball's location. Attackers are also the first line of defense. As soon as the opposition gets the ball, everyone becomes a defender. When members of her own team are looking to find the attackers, a good forward will be in constant motion, seeking to find the open space that will enable a pass to be made to move the ball forward.

CHAPTER 11

goalkeeping

THE LAST DEFENSE

A herd of players is charging. The crowd roars in anticipation. A coach shouts an order to his player: "Shoot!" The goalkeeper focuses on the direction of the ball and positions his body to face it. The shot is taken—a bullet toward his face. Instinctively, he puts his hands up with his fingers spread. He catches the ball, securing it by wrapping his arms around it and pulling it into his chest. His teammates and supporters cheer. At that moment, he is the single hero of the game.

Goalkeepers say that making a save is an experience beyond words. But missing a shot, resulting in a goal for the opposition, can be devastating. Blame and credit are the double-edged sword of goalkeeping. This is why the focus of goalkeeping in youth soccer must be not only on skills but also on tending to a goalkeeper's emotional health.

In addition to a strong, resilient character, a goalkeeper must possess special athletic abilities in order to make the moves required of him. The explosive nature of jumping and diving requires leg strength; good technique is needed to kick the ball well; the dexterous hand skills required are like ones needed in baseball and basketball; and lightning-fast reflexes and quickness are critical. The goalkeeper is probably the most versatile athlete on the field.

Goalkeepers think of themselves as individualists and as eccentrics. This is reflected in the colorful shirts that they wear, different than any other player on the field. (A flashy shirt can also cause an opponent to shoot at the keeper, as if drawn to a target.) They are able to withstand the pressure of their role as well as witness the game from afar for long stretches. They are brave—willing to put their bodies on the line without fear of the physical risks—confident and decisive. They are assertive and are not afraid to take on the leadership role that must inevitably be assumed by this position.

the decision to specialize

From the beginning, your child should be given the chance to experiment by playing in goal. He should not be immediately restricted to that position, however. While some children play only in goal from the beginning, it is a good idea for them

coach's corner

So much of goalkeeping is proper confidence building. A young keeper must constantly be protected and nurtured. Having a child play against older, bigger, or much better players when he is not prepared can be disastrous, but it commonly happens.

I began playing in goal at age 8. My coaches immediately recognized that I had good reflexes and a special ability for the position. At age 10, I was a guest in a scrimmage with U-13 players. In the second half, I was put in goal. I remember how totally intimidating it was. I felt like I was in an ocean in which I couldn't swim. I held my own by conceding only one goal, but the other team dominated possession of the ball and kept me very busy. The oncoming giants filled me with panic. I remember looking at one player who, realizing I was small, chipped the ball over my head for a goal. I went home crying and swore to my parents that I never wanted to play in the goal again.

The coaches did a foolish thing by putting me in that situation. From this experience, I learned how essential it is to get the right level of competition for youth soccer players, especially goalkeepers.

I believe that if I had stayed with goalkeeping, I could have made it to the big time. But because of that traumatic experience in a formative time, I'll never know.

to experiment with other positions, at least until the age of 12. This way, your child builds a base in physical fitness. A young goalkeeper does not do much running around, and it is too soon in his playing career for extra or specialty conditioning. Playing in the field emphasizes the foot skills necessary to play in goal. Practicing in the field also gives him the opportunity to gain a crucial understanding of other positions, and of the game.

Some children express an interest in becoming goalkeepers. They have experimented in the position and like the praise they get. They enjoy goalkeeping skills, such as diving and catching the ball. Other children are encouraged to play the position by parents or coaches. In the older ages, some children specialize because their physical size is a benefit (goalkeeping favors taller children), or they have reached a limit in their field play and feel that their chances to reach higher levels are better as goalkeepers.

Parenting a goalkeeper is both exciting and challenging. It is a singular, sometimes lonely, position that requires a lot of parental support and creativity. While other players make mistakes on the field, they are not so obvious. A mistake by the goalkeeper almost always brings one result: a goal for the other team. You must also accept the physical risks that a keeper faces. Particularly as players become older and play at higher levels, the play gets rougher and the risk of injury becomes greater. Typical goalkeeper injuries include sliding burns, bumps and bruises from getting kicked, and getting the wind knocked out of them from diving.

Parenting a goalkeeper is expensive and can be time consuming. Their equipment, which includes gloves, long and short pants, padded shirts, and a soft-billed hat for sun protection, is more extensive than that of the field players. You must be actively involved in their training and constantly seeking possibilities for goalkeeping training, camps, and other programs. It is also harder to find experts and role models because there are not as many goalkeepers as field players.

supporting your goalkeeper

A youth goalkeeper benefits by extra support and understanding necessary to play this unique position. You can foster this by following the tips below.

- Goalkeeping can be hard to pick up in regular practice. Try to send your child to specialty training and camps. Consider private lessons, if necessary.
- To most actively support your child, consider taking a goalkeeping coaching course or study videos and books. Contact the national youth soccer organizations or check out the Internet for courses. (For more information, see the resource list on page 207.)
- Emphasize on-field communication. Young keepers need to develop a comfort level with talking and shouting. Let them practice on you.
- Videotape your child so that he can see himself playing in goal.
- To see good keepers (and other players) in action, watch top teams. Also, see if your child wants to volunteer to retrieve balls at high school team practices.
- Find a goalkeeper mentor. An older sibling, relative, or friend can provide inspiration and useful hand-me-down equipment. Keepers often enjoy their rituals and special items, such as lucky gloves from another good player.
- Develop a well-rounded goalkeeper by encouraging him to participate in other sports.

- Invest in good goalkeeping gear (for more information on gear, see chapter 3). Short-sleeved warm-weather keeper shirts are available. Some experts feel, however, that especially for young children, long-sleeved shirts are more valuable for elbow protection. Particularly in colder climates and for young children, wearing long underwear is helpful. Younger children have less body fat and need help to keep warm during long stretches of inactivity.

levels of play

Unlike the field skills, which were broken down into five levels, goalkeeping is divided into only three general levels of learning: beginner, intermediate, and advanced. Most goalkeeping skills are introduced at the beginner level. Not all of them are immediately used or perfected. The expectations are different on every level. Skills such as positioning, shot stopping, and ball distribution are broken down into various types and categories, which are introduced at varying levels. An example is diving. While children are taught to dive from the beginning, only on the intermediate to the advanced levels do they learn such maneuvers as diving for air balls at various heights or diving forward or backward while punching or deflecting the ball.

Because a goalkeeper is the only player in soccer allowed to use his hands, an often-overlooked area of this position is the kicking. Particularly since FIFA (the international soccer federation) made the ruling preventing goalkeepers from taking a back pass or throw-in with their hands, good foot skills are more necessary than ever.

Today's goalkeeper is essentially like a sweeper (a roving defender who serves as the last line of defense before the goalkeeper), needing a mastery of field play. He must kick the ball in a variety of ways, such as stationary punting, drop kicking (dropping the ball from the hands to the ground, then striking it after it bounces), and kicking moving and bouncing balls. Eventually, tactical kicking is added—kicking the ball to specific points and kicking according to weather and field conditions as well as for accuracy. Very often, with younger players, the coach will have a field player with better skills take goal kicks and free kicks, which could be taken by the keeper. This is acceptable for the short term, but eventually, a keeper must take his own kicks. Therefore, kicking practice at the earliest possible age will be of great benefit. In addition, like all players, it is very important to practice kicking with both the left and the right foot from the beginning.

Goalkeeping is one of the most fun and satisfying soccer activities for parents to practice with their children. This is because the skills are so versatile, and it employs catching, a skill that parents are often more familiar with. Parents are particularly important in this task, as goalkeepers by nature will not have many like-minded peers with whom to practice. Also, team practices are centered around field play, which requires an extra time investment by keepers to practice their own skills.

Goalkeepers often need extra help because they are sometimes neglected by coaches. An article published by Soccer Association for Youth entitled "The Forgotten Player—Goalkeeper," by

Jeff Wander, reports that the three most common excuses for coaches not spending time working with keepers are lack of time, lack of manpower, and lack of knowledge about the position.

When practicing, always use age-appropriate equipment, including proper size balls and goals. This is not only for safety but also for learning skills that duplicate those used in competition.

beginners

Beginning goalkeepers should be grounded in the basics. This includes the ability to stand in the ready position (facing forward, up on the toes, feet slightly spread, hands out to the side); to understand and execute proper positioning in response to the ball; to catch, control, and secure the ball; to have some method of deflecting the ball; and to know how to use basic distribution techniques, which include punting, rolling the ball, underhand passes, sidearm throws (to the side), and javelin throws (overhead).

JAVELIN THROW

This throw is usually used as a high-speed, accurate method of distribution. The left arm is poised for aim. It then comes down to add momentum as the right arm launches the ball, much like a catapult. The feet should be several feet apart for balance. The keeper steps into the throw with the left leg and slings the ball over his head. The left foot points in the direction of the throw.

Just as with field players, onlookers often do not appreciate how complicated goalkeeping skills are. Jumping to save high balls, a skill introduced at this level, requires learning to time springs from one or two legs and retrieve a ball in midair, a difficult act of coordination. The basic diving save, done by stopping a rolling ball with the body, is another example. It requires perfect timing, a knowledge of body positioning, and good hand/eye coordination.

Here are some exercises to hone basic skills.

Side diving. An ideal way to get used to diving for the ball is to start from a sitting position. Have your child kneel and simply fall to the left or the right. When he becomes familiar with landing on his side (as opposed to his stomach, a common mistake among beginners that often knocks the wind out of them), add a ball to the exercise, which you roll to him. Work up to bouncing balls, then to balls off the ground entirely.

Quick reactions. Have your child turn with his back to you. Shout "Turn!" and as he turns, throw him the ball, which he should then try to save. Vary the service—high, low, middle, and to the sides.

Coming out. A common problem with youth goalkeepers is that they stay

TIP SAVE

A last-ditch effort, this can be done by tipping the ball over or around the goal. The keeper's eyes should remain focused on the ball. Extending the right arm allows for maximum reach toward the ball. A crucial aspect of this move is to get as close to the ball as possible before having to dive in order to make the save. Spread the body out to lessen the impact on landing. It is safer to land on your side than on your stomach. Try to land on the fleshy parts of the body such as the upper arms (instead of the elbows), thighs (instead of the knees), and the buttocks.

DIVING PARRY

Parry means to deflect. The parry can be done in any position, and it's used if the keeper cannot catch the ball. A parry gets more of the hands' surface on the ball than a tip save, so the keeper can better direct where the ball is sent. Ideally, the hands are formed in the "W" position, with the thumbs touching each other. Good form (the body parallel to the ground) allows the keeper to land on his side, with the impact absorbed by the entire body. A mat is used to practice this move.

rooted to the goal mouth. Instead, they should come out to meet attackers and take away shooting angles and make it harder to take shots. To practice coming out, dribble the ball toward your child. Vary the pace and the angle at which you approach him. He should come out of the goal in an attempt to stop your run. Start slowly, adding speed only as your child's skill level improves.

intermediate

On this level, strategy begins to play a bigger role. While a beginner just hopes to save the ball and distribute it in any way possible, an intermediate player begins to understand such tactics as positioning himself to narrow the angle to prevent goals and distributing the ball strategically. Distribution entails choices, such as whether to roll or punt the ball and to which player or part of the field.

An intermediate goalkeeper also begins the task of acting as an important set of eyes for the team, anticipating plays and thus supporting the defense. He speaks loudly and decisively, directing his defenders to different areas of the defensive zone or to guard specific opponents. He begins to organize the defense for set plays (such as corner kicks, free kicks, and goal kicks), by instructing them where to stand to defend corner kicks and how to set up a wall of players for free kicks. In order to do this, he must learn the technical language of his position. He may shout, "Keeper" (he intends to play the ball); "Support" (he can take a back pass), and other calls that are also used by field players, such as "Mark" (guard a player) and "Time" (a player has time to make a play because an opponent is not nearby).

Here are some exercises to hone intermediate skills.

Shuffling. Fast footwork enables a keeper to get to a ball quickly and have a better chance of preventing a goal. Shuffling from side to side gets a keeper to the ball faster than running forward and then turning to dive or save. Create a small maze of disks or markers around which the keeper can shuffle–side to side, backward, and forward. When he comes out of the maze, kick the ball to him. He must save it, return it to the shooter using a variety of distribution techniques, and go backward through the maze. He then receives another shot and returns it.

Wall ball. Once a keeper gets a ball, it is important that he distribute it to his teammates appropriately. Many times, this means kicking the ball to specific points where teammates are. Use a wall and practice either punting or place kicking (kicking the ball when it is stationary on the ground) the ball into a designated area on the wall. The keeper catches the rebound. To vary the exercise, change the distance from the wall and create restrictions on types of kicks. Two or more players can also play GOAL. Each player who misses the rebound gets a letter. The first one to spell GOAL loses.

Accurate kicking. This is a game for a group of goalkeepers and enhances throwing accuracy, placement of kicks, and distribution skills. Playing one versus one, or two versus two or more, set up two targets, 10 yards apart. (Garbage cans, representing the goal, are ideal.) Play regular soccer, trying to hit the target by punting, throwing, or regular kicking. If a ball hits the target by kicking, award one point; by throwing, two points; by drop kicking, three points. If the ball lands inside the cans by any of the above methods, add an extra point. When the hands are used for anything other than throwing, a player must constantly toss the ball up and catch it (practices hand control). One variation of this game is to flick ground balls up to the hands instead of picking them up.

advanced

An advanced goalkeeper dazzles onlookers with a variety of leaps, dives, and artful distribution techniques. (In fact, it is often advanced players who inspire younger children to try this position.) The keeper not only punts and takes goal kicks but he also does drop kicks, a technique where the ball is dropped and then struck immediately after it bounces. Kicks such as the drop kick take perfect timing.

People are under the impression that a goalkeeper's position is relatively sedentary, requiring little fitness. The opposite is true. To perform at this level, a keeper needs a high degree of physical fitness. At this level, there are no second chances. The ability to react at the highest level for 90 minutes requires exceptional fitness.

Unlike goalkeepers at previous levels who tend to kick, dive, or jump with the dominant side of the body, an advanced player moves adeptly off either leg or to either side. He punches the ball with one or both hands and makes tip saves—jumping high into the air and flicking high balls over the crossbar (the part of the goal that is parallel to the ground and directly over the goal line).

Tactically, he is skilled at anticipating the angle of a shot, and he uses psychology (intimidating looks or aggressive movements that could cause an opponent to panic) when dealing with opponents, even forcing them by his most subtle movements to shoot the ball to anticipated spots.

Now that he is comfortable with diving to make saves, it is important to hone that skill. To most fully develop diving techniques, have him try the exercises below. As he becomes more adept, the keeper should focus on the height and arc of his dives so that he meets the ball before it goes into the net.

Diving high jump. Have the keeper dive over soft objects, such as cones or propped-up mats, into a sand pit or other soft surface, such as a mat. Continue to raise the height of the object over which he jumps. Begin without a ball, then add the element of serving the ball.

"Ray Amato Splash." This was developed by a Bridgewater, New Jersey, soccer dad and former college goalkeeper. Young keepers love this activity. Have the keeper stand on a low diving board or on the side of a pool and do a goalkeeping dive into the water. Then, add a ball, first thrown at a fairly low height, for the diver to catch. Finally, toss the ball high, encouraging the keeper to spring up into the air before landing in the water. You can add another element by positioning a third person to hold a makeshift goal on the other side of the pool at which the server aims the ball. Always be sure to use caution when playing in a pool. Although the water is the unique aspect of this exercise, you can also try it with a soft mattress.

Precision kicking. Set up targets and have the keeper kick and punt balls to hit them. To isolate a skill, restrict the game, such as allowing only drop kicks.

3

THE SOCCER LIFESTYLE

12. nutrition 97
13. cross-training and conditioning 108
14. injuries and safety 116

CHAPTER 12

nutrition

EAT RIGHT TO PLAY GREAT

You are about to embark upon the most unexplored, yet perhaps the most important, aspect of youth soccer: nutrition. Why is it so important? Because through the tenets of proper sports nutrition, it is wholly reasonable to expect a mediocre team or athlete to discover a whole new level of play or for a good player to reach excellence. Then there's the added resistance to injury, the reduced recovery time between games, and the opportunity to create a lifetime of good eating habits. And to top it all off, the most essential tool that you'll need to make this happen is you, a conscientious parent.

Wanting your children to be well-nourished is one of the basic instincts of parenthood. You have that working for you. Plus, you have your common sense. Add those two together, and the game, as they say, is half-won.

As in all good battles, though, you have some worthy adversaries—namely, your kids. Convincing them to eat properly is every parent's struggle. Junk food abounds. Powerful marketing programs thrust the worst possible snacks at them. Ironically, this is especially true in sports like youth soccer.

Most games and tournaments have several things in common—nearby fast-food outlets, snack bars, and little time for proper meals. Here's where your foresight and planning come in. As a sport requiring strength, endurance, and concentration, soccer is an excellent vehicle for motivating children to eat well. When children see their level of play directly affected by their eating habits, the incentive is there. As a big added bonus, it can lay the groundwork for a lifetime of good nutrition.

look to the pyramid

One of the most interesting aspects of sports nutrition is that what works for athletes has been proven to work in daily life as well. Take the once-dominant pre-workout meal of steak and eggs. Sports nutritionists long ago tossed that out the window in favor of meals heavy on carbohydrates like pasta. Doing so turned out to be a good thing for the general population as well.

The point is, by educating your child in proper nutrition, you and the rest of your family will benefit equally. There's no better place to start than the U.S. Department of Agriculture/U.S. Department of Health and Human Services Food Guide Pyramid.

Chances are, you've seen it in a pamphlet, on a cereal box, or in a book. It's an illustrated version of the ratios and types of recommended foods. It is broken down into six basic food groups: grains (rice, oatmeal, pasta, bread, and the like), fruits, vegetables, proteins (meat, poultry, fish, eggs, and nuts), dairy (cheese and milk), and fats (oil and butter). The daily recommendations for a good diet are:

- 6 to 11 servings of grains
- 2 to 4 servings of fruits
- 3 to 5 servings of vegetables
- 2 to 3 servings of dairy foods
- 2 to 3 servings of proteins
- Fats and sweets in small amounts

Although this may seem like a substantial amount of food, it is only 1,500 to 1,800 calories per day. The average active adult needs between 2,000 and 2,500 calories. Note that a serving size is relatively small; a single protein serving is a three-ounce piece of meat, approximately the size of a deck of cards. Illustrated another way, one large bowl of cereal equals two to four servings of grains, one large apple is two servings of fruits, and a big bowl of salad is a whopping three to four servings of vegetables.

Calculated with your young soccer player in mind, the American Dietetic Association (ADA) says that an adolescent training diet should be made up of 55 to 60 percent carbohydrates, 12 to 15 percent proteins, and 25 to 30 percent fats. Before you drag out your calculator, the good news is that eating according to the Food Guide Pyramid will provide this balance.

children have different needs than adults

Use the Food Pyramid as a template, but bear in mind that a young growing athlete does have some special nutrition needs. For instance, children need more protein to support their burgeoning muscles. And while high-carbohydrate, low-fat diets are important for adults, parents sometimes overemphasize low-fat foods for their children.

The bottom line, according to the ADA, is that you don't need to worry if your kids sometimes indulge in higher-fat foods, especially if they're the kinds of foods that are high in unsaturated fat—nuts, avocados, and olive oil, for example. Fats are actually essential for an active child, keeping her well-fueled for endurance events like soccer. This is particularly true in colder weather, when energy needs are higher.

A few things to bear in mind: Adolescent athletes are at increased risk for iron deficiency because of their growth and because exercise depletes iron levels. Also, calcium intake reported by adolescents is often well below the Recommended Dietary Allowance. Adequate calcium is important to prevent stress fractures. Moreover, growing bones can't form solidly without adequate calcium.

These two nutrients and their deficiencies are especially significant for females. Calcium prevents a common condition among older women—osteoporosis, a dangerous thinning of the bones. Iron is important because many girls and women lose this nutrient at higher rates through menstruation.

Some signs that your child may be iron deficient include anemia (marked by very pale skin) and chronic fatigue. Sometimes, the whites of the eyes turn bluish or grayish. Calcium deficiency is harder to spot, as it may not result in symptoms. That's why milk and other calcium-rich foods are such an important part of your athlete's diet.

Even if your young athlete could stand to lose a few pounds, it's not recommended that you put her on a strict diet. Rather, focus on eating appropriate whole foods such as baked potatoes rather than french fries and whole apples rather than apple pie.

calories and more calories

Youth soccer players are calorie-burning machines. Consider that an average youth player probably runs anywhere from 2 to 4 miles per game. If your child plays in a typical two-day tournament, that could add up to 10 to 15 miles a day. Also consider that running, by itself, burns about 100 calories per mile (the equivalent of a medium banana). Toss in the practices and caloric requirements of just growing, and you can appreciate that playing soccer requires an enormous energy expenditure.

In one British study of top 14-year-old swimmers, soccer players, and track athletes, all three groups failed to meet the recommendations for caloric intake (at least 3,000 calories per day for active young athletes). Soccer players were also deficient in vitamin D, zinc, calcium, magnesium, and iron. Nutritional knowledge was also low, as a questionnaire revealed. From a possible score of 56 points, soccer players averaged 15.5.

Since the recommended numbers of servings from the Food Pyramid do not provide sufficient calories for active teenagers, they should eat more servings while adhering to the ratios laid out in the Pyramid.

Getting those extra calories into your young athlete means facing an additional hurdle. A physically active child often has a depressed appetite due to elevated body temperature or the excitement of competition. Often, a child will not stop to notice that she is hungry. This is compounded if food is not available or not offered. That's where you come in.

If you have concerns about the adequacy or quality of your child's food intake, be sure to consult with a registered dietitian who specializes in sports. Nancy Clark, R.D., author of *Nancy Clark's Sports Nutrition Guidebook* and the director of nutrition services at SportsMedicine Brookline in Massachusetts, provided advice for this chapter and recommends calling the ADA referral network at (800) 366-1655 or visiting www.eatright.org to find a local registered dietitian according to ZIP code.

become a pushy parent

If there was ever a time to be a pushy parent, now is it. Feed your players often and well. Choose from among the foods mentioned in this chapter. Even young children who compete casually need special attention. Think of young soccer players like the video game character Pac-Man; they need to be munching all the time.

Be forewarned that players may initially push food away, claiming that they are not hungry. When they begin to eat, however, they usually find their appetites. Eating often is a habit that a parent must facilitate. Get used to carrying food with you everywhere. Do not rely on being able to purchase something near the playing fields or at a game. The foods typically sold at convenience stores or tournaments (candy bars, chips, hot dogs, and hamburgers) will not facilitate good performance or good eating habits. It is also risky to rely on buying food nearby. Particularly when feeding children during or between games, you don't have time to run to a store that is several miles away.

Here are a few tips to keep in mind.

- Make sure that your child eats a good meal before she plays. A rule of thumb is to have a meal an hour or two before an event. Some players, however, can eat right before playing and suffer no ill effects. Each player needs to experiment.

- Take your own supply of meals and snacks everywhere, every time. At worst, you'll have to take your supply home (which probably will not happen, as you'll be surrounded by other hungry players).

- Be flexible and creative. Give your child snacks in the car on the way to or from a game. Carry a cooler or a lunch box.

- If you cannot be around to prepare food for your child before practice, pack extra food in her school lunch for both pre- and post-play snacks.

- Organize group nutrition. If your child's team does not already have parents who share rotating snack or drink duties, volunteer to draw up a plan for doing so.

- Pack nonperishables such as pretzels, crackers, or sports bars in your child's soccer bag. Replenish them immediately after they are eaten, so there is always a supply.

- Carry foods that players are familiar with and like. A game or practice is not a time to try out something new.

- If your child insists that she has no appetite, have her drink calorie-filled sports drinks, fruit juices, yogurt shakes, or milkshakes.

- Don't forget recovery foods and fluids. Muscles need to replenish (see "Postgame Recovery" on page 104 for more information).

- There is a time and a place for treats. Save candy, ice cream, or fast food for after the games.

Of course, there are limits. Well-fed does not mean overfed. Some parents erroneously believe that strength and endurance are built at a quicker rate by eating enormous amounts of food. All this does is add body fat, especially if it's the wrong kind of food.

Eating a pregame meal with the team is a great way to build team spirit and camaraderie. If necessary, volunteer to help the team arrange communal meals. Good habits are contagious. When the

MOM'S VIEW

The coach shook his head. "I guess we're just not an afternoon team," he lamented. He had good reason to feel that way. It was the summer of 1997. In their first tournament, the girls of the mid–New Jersey Select U-10 team, the Stampede, narrowly lost a 4:00 P.M. final. Over the two-day series of games, performance had regularly slipped in late-day competitions.

The next weekend, with verve and pep, the girls triumphed in an 11:00 A.M. game. "Uh-oh," I overheard the coach say. "Our next game is in the afternoon."

Perplexed, I found myself saying, "There is no such thing as being a 'morning' or an 'afternoon' team." Suddenly, the proverbial light bulb clicked on.

"Money!" I yelled at the coach. "I need cash!" Time was of the essence. In a strange town, on a busy Saturday, I raced the supermarket aisles, grabbing bananas, bottles of sports drinks, cups of yogurt, and other high-energy snacks.

I arrived back at the field and fed the girls with barely enough time for the food to settle in their stomachs before the next game. The result? The Stampede triumphed, becoming both a "morning" and an "afternoon" team.

Throughout that summer, the team began a process of education and preparation. Pages of information, much of which appears in this chapter, were handed out. For two summers, I carried bags of food with me everywhere (the jokes were aplenty, but I remained undaunted).

Before each game, I asked the same questions of each girl. "Did you eat? What, and how much?" Then I passed the pretzels, graham crackers, and raisins.

It caught on. We ate separately as families and together as a team. Enlightened, we looked around at our competition over the two-year period that our team was together. Forced to spend hours together in the same places, we saw what other teams ate and drank. Sadly, it was usually a case of what they did not eat and drink.

Over two summers, the Stampede amassed an astounding record of 55 wins, 5 losses, and 5 ties. Did food make the difference? One example provides the answer. In the penultimate loss, in which circumstances forced the tired girls to play without accustomed snacking, they went down 2–0. Two weeks later, against the same team in a final, the parents passed the snacks. The girls were ravenous and had the equivalent of a small meal each. The result: a 2–1 victory.

Remember, soccer is a game of endurance as much as of skill. The team that still has steam in the second half of an afternoon game is generally the one that wins, on the field and off.

team sees and feels the benefits of being well-fueled, they will associate eating properly with success.

different energy foods

Glycemic index (GI) refers to a food's ability to supply glucose to the bloodstream. Glucose is the primary fuel your body uses. Foods that are digested quickly and soon appear in the bloodstream have high GIs. Conversely, foods that are digested more slowly before providing energy have low GIs.

Foods can also be referred to as quick-release foods, which provide instant energy, and slow-release foods, which distribute energy over a longer period of time. Basically, quick-release foods are best during halftime and immediately after a game. Slow-release foods are best well in advance of the event, including the evening before and breakfast.

Moderate-GI foods are good up until about a half-hour before activity. If your

GLYCEMIC INDEX

Glycemic index (GI) refers to a food's ability to supply glucose to the bloodstream. Different foods provide varying amounts of energy (glucose) at different rates. Foods that are digested quickly and soon move into the bloodstream have high GIs. Conversely, foods that are digested more slowly before providing energy have low GIs.

Try choosing high-GI foods right before, during, and immediately after games. Choose low-GI foods the night before or at least two hours in advance of games. Moderate-GI foods make good snacks on the way to the games or between games. Note that these are only guidelines. Experiment with your athlete to see what works best for her.

HIGH	MODERATE	LOW
WHEAT BREAD	PASTA	APPLES
POTATOES	GRAPES	BAKED BEANS
HONEY	ORANGES	ICE CREAM
RICE	BANANAS	PEANUT BUTTER
MUFFINS	WAFFLES	BRAN MUFFINS
PANCAKES	DRIED APRICOTS	SKIM MILK
YOGURT	RAISINS	RAW CARROTS
PLUMS	PINEAPPLE	GREEN BEANS
PEARS	BREAKFAST CEREAL	POPCORN
CHERRIES		
WATERMELON		

athlete has a history of getting too anxious to eat properly before a game, make sure that the night before she has an extra-large meal rich in low-GI foods. Toss a nighttime snack in on top of it.

meals for game day or practices

Here are some ideas for meals on days when there are games or practices.

Breakfast. Look to low-GI foods such as oatmeal, orange juice, bananas, apples, cereal and milk, and bran or corn muffins. (Commercial muffins are usually loaded with unhealthy fats. If you bake, make muffins with canola oil. If not, choose something else.) Forget waffles and pancakes; they're better for a postgame recovery brunch. If your child is battling a case of pregame jitters and can't bring herself to eat, have plenty of fruit on hand on the way to the game. Have her munch little bits as she's able.

Lunch. If you choose a sandwich, it is best if it is more bread than filling. Good fillings include turkey, cheese, or peanut butter. If pizza is on the menu, go for a thick crust instead of thin. Skip pepperoni or sausage in favor of vegetable toppings.

If you eat at a fast-food restaurant, choose a broiled-chicken sandwich over a burger, and choose a salad if your child will eat it. (Go sparingly on the dressing and croutons.) Forget the french fries and chips. Replace fried potatoes with baked potatoes or choose extra bread, rice, or pretzels.

Dinner. All meals are important, but a relaxed dinner is an excellent chance to refuel after a game and to gear up for the next day's game. Prepare a meal that your child enjoys.

Think pasta and tomato sauce, or baked chicken and rice or potatoes. Go for a dessert with a fruit base, like apple crisp, over, say, chocolate.

If you are on the road, choose a restaurant with healthy menu choices. Order food steamed or baked, not breaded or fried. Have extra water and rolls or bread.

EATING ON THE ROAD

Youth soccer often requires extensive travel. Since you don't know what you'll find on the road, it's best to take food with you. Here's what you want in your cooler.

- A plentiful stock of nonperishables, such as cereal, crackers, and dried fruit
- At least one meal (sandwiches, fruit, and a drink, for example)
- Napkins, cutlery, and a small cutting knife

Don't get caught between games with little time and nothing to eat. (This happens with regularity to youth soccer families.) Also, when arriving at a new site for an extended day of play, scope out the nearest restaurants or look for a supermarket. And remember that you can never overstock. Being part of a team often means feeding a team.

postgame recovery

The game is over. But the next day's match is fast approaching. Don't end your efforts with the final whistle. Refueling a player's tired muscles is as important as feeding her well before the game.

Postgame nutrition is often overlooked. That's unfortunate, because nutritious foods speed muscle recovery by supplying glycogen, the muscles' fuel, in the form of carbohydrates. In fact, the muscles absorb carbohydrates more quickly than normal for several hours after playing. Failing to replenish muscle glycogen, in fact, can leave your player stiff and tired the next day.

After strenuous exercise, a player can recover best by eating a small carbohydrate-rich snack (such as a bagel or banana) immediately after playing and continuing to snack until the next meal. If a player complains that she is not hungry, start with fluids. Encourage her to eat even a small amount of food to renew her appetite.

The same is true of replenishing fluids. It's critical to restore what was lost. If your child needs pit stops on the way home from a game, you'll know that you've done your job.

nutritional needs for girls

Adolescent athletes are at increased risk of iron deficiency. Female adolescents have additional iron losses through menstruation. The ADA states that it is important to monitor iron stores in female athletes. You can do this through simple blood tests performed by a family doctor at your daughter's regular checkup.

The lack of calcium intake is also of special concern for female adolescents, particularly those who have ceased to menstruate or who have irregular menstruation. The hormones that cause menstruation are also responsible for functions associated with building strong bones. If your child is prone to stress fractures, have her calcium levels checked by her doctor.

Compulsive eating behaviors, such as endless dieting, anorexia, or bulimia, are present in some populations of female athletes. Although soccer is not a sport singled out by experts as placing an emphasis on slim body size that may result in destructive dieting patterns (the way that gymnastics or distance running is), no sport is immune from eating disorders. Parents should pay special attention to their daughters for signs of these disorders.

Anorexia can be marked by significant weight loss, hyperactivity, an intense fear of becoming fat, cessation of menstrual periods, loss of hair, and extreme sensitivity to cold temperatures. Some symptoms of bulimia include binge eating, self-induced vomiting, and rapid weight fluctuations of more than 10 pounds. If you see signs like these, get help from a professional.

Girls are not the same as boys when it comes to food. They are generally smaller and, hence, they need fewer calories to maintain lighter bodies. They cannot get away so easily with consuming junk food. A seemingly innocent bag of chips, for example, if eaten every day, makes up a larger percentage of a girl's daily overall food intake than it does a boy's. Adolescent girls need to be educated on good nutrition and proper food choices so that they get the most nutrients possible in everything they eat.

the importance of fluids

No discussion of sports nutrition would be complete without talking about the importance of drinking enough fluids. It is arguably the single most important aspect of youth soccer, for safety and performance. The American College of Sports Medicine recommends that a person drink 4 to 8 ounces of fluid for every 15 to 20 minutes of vigorous physical activity (like soccer). Active players should also drink 16 to 20 ounces just before playing and again immediately after.

Here's a good way to make sure that your player drinks enough. Children under the age of 10 should drink until they're no longer thirsty. Then give them half a cup more. A full cup is recommended for older children. If your child is unclear about the necessary amounts, let her fill a plastic cup from a drink bottle to get the idea.

Research has shown that even when children are offered water during prolonged exercise in the heat, they do not drink enough. Even with drink breaks, children sometimes just take a sip or two. Insist that your child drink more. Explore the possibility of placing personal drink bottles along the sidelines to use during breaks in the game.

Most teams ask players to bring their own water bottles. Go for a large size, in case refilling close by is not an option. It is a bad idea to have players drink from a communal bottle or from each other's bottles, as strep and other infections can be spread this way.

Some children prefer sports drinks, which can be a good addition, especially because it has been proven that children will drink more of something they like. Diluted fruit juice is also a good option. Nondiluted juices don't get absorbed as quickly and don't contain as much water. Although sports drinks are most useful for endurance activities over one hour in duration, there is evidence that they can aid performance in shorter bursts of intense sports. Fortunately, soccer contains aspects of both. The extra calories are useful to a player, helping to provide energy and maintain a normal blood sugar source.

Sports drinks are practically an institution in youth soccer. Some players, however, find them too sweet or heavy, and get stomach cramps. If this happens, dilute them with water. Be sure to experiment during training to learn which formula your child likes best. The products that are best absorbed have 50 to 80 calories per eight ounces. Here are some other fluid tips for your child.

- Have her drink plenty of water the night before playing. Add to her reserves by having her continue throughout the day of playing.

- Have her drink warm fluids in cool weather if she is chilled. Drinking icy-cold fluids in warmer weather will keep her body temperature down.

- For added flavor, freeze fruit juice in ice trays to add cubes to water. Or mix fruit juice and water.

- Pack a water bottle filled with ice to keep the water cold. Some players like to freeze water or sports drink bottles the night before. (Make sure they are made of plastic.) Take them out just before you leave for the game. They'll thaw nicely by the time they're needed.

- Avoid sodas during games. In addition to being too high in the wrong kind of sugar for sustained physical activity, colas and some other sodas contain caffeine, which causes frequent urination and contributes to dehydration.
- Stock up on foods with high water content, such as fruits and vegetables. For a tasty treat, try freezing fruit chunks.
- A player is well-hydrated if she urinates frequently throughout the day. The urine should be clear and of significant quantity. If urine is dark in color, get some fluids into her.

VITAMINS AND SPORTS DRINKS

There is no scientific evidence that supports the general use of vitamin and mineral supplements to improve athletic performance in properly nourished athletes, according to the American Dietetic Association. Although these supplements may improve poor nutritional status or deficiencies from an inadequate diet, the indiscriminate use of supplements is generally a waste of money.

Overuse of vitamins may also lull your child into thinking that she's eating properly when she's not. For example, a multivitamin and a can of soda do not make a healthy meal.

Your child should be getting necessary vitamins and minerals from foods first. While there is nothing wrong with taking a daily multivitamin as low-cost health insurance, our bodies absorb nutrients best from food. Bear in mind, too, that many popular foods like cereals and energy bars are enriched with extra vitamins already. Your child is likely to be getting more vitamins than she realizes.

Here's another nutritional myth: While sports drinks are extremely popular in youth soccer circles, consumed on a regular basis, they are no better than soda. Many athletes drink them all the time, not just during games, believing that the drinks add some mystical sports-friendly substances to their diets.

Sports drinks are largely just sugar water with a dash of salt. They have their place in sports during vigorous activity or if players simply consume more sports drink than water because it tastes better to them. But don't bother spending the extra money for your child to drink them all the time.

Sports energy bars are a matter of taste and finances. They're more of a marketing program than something essential to improving performance. A banana or a few fig bars are the energy equivalent of a sports bar, and to many children, they taste a lot better. To you, they're a lot cheaper.

dehydration

Now you know why proper hydration is so important. Let's take a look at the opposite end of the spectrum: dehydration.

Children are at increased risk of dehydrating because they do not tolerate temperature extremes as well as adults do. Their body-core temperatures rise faster than adults' because of immature sweat glands.

Here's another surprising fact to keep in mind. Thirst is not an adequate indicator of the need to drink. By the time your player feels thirsty, she is already dehydrated.

Watch for signs of dehydration, including infrequent urination, headache, or unusual crankiness. Heat cramps, usually in the abdomen or the legs, are also warning signs of dehydration.

Heat exhaustion is more serious. The signs are cool, pale, moist skin; profuse sweating; dilated pupils; headache; nausea; or vomiting. If heat exhaustion occurs, move the player to a cool location and have her lie on her back with her feet up. Remove excess clothing and loosen what's left. Give her water or a sports drink.

Heat stroke is the most serious of all; it is possibly life-threatening. It can happen if heat exhaustion is left untreated. The symptoms begin the same as heat exhaustion but then the person stops sweating altogether. Her skin turns red and hot. She's confused, perhaps agitated and irritable. Severe symptoms include seizures and unconsciousness. Call an ambulance and get her to a cool area. Get her body temperature down by removing excess clothing, fanning her, and applying cool compresses. Get her to drink small amounts of fluids. Give her too much, and she may vomit.

And remember this: Seasons may change but the need for fluid doesn't. Don't let your guard down in cooler weather. Dehydration is not as noticeable then, but it can happen. Keep the fluids flowing year-round.

CHAPTER 13

cross-training and conditioning

ACHIEVING TOP FITNESS FOR MAXIMUM PERFORMANCE

Let's say you love bananas. You eat them all the time. In fact, they're all you eat. Bananas are a perfectly healthy food, as long as they are coupled with other perfectly healthy foods. That's the catch. To a similar degree, it's the same with sports.

Your child may be perfectly healthy playing only soccer. But he'll be even healthier and more well-rounded if he couples it with other sports. And, it'll make him an even better soccer player.

Quite simply, the definition of cross-training is to engage in two or more sports or exercise activities. Cross-training became popularized with the advent of the triathlon, an event involving swimming, cycling, and running. The multi-sport practice quickly spread to include a number of activities in various combinations. Other athletes then began the useful and enjoyable habit of combining activities, too. Often, they found that their primary sport was improved by their forays into new fields.

Although cross-training has not specifically been applied to youth activities, children actually are its main proponents. They cross-train naturally on their own. How often do you see a child just jumping rope or refusing to play anything except tag? They naturally shift from one activity to another.

the value of variety

Your child's schedule is booked solid with soccer practice and games. In addition to schoolwork and other activities, it is no wonder that parents ask, "Isn't soccer enough?" While soccer is certainly varied enough to provide excellent overall fitness, other sports have their own benefits to offer. There are many reasons—and many ways—to engage in other physical activities. In addition to providing variety, other activities can make your child's soccer better, make him less prone to injury, and remind him that, above all, sports are fun.

Balanced fitness. Think of the term *natural athlete*. It signifies someone who can pick up any sport and almost immediately be good at it. Chances are, that natural athlete had a good grounding in balanced fitness. In his early years, he probably played games and sports that developed all of his physical skills.

Soccer, broad as it is, still only develops a certain skill set. For example, it teaches tremendous foot-eye coordination but not hand-eye coordination (except for goalkeepers). Teaching broader skills is especially important in childhood. Similar to acquiring a foreign language, if physical skills are not developed early, the ability to do so later on becomes limited. Children may also lack the confidence, particularly in adolescence, to experiment. Teens hate to look bad. Early learning lasts—acquiring broad skills at a young age sets the stage for lifelong abilities in those areas. In short, it makes for a natural athlete.

Variety. Children are intuitively in touch with their bodies. They usually protect themselves—physically and emotionally—from overdoing one sport. They are quick to realize that they are bored, and they express it. If this describes your child, you know that it's time to back off the soccer a bit and turn him on to new activities. Engaging him in a variety of new activities takes the emphasis off soccer and, paradoxically, helps him rediscover what he liked so much about it in the first place.

Injury prevention and rehabilitation. One of the major reasons to cross-train is to prevent repetitive-use injuries. Think of a piece of wire. If it gets bent back and forth enough times, it breaks. That's basically what happens with a repetitive-use injury. Use the same muscles or body parts over and over again in an activity, and the likelihood that they will become injured increases.

Examples of repetitive-use injuries

A LOT GOING ON

If you think that soccer is a boring game, then the facts below should change your mind. Soccer is a game of constant motion, and to be successful as a player, you must be in good physical condition. Here are some facts from the *U.S. Soccer Sports Medicine Book*, compiled by *Performance Conditioning for Soccer Newsletter*, a periodical dedicated to conditioning soccer players.

These figures apply to older teenage players but give a good overview on the abilities required for all levels of soccer.

- The distance covered during a game is between 5 and 6.5 miles (2.5 miles for goalkeepers).
- The distance that a player covers in a game with possession of the ball is less than 2 percent of the total distance, or only about 200 yards.
- There are about 1,000 activity changes in a game, meaning a change of speed or direction every 6 seconds.
- Games are typically played at 75 percent of a person's physical limits.
- Rest pauses are for about 3 seconds every 2 minutes.

common to soccer include groin strains, shinsplints, knee strains, and Achilles tendon injuries. Other sports allow soccer players to stress different sets of muscles than those used in their primary sport.

Over the years, both world-class and recreational athletes have become smarter and more successful by supplementing their primary sports with a cross-training program. If and when athletes do get injured, they no longer resign themselves to passive healing. Cross-training allows them to maintain their fitness level by concentrating on another activity that uses different areas than the injured one.

cross-training activities

Virtually any sport can be combined with soccer. But remember one thing: Decide which one takes priority. Sure, you can have a part-time job, but you can devote yourself to only one full-time job. Try to do two, and you'll burn out. The same goes for sports. Obviously, with sports often running by season, your child can devote himself to different ones over the course of the year. Here are a few extracurricular sports to consider for cross-training with soccer.

Basketball. Basketball mixes well with soccer. One reason is because it traditionally takes place in the winter. In many ways, basketball resembles soccer—dribbling, passing, and shooting. But hands are to basketball what feet are to soccer, and basketball builds up hand-eye coordination that soccer doesn't.

Plus, in one way, basketball can be a more intense sport than soccer. Fewer players in smaller space means that your child may be more involved in the play. This builds up the cardiovascular fitness that is so necessary to soccer. The physical contact and aggressiveness in basketball greatly resemble soccer, too.

Cycling. Cycling is a great complement to soccer. It's a low-impact activity, which means that it is easy on a soccer player's knees and shins. Cycling is also tremendously easy to work into a busy schedule. It's a simple matter of biking to school instead of taking the bus or riding to a friend's house instead of having you drive.

Cycling relies heavily on the quadriceps muscles (front of the thighs) and your child just might find that he becomes a more powerful soccer player because of it. For the serious cyclist, the lower back also gains strength from riding in the tuck position, which is valuable for preventing back injuries on the field.

Running. Endurance running is an obvious complement to soccer. Endurance is what keeps a player strong throughout the game.

The school track season starts in the spring—an ideal precursor to summer soccer. If your child doesn't want to get that deeply into competitive running, training for a 5-K or shorter-distance fun run is a good goal.

Make sure that your child trains on softer surfaces—a track, grass, or even asphalt. Anything is better than concrete sidewalks, which can lead to painful shinsplints and sore knees. Younger runners (those under age 14), however, should restrict the distance to a mile or two at most.

Running does not necessarily mean one-pace monotony. Children can enjoy the variety of mixing it up on the run. After warming up with an easy jog, they can alternate faster jogging and sprinting, a workout known as fartlek (Swedish for "speed play"), that entails choosing a distance—say, the distance between three telephone poles—over which they can pick up the pace. Vary the markers or distance, allowing for a recovery jog or walk between efforts.

other activities

Other good cross-training activities include hockey, tennis, and other racquet sports. All of these include the short bursts of activity and rapid lateral movement that is so important to good soccer. And don't forget baseball. Many good goalkeepers come from a baseball background, which develops high-speed throwing and catching skills. Swimming is also excellent for staying in shape while in an impact-free environment. Dance and gymnastics provide muscular strength and develop great balance, flexibility, and agility.

If your child is looking for something a little more physical, martial arts like judo and karate are excellent crossover activities. Martial arts also put a heavy emphasis on mental discipline and good flexibility, both great tools to develop for soccer.

IT COMES DOWN TO RUNNING

Take a close look at what a player does in the course of a soccer game, and you'll realize that most of it consists of running in one form or another. At the end of a professional game, a player may have covered up to eight miles, according to staff members from John Moores University in England, authors of *Umbro Conditioning for Football*. While these numbers apply to pro players in a 90-minute match, the point is still clear that running ability is vital at all levels.

Out of those 90 minutes, that player spends 18 to 27 minutes (20 to 30 percent) walking, 27 to 36 minutes (30 to 40 percent) jogging, 13 to 23 minutes (15 to 25 percent) running, 9 to 13 minutes (10 to 15 percent) sprinting, and 4 to 7 minutes (4 to 8 percent) moving backward.

year-round fitness

It's the beginning of the season. "Coach, can I come out?" an exhausted child begs as he limps to the sideline. It's the inactivity of the off-season that has caused the player to make the plea. He's not alone. There is often a general pattern of player fatigue at the beginning of the season. As the season progresses, players gain stamina. At the end of the season, they have gained a fairly high level of conditioning, only to let it slip away during the off-season. By maintaining fitness year-round, players are more consistent. They also enjoy the game more. And they experience more success and enjoyment in early-season games.

Charles Hughes, in his book *Soccer Tactics and Teamwork*, writes that, in an analysis of 30 matches, in which 76 goals were scored, 23 goals (30 percent) were scored in the last 15 minutes of the game. Seventeen goals (22 percent) were

coach's corner

"How much pain will there be?" "Can my body survive?" "Just get it over and done with." That was the message that I got from my high school team the first day of preseason practice. It was the abject look of fear and loathing on their faces that made me rethink the customary practice of two-week torture sessions.

I realized that no matter how I spiced that training up, the attitude of the players was clearly one of drudgery. "We had the summer off, now it's back to work."

In order to promote year-round fitness, I began by ensuring that the players were involved in spring sports. Any physical activity was fine as long as they were not sedentary, which was their custom. Then, I began the preseason program 10 weeks, instead of 2 weeks, prior to the fall season. Most good high school players are now encouraged to train year-round.

Since beginning the conditioning program, there has been a dramatic improvement in the team's play. It appears that in almost every close game, we prevail in the second half. A lot of our goals are scored in the final stages, when we are clearly outlasting the other team. We have moved our way up to becoming a yearly contender for the state championship in our class. Some teams with better skills may have beaten us, but they have never "run us off the park," as we say in England.

scored in the last 5 minutes of the game. It's evident from this that the better-conditioned team can roll over their opponents in the final stages of a game, virtually running them off their feet.

Once it is understood that conditioning is important, and that it can be enjoyable, there are many ways for parents to set the tone.

Get into shape and stay that way. There is a cumulative effect of fitness. It is much easier to stay in shape and build on that than it is to drag yourself to a decent level of fitness from a sedentary state. But once you stop, you lose it. This does not happen immediately, but after several weeks, there is a marked decline in fitness. Breaks between soccer seasons are enough to lose most conditioning benefits.

Beware of fitness as a punishment. Watch out for programs or coaches that force players to run laps or do pushups if they misbehave or do not perform up to expectations. Children might learn to associate fitness with negative behavior and thus not want to engage in it.

Combine skills with conditioning. Have your child practice soccer skills while improving his physical fitness. For example, instead of running several miles, encourage him to dribble the ball for a set distance or time.

For children under 14, an organized conditioning program is usually not necessary because they are generally active enough in their daily lives. If your child is playing soccer year-round or is cross-training in a soccer-related sport (like basketball), encourage his continued interest. Here are some other low-key, fun ways to ensure that your child stays fit.

Make it a family affair. Most children respond positively to involved parents. Take a jog with your child or challenge him to a sprint race. If running is not your thing, try other sports or activities such as cycling or hiking.

Keep it fun. Games are the best way to add zip to a conditioning program. Kids love to be challenged, so try making an obstacle course and have a running scavenger hunt. Or, time them running a lap around the house while dribbling a soccer ball. At this stage, do not focus on running form.

Turn to specific exercises. For the motivated child, introduce general conditioning exercises, such as situps and pushups. If he's between the ages of 8 and 10, have him work his way up to 10 of each, three to four times a week. From 11 to 14, double it to 20 pushups and 40 situps. It is not recommended that children under 14 train with weights, so they should devote any extra time to playing more soccer or other sports.

Make it a habit. A little exercise done frequently is better than a lot done occasionally. The key is to develop the fitness habit. It is more important and beneficial to run around the block once and jump rope for one minute on a regular basis than it is to do a longer, more rigorous workout only occasionally.

serious conditioning

Serious soccer players over the age of 14 need to crank up their training a notch. Consistency is the key, and although the program is serious, it does not mean that it can't be fun. Socializing and camaraderie provide enjoyment when training is done as a team or with friends. These programs are often tailor-made and should be developed by qualified professionals.

Higher-level soccer consists of continuous running with bursts of explosive speed. In addition to the need to develop high levels of endurance, players need good sprinting and jumping form and agility. No significant further work on any area of conditioning can take place, however, until players have built a solid foundation of aerobic, or cardiovascular, fitness. Now is the time when players need to understand that running is an integral part of soccer practice. Individual running programs, especially off-season, will keep players in optimal shape.

Here are some tips for players interested in advanced conditioning.

Don't train for a marathon. Being able to run continuously for 20 to 30 minutes is adequate for serious soccer players. It's important to gradually build up to this length of time, though, and not attempt it on the first few runs. Once this can be done comfortably, intersperse short sprints into the run.

Work on getting faster. Speed is essential to advanced soccer play. And everyone can improve on speed by concentrating on running technique, leg strength, and power. Weight training, jumping drills, and running uphill will also help.

Strengthen the rest of the body. Abdominal and upper-body strength is vital. A strong upper body is important because high-level soccer is a very physical game, manifested in pushing and shoving. Strong abs also protect the back. Advanced players over the age of 14 should work their way up to at least three sets of 20 pushups and 30 situps per day.

Lift weights when the time is right. Once a player is past the age of 14, significant strength can be gained from weight training. If a player is interested, it is highly recommended that weight training be supervised by someone with experience.

deep-water running

Water workouts are a great addition to the conditioning program for advanced athletes, especially those coming back from injuries. Deep-water running is exactly what it says—running in deep water. The information below is from deep-water running instructor Doug Stern, a former high school teacher for 32 years who devised a deep-water running curriculum for the New York City School District.

Water has benefits that make it ideal for conditioning. In water, an exerciser encounters tremendous resistance, which strengthens muscles and joints without the harmful pounding that other activities, such as running, produce. Deep-water running also allows for faster recovery from injury, since return blood flow to the heart is more efficient (on land, gravity causes blood to be mainly directed to the lower body). Better blood flow to injured areas means faster healing.

Deep-water running is ideal for injured players, who can recuperate while maintaining cardiovascular fitness, muscle strength, and flexibility. It is also a good way to go the extra mile, developing extra fitness without risking injury from overdoing soccer or other land sports.

All you need to make deep-water running comfortable is a flotation device. While there are several types of flotation devices, a belt is most helpful and can be purchased through swimming-gear distributors or in specialty or sporting-goods stores.

To start, stand in shallow water. Swing your arms as you would for running. Then, begin high-stepping. Move your way down to deeper water until your feet can no longer touch the bottom. Focus on good form and keep your posture upright. Don't let your arms and legs splay out to the sides. Imagine yourself running on land and emulate that form. As you run suspended in the water, it doesn't matter if you move around the pool. That will likely happen.

Once you have achieved good running form, try to increase the time that you run. Running in water is very tiring at first. Start by running for 5 minutes. An experienced athlete can eventually go for 45 minutes to one hour. Variety is important, though, since boredom can set in. Once you warm up and are accustomed to the activity, try running intervals (quicker-paced segments interspersed with the normal running).

Here are a couple of good water exercises for soccer players. These can be done on their own or preceding a longer water run. In either case, warming up first by water running for five minutes is a good idea. As with any workout, don't forget to do the cooldown and stretching afterward.

Leg scissors. Groin strains are a common problem in soccer. These exercises strengthen groin muscles. They also facilitate the rapid changes of direction that soccer players frequently make.

With your back against the pool's wall, extend your arms out to the sides and hold on to the side. Put your legs out to your sides as if you were in a jumping-jack position, with straight knees. Pull both legs together and cross your ankles. Push your legs out to the original position. Pull them in again, alternating the foot that crosses in front. Do this exercise for two minutes.

Leg crossovers. This exercise will strengthen the quadriceps (front of the thighs) and the inner thighs and stretch the hip flexors (muscles that flex the hips) and shoulders. It's ideal for targeting the muscles used often in soccer.

Take the same position as above, with your hands on the side of the pool. Extend your legs straight under you, toward the bottom of the pool. Pull your right leg across your body, with your knee straight, reaching as far as possible toward your left hand. Rotate your hips to facilitate the swing. Return to the starting position and switch legs, swinging your left leg toward your right arm. Do this exercise for two minutes.

You can also try practicing useful soccer skills in waist-deep water, such as jumping and heading, for more beginning players, and for the advanced, goalkeeper saves, diving headers, or scissors kicks.

We've given you an overview here of the wealth of complementary sports that are available to your child. Now comes the important part: trying them and enjoying them.

CHAPTER 14

injuries and safety

PREVENTING AND TREATING SOCCER'S HARD KNOCKS

Few things chill the blood of a parent like the sight of an injured athlete lying on the field. Your breath catches and time stands still until you see her slowly get to her feet and shake it off.

Sports and injuries, unfortunately, go hand in hand. But with a little bit of foresight and a solid commitment to safety, you and your child can reduce both the number and severity of injuries. Soccer, in its own way, can help. Due to its low-contact nature, it has one of the lowest injury rates of any youth sport.

Here's an overview of some of the more common soccer-specific injuries and what you can do to treat and prevent them. The medical advice is provided by Edward M. Decter, M.D., an orthopaedic surgeon in Livingston, New Jersey. Dr. Decter, a veteran soccer dad, is the team physician for St. Benedict's Prep, the number one–ranked boys' high school soccer team in the country in 1997 and 1998. He is also a former team physician for the Metrostars professional Major League Soccer team.

foot problems

Overpronation. Babies and preschoolers are naturally flat-footed. Their arches don't usually develop until the age of five or six. If they remain flat-footed after that, it is likely that they will be overpronators. Pronation is the natural tendency to roll your foot inward as it strikes the ground. People who overpronate roll their feet inward too much, causing excessive stress on the tendons in their feet and resulting in pain.

Flat-footedness is an inherited trait. If one or both parents are flat-footed, there is a higher likelihood for a child to be flat-footed. Putting inserts into the shoes to raise the arches somewhat alleviates overpronation.

Accessory navicula. Another condition that can cause pain is an accessory navicula, in which certain bones in the center of the foot do not mesh properly. In the young, rapidly growing child, this is usually treated with a navicula pad placed inside the shoe, which is a less expensive treatment than purchasing specially designed footwear. When growth of the child's foot starts to slow down, you could consider purchasing an orthotic (custom-made shoe insert). An orthotic is a more expensive option than a simple navicula pad. Fortunately, the simple treatment often works just as well and you don't need to bother with an orthotic.

Heel injuries. Heel pain usually occurs in children under 13 years of age. A fatty pad covering the heel protects it from injury. In younger children, this heel pad isn't fully developed. Soccer players pounding up and down a field in a pair of undercushioned cleats can find themselves hobbled by heel pain.

Dr. Decter is in the process of developing modified soccer shoes to prevent heel pain. You can also use custom-made or store-bought inserts in cleats.

The most effective treatment for heel pain is to keep your child off the field for up to 10 days while her bone heals. While your child is sidelined, get some heel pads to place in her street shoes to reduce the impact that walking has on her heels. You can also use ice treatment for the first couple of days to reduce swelling. Follow up with some anti-inflammatory medication.

If your child is having heel pain on a regular basis, it may be a sign of overtraining or poor running technique. Get a sports physician to examine her.

Seaver's syndrome is a condition that is caused when two parts of the heel bone don't properly fuse in a growing, active child. The repetitive pounding in soccer, coupled with the pull of the Achilles tendon, can lead to some pretty severe discomfort in the heel area.

If your child has Seaver's syndrome, she won't be alone; this is a very common problem among youth athletes. It's treated with rest, heel lifts (plastic or rubber shoe inserts), and as the child starts to feel better, even supportive taping of the heel as a preventive measure.

The worst-case scenario? Sometimes, this condition can keep your child from playing the entire season. If that's the case, it's important to make sure she rests, or she will delay healing for an even longer period of time.

ankle injuries

Ankle injuries are probably the most common type of injury seen in soccer. Take a group of kids hacking at a ball, add a lot of stop-and-start action, and toss in a dozen or so high-speed directional changes, and you have a recipe for ankle injuries.

Step number one is to make sure that your child's shinguards are the type that have ankle protectors. A direct kick to an unprotected ankle can sideline your child for the season.

When ligament injuries occur, they're generally caused by a child rolling an ankle on the field. Fortunately, the younger a child is, the easier it is to treat ligament injuries and the less likelihood there is that she'll need surgery. These injuries can usually be treated with a cast and a crutch.

Ankle fractures, however, are another story. A broken ankle is often characterized by a lot of swelling around the injury as well as disfiguration of the ankle joint. In serious fractures, there will be an obvious deformity and the foot will stick out at an odd angle. Recognizing this is usually quite simple; the ankle will just look broken. Get the child to a hospital.

Someone should also check to see if the area beyond the break is getting enough blood. You can do this by taking the pulse of the foot on the top of the midfoot. The area should also be a normal skin tone. If it looks pale or blue, the blood flow is cut off, and it is absolutely necessary to get medical help as quickly as possible.

It is also essential that a medical kit be on the sideline. One of the important pieces of equipment in this kit is a splint to secure the extremity in the position in which it lies. (Other items in the medical kit should include a bee-sting kit, smelling salts, ice packs, adhesive bandages, latex gloves, Ace bandages, and gauze.)

Preventive measures are to wear proper shoes, avoid uneven playing surfaces, and strengthen the muscles around the ankle by doing controlled ankle rolls on a regular basis. It's a good idea to take a walk over unfamiliar fields to check for things like potholes, trash, and other ankle hazards. If your team is playing in rain, have someone trudge through standing water to make sure there are no surprises underneath.

shin injuries

These types of injuries are very common problems in young athletes.

Shinsplints. Shinsplints are inflammations of the muscles surrounding the shins and are caused by repetitive running on hard ground. The pain is usually localized from the mid to lower portion of the outside of the lower leg.

Treatment for shinsplints often includes physical therapy, but the injury will generally heal on its own if the child rests long enough, which is generally three to six weeks. In the initial phase of healing, ice treatment and anti-inflammatories, such as ibuprofen, aspirin, or naproxen sodium, can be used with some success. Don't use acetaminophen, as it has no anti-inflammatory properties. Apply ice for 15 to 20 minutes three or four times a day.

One exercise to help prevent shinsplints is toe raises. Put both feet flat on the floor and roll your toes and feet upward as far as you can, repeating until exhaustion. This builds up the front shin muscles and prevents them from further injury. Other preventive measures are similar to those that are described for heel pain.

Stress fractures. Another common problem in the shin area is a stress fracture, a microfracture in the front lower-leg bone (tibia). It usually happens along the lower third of the tibia, and its symptoms are similar to those of shinsplints. These fractures are rarely picked up by conventional x-rays because they are so small. A physician may have to resort to more sophisticated diagnostic tests, such as a bone scan or magnetic resonance imaging (MRI).

Stress fractures are usually treated by resting until they have healed. This may take anywhere from 6 to 12 weeks. A cast is usually not required. Instead, crutches may be necessary to take the weight off the leg.

Fractures. A more serious type of injury is a fracture, which can result from a direct traumatic blow to the shinbone. A fracture of the tibia can be very debilitating. It may take several months to completely heal, and it usually spells an end to the season for your child.

The two types of fractures are simple

and compound. A simple fracture is one in which the broken bone does not protrude through the skin, and is characterized by swelling, deformity, and unusual movement of the broken bone. A compound fracture is one in which the bone protrudes through the skin, and it is more serious because of the risk of infection from foreign material like dirt.

Besides ankle and stress fractures, if a youth soccer player breaks a bone, it is usually one of the long bones in the legs or arms. Fractures involving a long bone with an obvious deformity, such as a bone protruding through the skin or a limb that is oddly bent, need to be splinted immediately and checked to be sure that blood circulation below the break is okay. If it is an arm fracture, the child can usually be transported by car to a local emergency room. If it is a fracture to a long bone in the leg, such as the femur or tibia, you should call an ambulance.

If there is not an obvious deformity, then it can be difficult to tell if a bone is broken. Most of the time, there will be pain, swelling, and discoloration around the break. If the pain continues, see a doctor.

One thing to also be on the lookout for in any leg injury is a tear in the lining that holds muscle mass in place (the fascia). This injury can happen if a player takes a swift kick directly to the muscle. Then, as the athlete starts to run, the muscle will protrude out through the fascia with a considerable amount of pain. In addition to the localized pain, there will be bulging.

When any of these injuries are suspected, it is recommended that an orthopedic surgeon or sports physician be consulted.

knee injuries

The knee undergoes tremendous amounts of stress just from normal walking, let alone from strenuous sports like soccer. That it holds together as well as it does is a testament to the amazing design of the human body. But because of the rapid acceleration and deceleration that is part of soccer as well as because of the twisting and turning that goes on during play, knee injuries are relatively common.

ACL injuries. With knee injuries, you may hear about something called the anterior cruciate ligament (ACL). This is a ligament that provides stability to the knee. For reasons unknown to doctors, there is a higher risk of ACL damage in female athletes than in males. The most telltale sign of ACL damage is instability in the knee, such as buckling while running or turning.

An ACL injury is usually very serious. It used to be a career-ending injury. But now, the ACL can usually be reconstructed with the use of arthroscopic surgery, in which a camera is inserted through a very small incision to allow the surgeon to see the whole knee. Children under 15, though, are generally not candidates for this type of surgery because their bones are still growing. Children this age are treated with alternate means.

The youngest soccer player whom Dr. Decter has seen with this type of injury was 7 years old. The boy was treated by immobilizing his knee with a brace, coupled with physical therapy. At age 14, the boy was playing competitively at a very high level.

This boy's treatment followed the

general recommendations for youth ACL injuries–bracing and physical therapy. If the patient has good muscle control, Dr. Decter usually allows the child to play soccer while wearing a brace. If the child's knees are unstable and it's likely that he'll injure himself further, Dr. Decter will not allow the child to play until the ligament is reconstucted, at around the age of 15.

HIGHER RISK FOR GIRLS

Why do women experience tears of the anterior cruciate ligaments (ACL), the ligaments that help support and stabilize the knee joint, at a rate two to six times greater than that of men? Some experts speculate that there is a connection between this injury and women's menstrual cycles.

One study found that more injuries happen during a woman's ovulatory phase, when estrogen is high, and fewer occur during the menstrual phase, when progesterone levels increase, according to Ed Wojtys, M.D., a professor of orthopedic surgery at the University of Michigan in Ann Arbor, who conducted the study.

Other theories speculate that something innate or structural makes women more prone to this injury. While experts cannot completely agree, one thing is certain. The risk can be greatly reduced by strengthening the supporting muscles–the thighs, hips, and calves–by lifting weights and doing other conditioning exercises.

Torn knees. Another injury you may hear about is a torn knee. This refers to damage to the meniscus, a C-shape structure that acts as a shock absorber. At the moment of injury, the athlete will usually feel something tear within her knee. Fluid will accumulate in the knee, which will usually become apparent about six hours after the injury. With fluid accumulation, there will be swelling and sensitivity to increased pressure. Also, the knee will feel tight when flexed.

This type of injury should be treated by an orthopedic surgeon. Treatment may run from arthroscopic surgery to, possibly, removal of the meniscus. Doctors try not to remove the meniscus in young athletes, as they feel its absence may lead to arthritis later in life.

Chondromalacia. Elsewhere in the knee, patellar, or kneecap, problems can be especially troublesome among teenage female athletes. Players can develop a condition called chondromalacia, a softening of the cartilage around the knee. This is often felt as pain while running and going up and down stairs. While overtraining and running may do the actual damage, many experts feel that the original softening of cartilage may be caused by the hormones of early female puberty.

The treatment for chondromalacia is usually rest, anti-inflammatory medication, physical therapy, and quadriceps-strengthening exercises, which include lifting each leg up and down with the knee locked. Usually, this condition resolves itself and the athlete is able to again participate in soccer.

Another knee injury is the growth-related Osgood-Schlatter disease, which is the pulling away of the knee tendon from the growth area of the knee. This causes pain until this area fuses and the tendon attaches to the main bone. This is a very common injury in 12- to 14-year-old boys, but girls often get it as well.

It usually resolves itself when the knee is rested for several weeks. Parents can rest assured that this is not a serious problem within the knee joint proper, and that rest as well as knee immobilization for several weeks usually alleviate the problem.

Players can continue with soccer after the initial swelling goes down. Playing through pain so severe that it hampers running form is not recommended, however. Strengthening the supporting upper-leg muscles can be helpful in providing support to the knees.

groin and testicular injuries

Groin pulls can affect either muscles or tendons. They're more common in boys because boys usually have tighter ligaments than girls. They are common injuries and can best be prevented by adequate stretching and warming up before playing. Treatment is rest, ice, physical therapy, and stretching and strengthening the injured muscle or tendon.

Injuries to the testicles that occur in soccer are always the result of blunt trauma, according to Bernard S. Strauss, M.D., an attending surgeon and former director of the section of urology at St. Barnabas Medical Center in Livingston, New Jersey. These injuries are relatively infrequent, though. When injury does occur, the intensity of the pain varies from mild discomfort, which passes in a matter of minutes, to severe pain, which may last for hours and may be accompanied by nausea and vomiting. More severe cases may require the use of pain medication and ice. With more significant trauma, swelling and discoloration of the testicles may occur and may last for as long as one to two weeks. Even-

SKIN PROTECTION

Protection from the sun is especially important for children since severe sunburn in early childhood has been linked to skin cancer in later life. All players need protection, including those who are already tanned or dark-skinned.

Although it is especially important on sunny days, don't neglect sunscreen just because it's overcast. Up to 80 percent of the sun's damaging rays get through on a cloudy day. A sunscreen with an SPF (skin protection factor) of 15 is usually enough. Products with higher SPFs are geared to those with sun-sensitive skin and those who are exposed to the sun all day.

Apply sunscreen liberally at least 15 minutes before sun exposure. And be vigilant. Young players who apply their own often do so sparingly and don't cover all areas. Make sure they get the tops of their ears, neck, and exposed scalp, places often forgotten and easily burned. Reapply every one to two hours or after heavy perspiration. Special sweat-resistant products are available for active people.

tually, though, the problem almost always resolves itself.

The only worthwhile preventive measure is a cup. The inconvenience and discomfort associated with its use, however, coupled with the low incidence of significant testicular injuries, results in most players refraining from using it.

hip injuries

A very serious problem in the hip area is called a slipped capital femoral epiphysis. Yes, it's as bad as it sounds. It occurs in a child when the head of the femur (the upper leg bone) has not yet fused properly to the rest of the femur. The head can actually slip out of the ball-and-socket joint where the femur rests.

The child usually experiences pain in the groin and an inability to run. The most important thing to recognize is whether the pain is in the groin and thigh areas. Anytime a child complains of pain in the groin, thigh, or inside of the knee area, a specific hip evaluation should be made to ensure that this is not a slipped capital femoral epiphysis. A child with this condition would walk with a noticeable limp. The condition is more common in heavier children.

Treatment of this injury usually requires pinning and surgical repair. If a child sustains this injury in one hip, there is a 25 percent chance that it will happen in the other hip, too.

Inflammation of the hip joint is another problem seen in youth soccer players. It is characterized by persistent pain in the hip. This occurs primarily due to repetitive running on hard ground. It can be treated with rest and anti-inflammatories.

shoulder injuries

Sometimes, it seems that a soccer player is on the grass as often as she's on her feet. Muddy fields and sliding tackles conspire to keep her on the ground. With this can come shoulder injuries.

Usually the result of a fall on an outstretched arm, shoulder injuries can range anywhere from a dislocation to ligament damage. It all depends on how the player breaks her fall and at what angle her arm hits the ground.

Unfortunately, if an athlete dislocates her shoulder, it sometimes causes damage to the surrounding ligaments. This can leave her prone to future dislocations of the same shoulder, even if she's not hit as hard as the first time.

The first time a child dislocates a shoulder, she is usually immobilized in a shoulder sling for a period of three to six weeks. Dr. Decter usually does an MRI to see if there has been any associated ligament or tissue injury as well. This can sometimes show if future dislocations should be a cause of concern to you and your child.

neck and spine injuries

Neck and spine injuries are fairly rare in soccer, but you still need to be extremely careful when assessing a child who may have suffered an injury of this type. Unnecessarily moving someone with a spinal injury can cause permanent paralysis.

If a child loses consciousness, Dr. Decter firmly believes that the child should be taken to a local emergency room to be evaluated to make sure that there is no internal bleeding or associated neck injuries.

Slightly less serious injuries to the muscles surrounding the spine can result from a solid impact with another player or from twisting violently to one side. Sometimes, muscle pulls around the lower spine are misdiagnosed as pulls of the hamstrings, so have a doctor check both areas.

If a congenital spinal deformity is contributing to an unusually high number of spinal muscle pulls, a player may still be able participate in soccer while wearing a custom-made brace. Dr. Decter has treated many young people who are playing at a high level with these types of braces. Only a doctor will be able to tell you if this is a possibility.

To help prevent muscle pulls in her back, your child should develop strong stomach and hamstring muscles through such exercises as stomach crunches and adequate stretching before and after play.

head injuries

Although soccer has an injury rate one-fifth to one-half that of American football, head injuries, such as concussions and bloody and broken noses, do occur. Players knocking heads, catching a ball in the face, or misjudging a goalpost are all potential dangers.

Concussions. A knock on the head, often accidentally from another player, is not uncommon in soccer. This may result in a concussion, which is a bruising of the brain. In the event of a possible concussion, whoever is in charge should stabilize the head and call for an ambulance. The signs of a concussion are any loss of consciousness (although you may still suffer a concussion without this), short-term memory lapses, dizziness, loss of balance, persistent headache, and nausea or vomiting. If in doubt, get the player to a hospital.

Bloody noses. To treat a bloody nose, put the player in a sitting position and pinch the nostrils closed for about 10 minutes, or until the bleeding stops. Have the player keep her head forward. If possible, put ice on the bridge of the nose to slow the bleeding. If the bleeding doesn't stop, apply pressure on the upper lip just beneath the nose. If these measures do not stop the bleeding, take the player to the hospital. (Make sure the player does not blow or pick her nose). Later, you may also apply petroleum jelly to the nostrils to keep them moist.

A broken nose is apparent by a misshapen appearance or by bruising around the eyes. Put ice on the nose to reduce swelling and seek medical attention.

Here's a bit of good news. A scare has been circulating that heading the ball may cause brain injuries over the long term. To try to get to the bottom of the issue, Michael J. Asken, Ph.D., a rehabilitation psychologist in the department of physical medicine and rehabilitation, and Robert C. Schwartz, M.D., an attending physician in internal medicine at Community Internal Medicine Center, both at Pinnacle Health at Polyclinic Hospital in Harrisburg, Pennsylvania, reviewed the current literature on the subject. They concluded that, while the evidence does warrant a closer look, there is no clear link between brain injuries and heading.

The current position of the U.S. Youth Soccer Association (USYSA) is that it is highly unlikely that chronic brain damage and intellectual impairment occur from heading a soccer ball. According to a 1995 statement by then–USYSA chairman Bob Contiguglia, the USYSA Sports Medicine Committee "studied the situation very closely. . . . Our findings are that repetitive heading does not cause head injuries."

But as a precaution, Dr. Asken and Dr. Schwartz recommend four steps.

1. Education should be provided to increase awareness of the potential for injury from heading a soccer ball.
2. Correct heading technique must be emphasized to prevent injury.
3. Rules that protect players should be enforced by referees and supported by coaches, parents, and fans. (Referees should ensure that defenders maintain the full required distance from the ball on restarts, such as free kicks, to prevent taking a fast-moving ball in the head from a short distance.)
4. Team physicians or trainers should continue to be aware of this issue, and appropriate sideline evaluation of athletes for concussions should be part of every game.

KEEPING TEETH IN THE MOUTH

Mouthguards, or mouth protectors, for sports have been in use for several decades. Although the importance of these protectors in preventing dental trauma has been well-established, organized football and ice hockey are the only sports that have documented mandatory mouth-protector rules.

Many modern mouthguards are nearly 100 percent effective in protecting athletes from losing teeth. It has also been shown that properly made, custom-fit mouthguards can reduce the rate of head concussions.

Mouthguards are divided into three general types: the ready-made or stock version, the mouth-formed protector (placed in the mouth, molded, and allowed to set), and the custom-made mouth protector. Studies have shown that all types are effective in reducing the number of dental injuries. The more expensive custom mouth protectors, however, have been shown to be most effective. Also, it's easier to speak and breathe with this type of guard. Anyone with braces should use a custom-made guard.

Here's some advice on what you should you do if your child's tooth is knocked out while she is playing soccer, adapted from information provided by the American Dental Association and the American Association of Orthodontists. If the tooth is dirty, gently rinse it with water, but do not handle the root. If possible, reposition the tooth in the socket. If it cannot be replaced in the socket, put it in milk, or in the child'smouth next to the cheek. Water, with a little salt if possible, is the next best choice if no other option is feasible. Get to the dentist as soon as possible. If it's a baby tooth, do not try to replant it, as it could damage the permanent tooth in formation.

EYEGLASSES AND SOCCER

Playing soccer in regular prescription glasses is an accident waiting to happen. To help prevent eye injuries, soccer-playing children should use protective athletic eyewear. One-piece plastic sports frames with polycarbonate lenses allow for high visibility as well as protection. Some special features that parents and children may want to consider are padded or rubber bridges, which add extra comfort; deep-grooved eyewires, so lenses will not fall out if the frame is hit hard; a face-formed shape for a wider field of view; and headband attachments to secure the frames on the player's head.

The American Optometric Association (AOA) states that contact lens wearers need protective athletic eyewear also, as contacts alone do not provide sufficient protection. Sports glasses come in prescription and non-prescription types because the AOA feels that children should use protective athletic eyewear regardless of whether they wear prescription glasses or contacts.

As sports glasses are a significant financial investment, devise some protection against loss. Provide a safe place to keep glasses before and after playing and educate your child on the importance of caring for the glasses. If possible, mark your child's name and telephone number on the glasses.

What should you do if a child gets hit in the eye? Take the child to a hospital emergency room or to an eye doctor for immediate care. Some children may see stars or spots or notice a change in their vision, but damage from a blow is not always so apparent.

prevention

Dr. Decter feels strongly that it is incumbent upon the coaches not to overtrain youth players. Sometimes, there is a tendency among coaches to push even young players beyond their age-appropriate capabilities. Complete fatigue after practice and persistent soreness the next day are sure signs that a child is being overtrained.

Appropriate footwear is vital. So is a safe playing surface. Children should not be allowed to play on fields that are uneven or pocked with holes.

To help avoid injuries, children should also be encouraged to improve their fitness levels before coming out for a sport. It would probably be a wise idea for a coach to give an off-the-field training program to players from age 14 on, so they will have reasonable levels of fitness when they begin the soccer season. Children younger than 14 should be active enough that they don't need an off-season training program.

It is also important that children have a preseason physical by a doctor to make sure that they have no hidden health problems. Dr. Decter believes that an orthopedic screen should be done as well.

The vast majority of children go through sports with only minor nicks and bruises. You don't need to be over-anxious for their safety, just prepared.

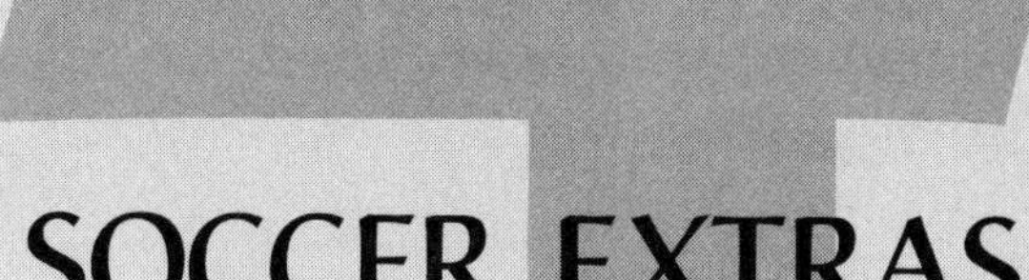

SOCCER EXTRAS

15. levels of play 129
16. camps and special programs 136
17. serious soccer 143
18. parents as coaches 150

CHAPTER 15

levels of play

DECIPHERING THE COMPLEX WORLD OF YOUTH SOCCER

Your child loves to play pickup games of soccer but seems bored when he's on the field with his team. Or he is highly skilled but his level of play during games seems to have plateaued. Or he's one of the stars of his league, outclassing most of the people he plays against.

Do any of these scenarios sound like they apply to your child? If they do, it could be time for him to move up to another level of play.

There are many levels in youth soccer, and a child can progress through them depending on age, ability, motivation, and goals. But to help your child make the right choices at the right times, you have to understand the system. Once you do, you can ensure that he develops as a player and, most important, continues to have fun.

the options

You'll learn one thing quickly when you start to seek out a new level of play for your child: There's a confusing array of options available. The names, categories, and style of youth soccer play are not consistent nationwide. In fact, you won't necessarily find all the levels of play mentioned here. Given these variables, here are descriptions of the six basic categories.

Recreational. This is also known as town play. This is the level of play where children usually start. Recreational leagues are open to all children, often beginning as young as four years old. Children don't have to try out for teams or be invited to join. They're just assigned. Play at this level should be fun, educational, and low-key. Often, an abiding feature of this level is a policy of equal playing time. While some recreational leagues are, in fact, quite competitive and do keep track of wins and losses, the emphasis in recreational play is noncompetitive. Some recreational leagues do not even keep score.

There is usually limited pressure on the players and minimal time investment, usually with training once per week and one game per week. Recreational play may be conducted part of the year and coached by parent volunteers, who may, but probably don't, have coaching licenses or other training. Typical groups who run these leagues include town parks and recreation departments, nonprofit soccer clubs run by parent volunteers, or professional organizations that are hired to run the league. There is usually a fee to play.

BENEFITS: Less competition and pressure; less time commitment; less travel; fewer costs; players often get equal amounts of playing time.

DRAWBACKS: Possibility of lower-quality instruction, wide variance in children's playing abilities, inexperienced referees, and lower-quality facilities and equipment.

Classic. Also known as competition, travel team, or town select. Classic teams are openly competitive and represent a club and/or a town. Usually, a child has to be selected for a team through tryout, invitation, or recruiting. Unlike recreational, this level is not characterized as low-key, although fun, fairness, and equal playing time might still be stressed. Depending on the league schedules, it is possible for children to participate in both recreational and classic play.

Coaches at this level are more likely required to have at least the introductory U.S. Soccer Federation F license or youth license modules. There may be a professional organization involved in

TIME TO MOVE UP THE LADDER?

Some talented children who flounder when playing on a recreational team blossom when they are encouraged to advance to higher levels. Conversely, children placed on competitive teams may struggle because, playing ability aside, they are not ready or willing to give the necessary physical and emotional commitment to the game.

How can you determine whether your child falls into the first group and not the second? Here are some signs.

- Your child expresses the desire to change levels.
- Your child is enthusiastic, always ready and willing for soccer training and competition.
- Coaches, players, and parents talk about the ability of your child.
- Your child plays soccer even when not around his regular team (for example, he plays around the house or with friends).
- Your child expresses boredom with his current team because he has outgrown the skill level of teammates.
- Your child understands and deals appropriately with failure.
- Your family enjoys the current commitment, handles it well, and would not mind having greater involvement.

While it is impossible to guarantee that a change—and a move up the ladder—is right, consider your choice carefully. It can be difficult to move again, or to go back, both of which are emotionally stressful on a child. If you're in doubt, remember that you can always hold off for awhile.

training or coaching. Teams at this level are flighted (placed in a level) in a division (age group) by ability, resulting in a flight champion. Clubs may have competitive or recreational teams, which compete within a league of other club teams similar in age and ability.

Teams generally belong to clubs, which in turn belong to the league of their choice, usually in their geographical area. They generally play for at least two seasons each year; in some cases, the teams compete year-round in additional tournaments or leagues.

BENEFITS: Better instruction; better quality of play; more equal playing ability; gives players a better sense of regional level of soccer play.

DRAWBACKS: More travel; more costs; greater time commitment; child faces possible rejection at tryouts; competitiveness can have negative aspects.

Premier. This level includes most of the features of classic, including inter-club league play. The main difference is that premier leagues have a higher quality of play than classic leagues. Premier players are selected from a wider geographical range, but not an unlimited area, as with some forms of Select-level play. Premier teams play within premier leagues, which are flighted, as done in classic. Because premier teams draw from a wider area, the selection process, and thus the level of play, is more competitive. Some associations allow players to be duel-rostered; that is, they may play on both classic and premier teams. Premier teams, however, often stay together year-round, in which case they serve as a player's only team. Because of the way it is structured, premier may include many of the characteristics of Select.

BENEFITS: Higher level of instruction and competition; selection builds child's pride and status; trips and travel; possibility to be seen by higher-level coaches from Select teams and Olympic Development Program.

DRAWBACKS: Child faces possible rejection at tryouts; significant time commitment for the child and parents (can greatly impact family life); higher costs; more intense competition can have negative aspects; heavy practice and competition schedule may lead to injuries or burnout.

Select. Select (all-star) is the official team of the U.S. Youth Soccer Association (USYSA) or any of its regions or affiliated national state associations. There are teams for the various age groups. Players are drawn from large geographic areas, which means that making the team is very competitive. Select level develops players with an eye toward advancing them to higher levels, such as the Olympic Development Program, top high schools, and college.

Select teams can vary in who they play. They can play against both Select and non-Select teams.

Select play entails much higher stakes and is for the serious soccer player and his family. By the time a player reaches this level, he has developed skills that are permanently ingrained. In short, he has acquired the habits to make him a player for life.

Select play can be in addition to a player's commitment to a regular team. The Select team may be coached by someone appointed by the state association, implying that the person has higher coaching licenses or training experience.

BENEFITS: Higher level of instruction and competition; selection builds child's pride and status; trips and travel; possibility to be seen by higher-level coaches from Select teams and Olympic Development Program.

DRAWBACKS: Child faces possible rejection at tryouts; significant time commitment for the child and parents (can greatly impact family life); higher costs; more intense competition can have negative aspects; heavy practice and competition schedule may lead to injuries or burnout.

Independent Select. An emerging type of Select team is a hybrid. It is made up of a number of better-skilled and more-serious competitive team players, usually brought together by a private club, professional organization, or even assertive parents who are attempting to create a higher-level team for their children. These teams can be found at increasingly younger ages. The enticing features of this system are that the organizers have more control. For example, they can choose the best players regardless of where they live.

Because there may not be Select leagues (although these are on the rise) to accommodate them, independent Select teams have to play where they can. They must also find a host town or club to prevent independent teams from operating without a structure or a base. A host club or town provides liability insurance, helps teams gain credibility, and allows them to be part of a scheduled league. There are teams, however, that compete independently in a variety of leagues.

BENEFITS: Higher-level players and competition than regular league play; competitors drawn from larger area, so the player and coaching quality is better; at older ages, greater possibility to be seen by college scouts; because they compete year-round, these teams maintain continuity, both athletically and competitively.

DRAWBACKS: Since the organization works outside the regular soccer system, teams must create new league structure, leave their towns, and find host towns; strong emphasis on winning; less security for a developing player, who may more easily be cut from the team; because of drawing from wide area, likelihood of greater travel time for both practice and competition; significant costs and time commitment.

Olympic Development Program. The U.S. Youth Soccer Olympic Development Program (ODP) is a national program that identifies and develops highly skilled players. It is the highest level in the USYSA system. The age at which this program begins varies among state associations and regions. Some states have developmental ODP pools beginning at age 11, while others begin full-fledged state teams at age 14. The program first develops players to represent their state associations. If they succeed at that level, they may then progress within the program to represent their regions, and then the country (the national team). Pools of players are identified through a series of tryouts that are judged by coaches and soccer professionals. From observation over time, the pool is narrowed down to form the teams.

A permanent place on the team is not guaranteed, as the players are continually evaluated. The teams' emphasis is on training and, therefore, the game schedule (mostly against other states' ODP teams) is not too intense. ODP is an addition to, not a replacement for, a player's regular team.

BENEFITS: Opportunity to train and compete with the best players in an age group; highest level of competition available; most highly qualified coaches; exposure to regional and national team coaches and college coaches; pride in representing your area or country.

DRAWBACKS: Lengthy tryout procedure that is very rigorous, both physically and emotionally; continuous evaluation means that a place in the program is not secure; possibility of constant rejection (may remain in pool but not be chosen to compete); greater possibility of burnout; additional sources of stress beyond playing (high-level systems often include high-level politics); significant costs and time commitment.

choosing a level

Which level will be the best fit? You have to know your child and your family to answer that question. The choice you make should be a blend of both your child's and your family's needs. Play at a higher level can mean a major commitment on everyone's part. Your child may have to pass up other activities to play. Both parents may have to defer some of their interests so that they can provide transportation and support. Even other siblings may get less attention for a time. Ask yourself what the entire family would enjoy and benefit from and what is a reasonable amount of time, money, and emotional investment to make.

Also, before committing to a new level, do your homework. Speak to players and parents on your prospective team or in your prospective soccer organization. Read all available literature that the team puts out so that you understand the details of your commitment should your child make the team. Attend one of the desired team's practices or games. Request a meeting or conversation with the coach.

To get an even better feel for the team, you might ask if your child can participate as a guest player for the team, if it is allowed by the system's rules. Or you can request that your child be allowed to practice with the team. Do this as much as possible; the more he plays with potential teammates, the more confident you'll feel about a decision.

Finally, when you find a team that seems like a good fit, let your child try out only if you are serious about him joining. Don't try out at a level just to see if he can succeed. This is unfair to the team and to players who might have been chosen instead. Also, don't try out for more than one team just for the sake of the exercise. Invariably, one of the coaches or teams finds out, which can result in your child making neither team and developing a bad reputation.

trying out

Like aspiring actors standing on a theater stage, children attending a soccer tryout often feel the pressure of performing. Tryouts, during which a child is observed and judged by adults holding clipboards, can be exciting but stressful. And often, aside from arrival time, very little about the tryout process is explained.

A youth soccer tryout can be conducted in a variety of ways. Some teams test players in individual soccer skills, speed drills, and game play; some simply have children scrimmage. Some combine all of these tests. Tryouts can be conducted in one or more sessions, and a team may call back some or all of the players. Players are usually divided into groups by gender and age. There can even be a form of pre-tryouts, in which programs recruit players for a tryout or a team by sending scouts to regular league play or by soliciting recommendations from other coaches.

In a well-run tryout procedure, evaluators look for specific abilities. These include speed, ball control skills when in possession or trying to get possession of the ball, how well the ball is controlled when first touched, passing ability, tactics, and positional awareness. They also look for aggressiveness, hustle, enthusiasm, and strong communication skills (talking a lot on the field by calling out to assist and encourage other players).

An experienced evaluator recognizes a player with vision, who has the ability, for example, to make passes into open space, thus anticipating plays. The evaluator looks at a candidate when he is both on and off the ball. A good evalu-

TRYOUT SUCCESS

The week of your child's soccer tryout has arrived, and he's as ready as can be. Now it's up to you to take the final steps to make the test a success. Here are ways that you can help.

- Take a relaxed attitude so as not to put more pressure on your child.
- Make sure that your child gets a good night's sleep the night before the tryout.
- Make sure that he is nutritionally prepared, as tryouts can be long. (For more information on nutrition, see chapter 12.)
- Arrive early to familiarize your child with the facilities and to warm up.
- Bring a water bottle. Just as in practices or games, the evaluators should allow drink breaks.
- Help him visualize, seeing himself succeed at the tryout.
- Have him go to the bathroom before the tryout begins. (Even older children need reminding; they get nervous, too.)
- Have him wear proper clothing (basketball shorts and baseball cleats, for example, will make a poor impression on evaluators).
- Have your child wear something brightly colored so that he stands out to the evaluators.
- Prepare him emotionally for both success and failure.
- Instruct him to get on the ball a lot, but to be careful not to be a ball hog.
- Encourage him to speak up. Talking on the field to other players is a sign of understanding the game. Evaluators especially look for this.
- Encourage him to be cooperative and attentive, following the directions given by the evaluators.
- Instruct him not to horse around, which can make a bad impression on selectors.
- Reassure him to play the game that he knows. He should not attempt something new and flashy if it is not in his repertoire.

ator also knows how to spot and assess potential, which is crucial in a developing youth player.

As a parent, there are many ways that you can help your child do his best at a tryout. There are also things that you can do personally to keep yourself from becoming part of the process. While many parents do not stay to observe the tryout, they are usually allowed to sit at a distance and watch. If you choose this option, you may be seen, but you should not be heard. Never cheer or comment. Only speak to evaluators if you need information, such as when the tryout results will be released. Going beyond this can put undue stress on the selector and your child, risking an appearance of compromised objectivity.

Keep in mind that this is a subjective process, and there are cases in which children are deliberately not chosen based on the reputation, or inappropriate behavior, of their parents.

playing up

Playing up occurs when a skilled player joins a team of older players, usually one year older. Your child might do this for several reasons. One is lack of availability of an age-appropriate team, but often, the reason is to compete at a more advanced level. The decision to play up may be determined by the rules of the town or club. Some discourage it, some require that a player place near the top of the desired team in tryouts, and some have no rules.

The decision to play up should be made jointly by you, your child, and preferably, a coach. If your child is frustrated or bored with the ability of his team, this is an indication that playing up might be appropriate. If, however, your child is happy on the current team—even if he is far and away the best player—it may be reason enough for him to remain on that team.

Be sure that you are not lured to playing up for the wrong reasons. Have your child play up to challenge himself, not for the status that he'll get. Determine if he will be a constructive member of the new team and not just sit on the bench.

It is easier to acclimatize to playing up before children's growth spurts. The best ages are between 8 and 11. It is more difficult to make the transition when size and strength begin to become issues (particularly at puberty). By high school play, playing up often becomes a moot point, as players' ages can vary by up to four years. In this case, having previously played up can serve a player well. If your child's size is radically different from the players on an older team, or if he expresses fear of being hurt, playing up is not a good idea.

CHAPTER 16

camps and special programs

OPPORTUNITIES FOR MORE FUN AND LEARNING

Chosen well, a soccer camp or clinic can be an invaluable addition to your child's training. Chosen poorly, it can be a waste of your money and her time.

Finding the right camp, however, can present a particular challenge to both players and parents. This is because soccer camps have proliferated so quickly and without consistent guidelines. There are scores of camps, and it can take a lot of homework to make the best choice.

This chapter does a lot of that homework for you. If a local camp is your only choice, you can still use the guidelines here to ensure the quality of your child's camp experience. If it doesn't match up, you can look elsewhere.

Although there are no official figures (some camps are not even registered), soccer camps in the United States probably number well into the thousands. These camps come in every style. There are half- and full-day camps; residential, or sleep-away, camps; sports camps that include but are not exclusively devoted to soccer; soccer specialty camps, such as for strikers or goalkeepers, team training, and styles and philosophies of play; regional or national camps, which draw players from large areas; camps at universities, run by the collegiate soccer staff; and camps staffed by former players from soccer-strong foreign nations.

choosing a camp

It's summer, and the living is easy. That is how it used to be, anyway. Now, in addition to sunning and swimming in a general summer camp, there is soccer playing.

Choosing a camp is entirely dependent on the playing level of your child as well as what you and your child want from a camp. Under what conditions does she thrive? Is she a beginning player who would most enjoy developing skills in a low-

coach's corner

Before I began my own soccer camp, I had excellent training at a camp in Massachusetts. For seven summers, I worked at Camp Mah-Kee-Nac in Lenox, one of the oldest and largest residential camps in New England, which ranks among the top camps in the country. Mah-Kee-Nac believes in strict compliance with safety rules and legal regulations, and so do I.

In eight years of conducting my camp, the first order of business is always day-long seminars for all staff. We go over every rule: Staff members must properly maintain all equipment for safety; make sure players take frequent water breaks; walk the fields every morning to check for obstacles and impediments; take any child who asks for or needs medical attention to the full-time staff nurse; stop and question any member of the public who walks onto the field during camp hours—no matter who it is.

You could say that I am a fanatic about safety issues. Every year, I greet the state health-and-safety inspector like a diligent student, confident and ready for the final exam. I am the same way about the camp curriculum and about constant and open communication with campers' parents. I believe that this is the way a good camp ought to be run.

key atmosphere? Is she an older or more serious player who does not mind a full day of playing in an often competitive atmosphere?

Once you've decided that, word of mouth is always the best way to get a camp recommendation. Make enough telephone calls to friends and to friends of friends, and you can be sure to get plenty of opinions. Get a recommendation from campers themselves, if possible, rather than from their parents. Another possible resource to assist in your decision is to speak to your child's current coach. He probably knows best about your player's skill levels and areas that need work, and he may be able to steer you to an appropriate camp.

There are several annual comprehensive soccer camp listings that can be helpful. Because the largest number of camps are conducted in summer, these guides are usually published in the spring. Two national magazines that carry the listings are *Soccer America* and *Soccer Jr.* (See the resouce list on page 207.) Other good sources to narrow in on your area are regional publications, such as *Southern Soccer Scene* or *Soccer New England*.

You can also look up soccer camps on the Internet. Once you find a camp of interest, begin by calling to ask for a brochure or any other available printed material.

You may not always be able to judge the quality of soccer instruction at each and every camp you consider, but it is essential to evaluate the reputation of the camp, especially regarding safety. Below are some guidelines to help you assess a camp, provided by the American Camping Association (ACA), established in 1910, which accredits over 2,000 various types of camps nationwide.

Direct your questions to the camp director or other senior staff members. If possible, try to follow up any conversation with a visit to the camp before making your final decision.

- What is the background of the camp director? Look for previous experience running camps, soccer or otherwise. A background in education is also helpful.

- What is the camp's philosophy? For example, is it competitive or noncompetitive? According to the ACA, noncompetitive methods have been shown to encourage young people to learn more and retain information longer. (Keep in mind that youth soccer players usually get a lot of competitive experience in their regular season play.)

- What are the ages of the counselors? Eighty percent or more should be 18 years or older. Any counselors under 18 should be at least two years older than the campers they are supervising.

- What percentage of the staff returns each year? Some staff turnover is natural. Most camps have between 40 to 60 percent returning staff. If the rate is lower, ask why.

- How are special needs handled? If your child has special requirements, ask about provisions and facilities. Is there a nurse? Is there a designated place to store allergy medication or other medicines? The camp should have a policy in place for children with asthma or food allergies, both common among young people.

- How do the children get around the camp? Campers are often transported by vans or buses. Find out how vehicles are serviced, and inquire about the camp's driver-training and safety-awareness programs.

- Ask about the camper-to-counselor ratio. Get specific information about counselors. The given ratio should not include nurses, cooks, and other support staff. The ACA suggests the following ratios for residential camps: One staff member for every 6 campers ages 6 to 8; one for every 8 campers ages 9 to 14; and one for every 10 campers ages 15 to 17. Day camps should employ one staff member for every 8 campers ages 6 to 8; one for every 10 campers ages 9 to 14; and one for every 12 campers ages 15 to 17.

- Are references available? Generally, this is one of the best techniques to check a camp's reputation and service record.

While the ACA questions are all valid, Ashley's Soccer Camp has found that parents can really make sure they're getting the right camp for their child by asking some additional questions. Here is some more advice about information that you should ask for and also some tips to ensure that your child, and you, get exactly what you want.

- Be sure that a sports specialty camp is what your child wants. No matter what the prospective camp, share all information with your child and allow her to make the ultimate decision.
- Ask the camp about registration. In New Jersey, for example, by law, any camp or child-care organization must be registered by the state department of health. Even so, many of them are not. Be exceptionally leery of any camp that ignores the law.
- Find out what the emergency procedures are. Is the camp affiliated with a local hospital? Who is trained in first-aid? An on-site nurse is an added bonus.
- Is the camp insured, both with liability and medical insurance?
- If the camp is residential, what are the nighttime sleeping arrangements? Do counselors bunk with the children? Who supervises and provides security?
- Be aware that official certifications, licenses, or sponsorships do not automatically ensure quality. These designations do not necessarily mean that those who have licenses are good coaches. Reputation and return rates of athletes (in the range of 75 to 80 percent) are the best markers of a good camp.
- Make sure there is a good mix of both male and female staff. Female role models are especially important for young girls.
- Ask about the camp's growth rate over the years. Children don't return to a camp if they don't like it.
- Do not be swayed by glossy brochures. If the camp sells itself on a celebrity soccer player, owner, or coach, ask if that person will be at the camp full-time or if he will merely make occasional appearances.
- Check that the camp fulfills general soccer safety rules such as staking goals properly, checking fields for safety hazards, and making sure players wear shinguards.
- Ask for a daily curriculum. If a block of three hours merely says "defending," it is not specific enough. Ask for details. You want to know that the instructor has a complete lesson plan and isn't going to just have the players out doing vague drills for hours on end.
- Ask for a staff list with biographical information. Ask which staff are present during which weeks. Try to talk to some staff members. They are especially important since they serve as role models both on and off the field.

- If you choose a specialty camp, make sure the staff is qualified in that specialty. If it is a goalkeeping camp, for example, the coaches should be specially trained and should have played that position.
- All soccer camps, particularly higher-level soccer camps, should be staffed by experienced players.
- If the camp is coed, what is the girl-to-boy ratio? How will the players be grouped (by ability, by gender, by age)? Boys and girls sometimes gripe about playing soccer together, or they tease each other mercilessly. How does the camp deal with that?
- Will children be appropriately placed according to skill levels? If adjustments are necessary, will children be regrouped?
- Even if they are all soccer-related, activities should be fun and varied.
- If you are concerned about intense soccer focus, check to see whether other activities, such as canoeing or swimming, are offered.
- When signing your child up for camp, be conservative. Initially, you should sign her up for only one to two weeks of camp. You can always sign up for more time later. Often, camps will allow you to sign on for additional weeks. Try day camp first, then move on to residential camps. Save the very serious and rigorous camps for when your child is older and more experienced.

Many of the youth soccer camps and programs in the United States are staffed by players from other countries, including Great Britain, Brazil, and Germany. While there are many excellent camps, quality control is a major concern, according to Jim Buck, general manager of British Universities North America Club (BUNAC), which has headquarters in the United States and England, an exchange organization that brings thousands of overseas staff to serve as counselors and coaches in hundreds of camps in the United States and other countries. There is no national affiliation for soccer camps, meaning no national standard to which they must adhere.

Barring accreditation, be aware of several points, says Buck. Camps should meet certain standards, including health requirements. The overall concern should be whether the camp is a proper legal entity. If a camp is not registered with the state health department, it is not legal and is subject to immediate closure.

Soccer camps often go overseas to Europe or South America to recruit staff. First and foremost, you should determine if international staff are in the United States legally. (If not, the camp may be without liability insurance). Ask what exchange program they use to bring counselors into the country. They should answer with the name of an organization like BUNAC, Camp Counselors USA, Camp America, or Work America. Was the staff checked for special training or screened for ability to do the job and for a background check? A special visa program, such as BUNAC, guarantees that both the staff and camp have been screened.

advanced training

Higher-level camps, which are almost exclusively for older players, often serve one basic function–to showcase players to college coaches. Even if the camp is not located exactly at the college of your choice, if it is in the same college conference, you can be assured that a player's reputation spreads. If your player is interested in a specific college, have her call the soccer department there to find out which camps the school sponsors or monitors.

An elite camp recruits players from top programs and tournaments and also based on coaches' recommendations. At this level, more serious players have heard of a number of these camps and may have zeroed in on their choices.

Some advanced camps work with players of various levels. These offer a mentoring-type option; that is, a good younger player who shows promise may be able to play with older, more experienced campers.

Advanced camps can be extremely rigorous, long, full-day programs that include fitness running, soccer-skills training, and scrimmaging. One week of this type of camp is usually plenty. The cost can be steep, adding another incentive to consider this choice carefully.

after the choice

Having done the homework to choose a camp, you can use the same methods to prepare your child for attending it. Speak to the camp director, staff, and veteran campers for advice on how to prepare. Find out what to expect, what to do (or not to do), and what to bring.

Pack the small-but-necessary items you may not be able to get at camp. This includes extra clothing (some camps do not do laundry). Also, it's not a bad idea to pack favorite nonperishable food items such as crackers, cookies, cereal, or sports bars. Some camps, however, may have rules prohibiting campers from bringing food. Your child should not take new soccer cleats or other new shoes; she should break them in first. Many camps do fitness running or other activities that require different shoes.

special programs

To satisfy a soccer-hungry nation, year-round programs have proliferated in the United States. Special programs include clinics (sometimes called courses) and may feature individual or team travel and competition, either in the United States or abroad. Sometimes, your child's entire team won't want to travel, say, overseas, but many of the individual members might.

Many clinics and trips are even held during the off-season as well as during the regular season. Much of what to look for in any of these programs is similar to the guidelines for camps. You want to explore the staff qualifications, speak to other participants, and find out what the curriculum is.

Trips. A soccer trip can be the experience of a lifetime, filled with adventure and special bonding among family and friends. Because your player may be the only one from her area attending a program abroad, to get the most out of her trip, get good references, and consider having her travel with a friend.

For a travel soccer experience, especially abroad, be stringent about trip safety guidelines. At the top of the list, ask about emergency medical arrangements. Whether or not you accompany your child, ask for an explicit itinerary in nothing larger than two-hour blocks of time. ("A.M.: Sightseeing," for example, could be any time and any activity, and is not specific enough.) You need to know exactly what you are getting and how organized the trip staff is. Another important thing to consider: Do activities concentrate solely on soccer, or do they include a combination of soccer and local cultural activities?

The ratio of adults to children should be even greater than with other camps—six or seven to one. This is even more important if supervisors are not trained professionals, for instance, if they're other parents. If you are playing as a team on a U.S. trip, make sure the competitions have been approved by your state association for insurance purposes.

Make sure the level of playing ability is appropriate for your child. Finally, inquire about the rules on playing time. Will all children get an equal chance to play? You may not want your child to travel thousands of miles just to sit on the bench.

Clinics. Off-season clinics keep soccer going year-round. Many are often held indoors in areas with inclement winter weather. Clinics are usually specialized instruction on specific soccer techniques, or indoor games or tournaments. Clinics are a great way to keep skills fresh during the off-season.

If you are considering a clinic, try to visit first. Call your local recreation department, the YMCA, a local high school, or your child's coach to find out what's available. Keep in mind that the standard guidelines for other aspects of soccer play also apply to clinics. Make sure the level of playing ability and age of the children is consistent. (Clinics sometimes combine boys and girls of all ages and abilities). Check that the facility is safe. If you do sign up, it is a good idea to get the proper equipment, such as indoor soccer shoes.

indoor play

Indoor play differs from outdoor play in its style, rules, and features of the game. Indoor games have either regular boundary lines like an outdoor field or a version that allows balls to be played if they bounce off walls. Two types of balls are traditionally used: One is regular style and the other looks like a soccer-size tennis ball. Indoor play usually has fewer than 11 players per side and shorter games.

Indoor play has some uniquely positive features. It is usually faster. This type of play is good for developing certain skills such as improved touch, quick reactions, and speed. Also, smaller goals help develop more accurate shooting. Because each side has fewer players, they invariably play all positions, giving children the opportunity to develop both defensive and offensive skills.

The most important safety aspect of indoor play is the surface. If the surface is artificial turf, how hard is it? There should be no concrete showing. A wooden surface should not be slippery and should be free of protruding nails or splinters.

For personal safety, consider slip-on elastic pads for knees and elbows, or your child can apply a protective coat of petroleum jelly on her knees and elbows.

CHAPTER 17

serious soccer

GUIDANCE FOR THE GIFTED

As your child progresses up the ladder of soccer skills and playing levels, his world will get more intense. The competition will be fiercer; he'll need to be in better physical shape; he'll need more practice to stay proficient in soccer skills; and he'll likely have to make more choices about what teams to play on. But for all of this increased pressure, serious youth soccer can be very rewarding for both you and your child.

What turns an average soccer player into a serious one? Above all, it comes when a player takes a long, hard look at himself and says, "Yes, I may dabble in basketball, hockey, and baseball, but I am a soccer player."

Although ability, physical fitness, and skill have a lot to do with it, you can't be a serious soccer player unless you're motivated. Although wanting to excel and to win is definitely part of that motivation, it is not all of it. A player cannot reach the upper levels unless he loves the game. A significant quality of a serious player is that he plays soccer beyond practices and games because he wants to. No matter what happens with soccer, this passion will elevate all areas of a child's life. In fact, a remarkably high percentage of serious soccer players are also high-achieving, successful students.

Another sign of seriousness is goal setting. A serious player is spurred by both short- and long-range goals, constantly wanting to get better. A serious player is also willing to make sacrifices to play higher-level soccer. Whether it is accepting a no-parties-the-nights-before-games rule or tolerating the physical discomforts of practice and competition, he does these things willingly.

Serious organized play can begin as early as age 10. However, some children are under pressure to begin serious focus even earlier. It is notable that the Brazilian soccer star Pelé, speaking at a 1998 coaching conference in the United States, expressed his strong opposition to Select teams for children under age 14.

Other youth soccer experts and administrators echo this sentiment. Despite their avid interest, it is important for very young children to have other activities. They should be able to develop as players while maturing enough to decide, independently and responsibly, that soccer is their ultimate goal.

coach's corner

The Montclair Bombers of New Jersey began as a regular town team of nine-year-old boys. An ambitious parent-manager recognized the need to bring better players onto the team in order to become more competitive. In 1993, the Bombers reconfigured into a Select team—a type of team that was still relatively new in the area. I was hired as the coach of the team.

In the fall of 1995, we made it to the finals of the State Cup. This is an accomplishment that only a handful of teams can even dream of. We lost in overtime on a heartbreaking penalty kick. Although the players were fine, the parents were devastated. In fact, this game marked the beginning of the team's end.

By the end of the spring season of 1996, I ended my relationship with the team. There was too much unhealthy pressure to win and too much backbiting among the parents. Also, I was unprepared to cut players who had not yet developed physically. I left, stating that I would rather have accepted a diminished winning record in order to develop the quality of the team. The players split apart, going to other teams.

The moral of the story is that even serious players have to be guided by realistic and constructive expectations. That's why it's important to look for a team based on how your child will develop as a player, not on how many games he will win. As proof of my point, another team I trained, which began in the same system at the same age but which took a lower-key competitive route, produced two players for the USA national team.

high school soccer

Entering high school marks a huge transition for a young person who is interested in playing soccer. There is a lot that a conscientious and ambitious young player can do to prepare himself for the experience. This preparation will help not only for soccer but also for the rigorous combination of sports and academics.

The words *preseason training and practice* tend to make players shudder with fear. They imagine the notorious "two-a-days" (double training sessions), which are used to evaluate all incoming players. Although different schools have different policies, it is often from this two- to three-week period that players are selected for either freshman, junior varsity (JV), or varsity teams. Preseason training can be torture for the unprepared player, or it can be a manageable routine for the physically fit one. The hardest part is usually not the soccer but being physically prepared for the matchups against players who are up to four years older.

Give your child the following advice about getting ready for high school soccer.

- Go into freshman year in good shape. A player who does this is in the minority and has a tremendous advantage.
- Become familiar with the program. Go to the high school training and observe what the team does. Practice is often daily, usually after school for about two hours.
- Attend freshman, JV, and varsity high school soccer games in the fall of eighth grade to understand the level of play. He should note how it differs from his current level of play.
- He should introduce himself to the high school coach and tell the coach that he looks forward to playing for him.
- Ask the high school coach or trainer how to best prepare for the season. Ask if there are any standards that are used for selection, such as running times or specific fitness-test results.
- Seek out players who are already on the team for advice and support.

High school soccer represents a huge commitment that goes beyond many earlier programs. Expect your child to play two or three games a week. Practices may be every nongame day. Your athlete may have to contend with the possibility of being cut from the team, something that doesn't often happen in earlier years. If all goes well, he may decide to pursue the next level: college soccer.

college soccer

Many young soccer players aspire to play in college. They may be under the impression that a college scout or coach will somehow see them play and immediately sign them up, complete with a full scholarship. Unfortunately, the real world does not work this way.

Most athletes have to go looking for scholarship money on their own. Only the very top players are actively recruited by colleges. Immediately upon applying to a college, a player should write to the relevant coach and ask about what money is available. Schools offer different types of scholarships; some are given for financial need, some for athletic ability.

The benefits of a college scholarship are obvious. In addition to making it possible to afford an education, they offer prestige and honor. Remember, though, that scholarships come with strings. These include the stress of keeping up both athletic and academic performance and the insecurity of possibly not having them renewed. Make sure that you understand all the conditions attached to the scholarships, such as the requirements for renewal from year to year, and that your child is reasonably confident that he can meet those requirements.

Players and their parents need to become active participants in the college recruiting process, says soccer mom Ramona Barber, whose children play college sports, including soccer. Barber conducts workshops and counseling on college opportunities, both sports and academics, throughout the United States through her information service, CollegeInfo, in West Des Moines, Iowa. Based on her survey of 159 men's and women's collegiate programs, she offers the following information and advice.

- Coaches expect players to personally take the initiative and contact them. Not a single coach in the survey expressed a preference for being contacted by either a player's relative or a recruiting service.
- Players should make the initial contact with the schools of their choice sometime during their junior years or before the start of their senior years.
- Athletic scholarship money is limited. For example, the National Collegiate Athletic Association (NCAA) limits Division I programs (its largest programs) to 9.9 full scholarships for men and 12 for women at any one time.
- Players must assume the responsibility of finding the right schools for them. As a high school freshman or sophomore, they should start by making a list of 10 to 20 schools of interest. They should write for information on these schools. The list should be narrowed to 6 schools by the end of the junior year. Then, players should write each soccer coach a personal letter. Finally, they should visit each school and meet the coach.

Barber says players should always focus on their schoolwork and take the relevant national tests such as the Preliminary Scholastic Assessment Test (PSAT), Scholastic Aptitude Test (SAT), and American College Testing (ACT). Also, they should know the deadlines for all college forms and applications for scholarships or financial aid and complete them in a timely manner. For college preparation, she offers these additional tips for each year of high school.

Freshman. Continue high-level club play. Work on physical conditioning. Try out for your high school team. Try out for the United States Youth Soccer Association Olympic Development Program, or ODP (for more information on the ODP, see page 132). Learn about college soccer programs. Attend summer soccer camps.

Sophomore. Continue to play the highest club-level soccer available. Start collecting video footage and newspaper clippings showcasing your success. Keep a detailed record of your game statistics. Continue trying out for ODP if you didn't make it before. Look for ways you can be seen playing by college coaches.

Junior. Continue high-level club play and high school play. Travel with your team to recruiting events throughout the year. Write college coaches and arrange for them to evaluate your play. File with the NCAA Clearinghouse at the end of May or beginning of June, not before. This organization monitors players' grades, courses, and ACT scores to ensure they all meet standards to play at college level. Get applications for admission and scholarships during the summer before your senior year. Make informal campus visits. Attend a summer college-recruiting camp at a school that interests you.

Senior. Keep in contact with coaches from the schools that interest you. Prepare a personalized soccer video for coaches who show an interest in seeing one. Arrange to have your final high school transcript sent to the NCAA Clearinghouse. Use the summer to get physically and mentally fit for fall college soccer tryouts.

the mental aspect of excellence

A player heads toward the goal, the ball at his feet. The goalkeeper comes out in anticipation. Who will succeed? Even on the professional level, where both players have incredible skills, it is most often the player with the mental fortitude–who does not panic, who can psych out the opposition, who can hone his focus–who will emerge victorious. Such is the power of the mind.

"Athletic ability is 90 percent physical and 10 percent mental. But watch out for that 10 percent," Keith Henschen, director of the applied sports psychology program at the University of Utah in Salt Lake City, once told a top sports coach.

Your child is probably practicing mental preparation and focus without even being aware of it. It happens on the way to practice or a game, when a player discusses what he wants to achieve in playing that day. It happens when a coach talks to the team or when the team conducts a pregame cheer. It happens when a player is told to put on his "game face." Learning to consciously direct it, however, is much harder and much more effective.

Any parent, regardless of athletic background, can help a child develop the mental skills associated with sports. With the help of both coaches and parents, a player can strengthen his edge by developing these tools.

Relaxation. A player cannot play his best if he is not relaxed. Soccer is a fluid game, every aspect of which–from decision making to ball skills–can only be realized if a player is relaxed.

Every player needs to find a technique and a routine that works for him. Some athletes relax by sitting quietly, stretching, jogging or jumping in place, shaking out their arms, deep breathing, or repeating phrases. A parent can facilitate relaxation by ensuring that the child arrives at the game on time or, if necessary, engaging in casual conversation, distraction, or humor.

Positive thinking. There are some players who are said to have a "nose for the goal." In other words, they score a lot. Beyond their physical skills, they undoubtedly believe that they can score. Positive thinking builds self-confidence,

MOM'S VIEW

"The game begins now," I often told the Stampede, the mid–New Jersey Select U-10 and U-11 girls, as we began their pregame warmup, which included using an array of mental techniques. While the players were stretching, I had them focus, often with their eyes closed, on specific aspects of the upcoming game and their own play. This enabled them to concentrate so deeply that they were able to block out the usual noise and distractions.

I am absolutely convinced that this type of mental focus makes a difference. It was obvious to me that the team's success was due not only to athletic ability but also to concentration and focus.

One dramatic incident stands out. Often during this warm-up exercise, I walked the circle of stretching players, whispering key phrases or suggestions to each one. Once, during this exercise, I repeatedly told a player whom the coaches knew would be heavily guarded by the opposition, "There is no one near you." Sure enough, two girls, each at least a head taller than our player, were glued to her during the entire game. Despite that fact, she managed to score two goals. After the game, I asked her if the two girls had posed a challenge. She looked at me, genuinely perplexed, and asked, "What girls?"

a necessary stepping-stone to success. A player can practice this skill by approaching training and competition with a concrete goal, such as doing a certain skill or winning crucial tackles. Also, have him try to look at situations in a positive light. Instead of being crushed after a defeat, have him see it as an opportunity to correct mistakes.

Concentration and focus. The results of a high percentage of soccer games are determined in the final 15 minutes. This is when the physically and mentally fit players prevail. Your child should have a clear mind before he steps on the field. Encourage him to leave all other distractions in his life off the soccer field.

Visualization. Positive visualization is the ability to imagine a desired outcome and then make it happen. It may sound doubtful to some, but most top athletes use this technique. Children are naturally good at this skill; they daydream all the time. Parents just need to encourage and channel this habit.

Try this exercise. Ask your child to close his eyes and remember a particularly successful play or aspect of his game. Research shows that the more detailed the visualization, the more effective. Tell him to see himself succeeding in as much detail as possible: his foot touching the ball, the look and sounds of the field, the ball sailing into the goal. Try this as a pregame exercise, but do not reserve it just for competition. Whether he's drifting off to sleep or riding in the car, encourage your child to practice visualization whenever soccer pops into his head.

Knowledge of the game. Encourage your child to learn everything about the sport. Provide him with soccer magazines, videos, and tickets to professional games and take him to watch other teams of various ages. Watching the best play rubs off.

Reaching for the stars. Young players often express their desire to play high-level soccer. Encourage lofty aspirations. A dreamer is a winner, whatever he dreams, according to sports psychologist Linda Bunker, Ph.D., of the University of Virginia in Charlottesville. "Winners say what they want to happen. Losers say what they feel will happen," says Dr. Bunker.

Dealing with discomfort. This is not the same as pushing through pain from an injury, which should never be encouraged. Anyone who is serious about soccer needs to understand and accept physical discomfort. Learning to push through soreness and fatigue gives children confidence and enables them to extend their limits.

Intensity. Competitive situations call on reserves of physical and mental energy. And the amount of intensity differs depending on the level of competition. For example, getting pumped up for an important game requires more energy than does mentally preparing for a scrimmage.

Athletes cannot always summon up maximum mental efforts, because the result will eventually be burnout. This is why coaches and players who use mental preparation should vary the intensity to prepare for different situations.

CHAPTER 18

parents as coaches

WHEN CHEERING ISN'T ENOUGH

Many parents are called upon, or volunteer, to coach youth soccer. In fact, the majority of coaches in the system come from the parent volunteer ranks. This chapter will help you successfully negotiate the often complicated but always exciting task of coaching youth soccer players.

diving right in

Once you've made the decision to join the thousands of other parents as a youth soccer coach, there are some steps that you'll want to take. Here are some tips to make sure that you get off on the right foot.

Run it by your child. It's a good idea to talk about coaching with your child first. Explain to her that you're interested in coaching and see how she feels about it. You might want to reconsider or coach for another team if you can't overcome any objections that she might have.

Hit the books. Consider taking a course to get the U.S. Soccer Federation F license or the youth license modules. This is the initial requirement for coaches, and many leagues require licensing as well. Many towns and clubs offer these courses, and the national youth soccer organizations can provide further guidance about finding a course near you. (For more information on the national youth soccer organizations, see the resource list on page 207.)

Start out slowly. Volunteer to be an assistant coach at first. Approach your child's coach or officials of your child's league.

Become a student of the game. The most direct route is to watch teams and players of a similar age to your child. Do not restrict your study to that level, though. Watch older groups so that you'll know what skills your child will be learning.

Ask around. While watching, ask knowledgeable spectators what is going on. You will be surprised how much you can learn.

See how coaches do it. Sign up for a coach's clinic and inquire how to receive coaching lesson plans from which you can work. Ask your child's coach about clinics or contact the national youth soccer organizations.

Be prepared. Stay ahead of your players by being prepared and studying what they will learn.

Learn the language. Listen along the sidelines for how soccer terms are used and watch the referees to see how they conduct the game.

Use an expert. If you have never played the game, try to get a high school player to assist you in demonstrating skills.

Check out tapes. Watch coaching and skills videos, which are often easier to learn from than books since they visually demonstrate skills.

Go to the source. If a system of coach's training is not already in place, contact national youth soccer organizations. These groups offer coaching guidelines and guidebooks.

Find out the local rules. Study a copy of your local league's rules, which may have variations of FIFA's (the international soccer federation) Laws of the Game, the international rules of soccer. It is common for youth soccer leagues to have rules unique to their organization.

ABOVE ALL, BE FAIR

All that children really want is for a coach to be fair. This does not necessarily mean exactly equal playing time or that everyone plays every position; these things may depend on many factors. It does, however, mean consistency. Set rules and hold to them. If you say that missing practice without good reason will result in diminished game-day playing time, then stick by it, even if the guilty party is your best player. Although you acknowledge that your child is the main reason why you are coaching, you cannot allow yourself to show favoritism or, conversely, be extra hard on her to avoid the appearance of showing it. Hold all children to the same standard and be supportive of everyone.

good coaches are good teachers

To do a good job with children, see yourself first as a child educator and second as a soccer coach. With this in mind, you will be guided by the right instincts. To that end, the ABC's of Coaching that follow apply to any situation in which children are being instructed.

The following tips are a collection of useful teaching techniques that can be incorporated into your coaching. They were created by Ashley's Soccer Camp in Montclair, New Jersey, and have been adopted by thousands of coaches nationwide. By adopting these principles and using them on the field with your players, you can create effective and enjoyable practice sessions.

Each letter of the alphabet includes one or more teaching concepts. No single concept is more or less important than any other, but together they make a formidable whole.

"And stop!" This is the only stop command used by trainers at Ashley's Soccer

Camp. Every player they work with knows it. It is most applicable when the dynamics of a group require a verbal command rather than a gesture, such as when children are running around practicing a specific skill. Have one consistent stop command. Be loud and forceful.

Be firm, fair, and happy. Make the children do what you want them to, but always do it smiling. No group is beyond control, and if your standards are high but attainable, and you are consistent and fair, the children will respect you.

Coach what players do correctly. Always coach what is right. Do not worry about, and highlight, what is wrong. Never use exercise as a form of punishment (like running extra laps). Humiliation does not create happiness or proficiency. Emphasize the positive. For example, "That was a good pass because you made it quickly" or "I liked how you sprinted after that loose ball!" Praising behaviors that you want repeated will enhance success.

Demonstration. One demonstration speaks louder than a thousand words. If you cannot do it, have one of the members of the group do it. Insist on a good demonstration and show the correct way to do something. Never show the way not to do it.

Energy. Always be energetic and show plenty of enthusiasm. After a few weeks of training and games, this may become a challenge, but dig deep into your reserves. Children will respond well to activities if they know that you are putting in a lot of energy.

Fun and flexibility. Always try to inject an element of fun into your activities. Constantly ask yourself, "Are they having fun doing this?" or "Would others have fun doing this?" If not, be flexible and try something new.

Games. A Games Based Approach to teaching means that children learn better and have more fun from playing games, not by repeating exercises. (For more information on the Games Based Approach, see chapter 2.) Many skills are involved in games. The coach has to know how to use and develop games in order to focus on teaching a particular skill. This system does not rely on using drills. A package of activities is essential, and when that package is delivered through games, the results are fun and success.

Have control. Without control, teaching cannot take place. Children need some boundaries. It is best to clearly communicate your rules and expectations early in the season. A good coach then constantly enforces them. In most cases, a lack of control is traceable to inappropriate activities, such as skills that are too easy or hard for children. This leads to bored and frustrated children. If this occurs, look to yourself before you blame your players.

Eyes on the group. Constantly walk the perimeter of where your team is practicing and scan the group. Scanning means paying attention to all your players by frequently looking over the group from different places around the perimeter. This requires constant attention, but it really helps in identifying potential problems. Nonattentive children will monitor your movements and slack off when you're not looking. Players quickly realize, and respond well, when they are under constant observation. Speaking of eyes, when talking to a group, keep your eyes toward the sun. Always allow the children to keep their backs to the sun.

Join in. Every activity must be structured to achieve maximum participation.

Children want to kick the ball and be involved. Activities must include everyone, with everyone doing something. Organized chaos can actually be useful, because it simulates game conditions. Remember that children are easily bored and do not enjoy standing in lines.

Keep records and maintain high standards. Records enable problems and ideas to be properly logged and dealt with effectively. This ensures that after each session, you can better evaluate what works and what does not. You can then focus on the best approach at future sessions. As you maintain these high standards for yourself, do so as well for the children. If you ask them to complete a pass in a certain way, for example, accept nothing less than the right way. If you allow standards to slip, your control of the group slips.

Learn names. Everyone appreciates being called by their first name. Children love to be known by their coaches. Make a point of learning names as quickly as possible. Use games and a variety of other activities to enliven this process. Saying, "My name is Susie" is not as exciting as playing tag and having children shriek their names when they are caught. Although it does work for some children, the use of last names tends to be impersonal. The bottom line is to call children what they want to be called, not what you want to call them.

Movement. This is a fundamental teaching tip for all sessions. You must have activities that entail continuous movement by all players to mentally and physically awaken and then engage them. By warming up prior to stretching, your sessions have a solid beginning. Continue with lots of movement during practice and end every session with a cooldown and stretching.

No talking while the coach is talking. It reinforces basic good behavior to keep children quiet while you are demonstrating or explaining. This should be a rule of every coach. Some coaches can get carried away and drone on, though. Children key in on your voice, and droning on causes them to daydream. Breaking your speech with inflections and silence is crucial. Silence, and a look in the right direction, are powerful tools for keeping control.

Organization. A successful team needs to be well-prepared. Ensure that your paperwork is always up-to-date and accurate. To help your team be in the right place at the right time, a phone chain is a great idea. Frequent contact with parents is also recommended to build strong team spirit. This may be in the form of a short, upbeat weekly or bimonthly newsletter. Another idea is to organize a refreshments rotation for game days. Also, you should carry medical records and releases for players to games. The releases are signed waivers so that a child can be treated in the event of an emergency. You cannot be too well prepared.

Planning. A lesson plan for every training session is essential. Take into account the age and skill level in order to create an appropriate plan. Insufficient or poor planning leads to "Band-Aid coaching," in which a coach does not have a set plan but gets by through fixing the biggest problem. Organize your session to include a warmup (always with a ball), stretching, conditioning, individual skills work, group games and activities, scrimmage time, and a cooldown.

Questions. Questions should be asked to stimulate the children. When you ask your players questions, employ a tactic called wait time. This means always waiting at least five seconds before calling on someone to answer. Children process information at different rates, and by responding to the first child to raise her hand to answer, you might exclude a large portion of the group. More children will participate if this teaching skill is employed. By waiting, you will see an increase in the participation of the quieter, less impulsive children.

Regressive pull. As the season progresses, you may find yourself being constantly tempted to engage in the players' habit of arguing about everything. It is called regressive pull, or going back and forth. You have to be vigilant in guarding against this. Be cool, be adult, and be in charge.

Safety, safety, safety. This is the most important aspect at any time when working with children. The emotional and physical safety of the players is of paramount importance. Evaluate every situation with safety in mind. Consider the safety implications of the field, equipment, game organization, and emotional aspect of the coach/player interaction.

Time on task. A coach must evaluate how much time is spent practicing skills. Time on task is the ratio of a player's time engaged in activity compared with inactivity (things such as listening to the coach, taking a break, or standing around). Have someone with a stopwatch monitor your coaching to help you work out this ratio. Aim for at least 80 percent of time on task, but do not be surprised to find your figures much lower early on. Remember, the children are there to learn by playing, not by listening to your voice.

Understanding. Coaches must constantly check for understanding. Ask the children what they have learned from the skills, games, and activities. What can they tell you about what has occurred? This means taking a break between activities and asking questions. This should be done at least at the conclusion of a session and at the beginning of the next session.

Versatility. Be it snow, heat, behavior problems, or the arrival of a moose on the playing area, a coach must be able to handle a changing environment with ease and confidence. The most important aspect of this is modifying an activity from its original form to improve it. Whether this means changing a game or enlarging the area after a few minutes of cramped play, a coach needs to be thinking all the time. You should be willing to admit that an activity is unsuitable. If it doesn't work, then move on. It's okay to admit this to the children as well.

"When I say go" and "Ready, go." "Ready, go" is the opposite command to "And stop," and it is equally important. We use "When I say go" as a way of starting an activity. A coach needs to be consistent with this instruction. Strong emphasis should be placed on the word *go,* and children should learn to react only to this word, and not before it is said.

Explain activities clearly. Be simple, clear, and concise when asking players to carry out a command. An eight-year-old will not understand a college-level tactical game plan. Instead, make all requests appropriate to the age and ability of the players. Try not to spend more than 30 seconds continuously talking; otherwise, players tend to lose concentration.

Why is the coach always on the winning team? A coach is there to teach and not to dominate the game. It can be easy for a coach's focus to shift from the children to himself if he is not careful. Too often, a coach shows off while children become bored or unhappy. Do not be tempted to demonstrate to the children that you can dominate in the scrimmage or do the most juggles. If this happens, a coach is not doing a good job.

Zzz. This means that the children are drifting off. Why? As mentioned under "Have control," a lack of control can be attributed to inappropriate activities. Look at yourself, your planning, and the activity before you blame the children for being bored. If they lose interest, the game could be too difficult, too easy, or just not fun. All activities can be structured to challenge all players. Suggest to the group, "When you are ready, you can try this more difficult skill, but if you're not sure, continue to work at the level on which you're most comfortable." If the majority of children are not interested in an activity, chances are that it is unsuitable.

codes of conduct

Effectively communicating with parents is essential to successful coaching. It will make your job easier and more rewarding if you develop an open and

COACHING TIPS FOR GAME DAY

Preparation is the best way to ensure a successful coaching experience. If you are armed and ready, confidence will be your ally. Follow these tips to ensure that your team is ready to play their best.

- The key word is preparation. Come with a game plan.
- Be flexible. You must be able to adapt your plan. Know what to do if a player is not working in her position, does not show up, or has to leave the game because of an injury.
- Arrive at a game with enough time to prepare yourself and the players, both physically and emotionally.
- If yours is a beginner team, explain every position and its responsibilities clearly and in detail to the children.
- Allow time for a sufficient warmup and cooldown, including stretching.
- Ensure that there is a parent rotation system, or some other system, for providing adequate fluids and healthful snacks.
- Be the team's best cheerleader. If you have nothing constructive to say, do not say anything. Remember that instructions are hard for players to absorb in the heat of battle.
- Do not show your frustration with things such as poor field conditions or the referee's calls. Maintain your cool.
- Have a strong sense of yourself. Do not go into "crazy mode" the second the starting whistle blows.
- Relax and enjoy the game, and your players will, too. Players pick up on the mood of the coach.

supportive relationship with parents right from the start. In this regard, it is vitally important that you prepare parents as well as players. A team meeting at the beginning of the season is an ideal forum in which to do this. Explain your philosophy, the rules governing substitutions, and playing time. Below is a sample of material distributed by Ashley's Soccer Camp coaches at parents' meetings. You can use it as a guideline for preparing the parents of your team.

Code of conduct for players. Players should arrive, at a minimum, 10 minutes before practice and 30 minutes before games. Tardiness or absence without notification or good cause may result in reduced playing time.

Appropriate equipment must be worn for practices and games, including sufficient clothing in cold weather. (Practices are held in the rain. Call your coach if in doubt about the weather.) Shinguards must be worn at all times. A water bottle should also be brought to all practices and games no matter what the weather. Clean cleats should be worn to practice; cleats should be polished for games.

For safety reasons, absolutely no jewelry should be worn to play soccer at any time. This includes earrings, watches, necklaces, hair clips, and so on. Sports glasses are recommended for those who require glasses. Mouthguards are used according to the advice of a dentist or orthodontist. Long hair must be tied back.

Players must respect coaches and officials and exhibit good sportsmanship to all other players and any others involved in the game.

Code of conduct for parents/guardians. You are encouraged to support the team, but you should not instruct the players in any way. It confuses your child, hampers her ability to play, and undermines the efforts of the coach. To avoid confusion when cheering on the sidelines, do not say anything that is a command, such as "Boot it," "Pass it," or "Shoot." Positive encouragement would be such comments as "Way to go," "Nice effort," or "Stay with it."

Do not speak to officials, except to say thank you after a game. If you have questions or concerns about the referees, speak to the parent manager, who can then relay the information to the coach.

If you would like to speak to the coach about a specific concern, call him on the phone. If it is regarding a game, allow the issue to settle for a day or two, as waiting often helps clarify things. Do not try to speak to a coach directly after a game.

Send your child to both practices and games well-nourished. Parent managers should arrange halftime snack duty. If you are responsible for a snack, bring fruit and/or sports drinks or juice only. No candy, soda, or cookies are allowed.

Report to the coach all injuries, special medical conditions (such as severe allergies or asthma), or extenuating circumstances (such as lack of sleep, illness, or family crisis) that may affect the player.

moving up the ladder

Parent coaching for youth soccer can be quite challenging, particularly since most parents didn't play while growing up. A lifetime of playing, though, is not required to be a coach. A willingness, coupled with a methodical apprenticeship and course of study, can lead to advanced levels of youth coaching.

One parent is a good example. He

began humbly enough by volunteering to be an assistant coach in a recreational program. He didn't do much at first, but he did concentrate on learning as much as he could. When the head coach chose not to return, he took over for her. He later graduated to being an assistant in the travel program, which is an advanced level of play, and he eventually became a head coach there.

From the early days, he studied the game a great deal. He did this by attending a parent coaching clinic, watching numerous coaching videos, reading books, and watching as many games as he could. He went to recreational games and high school games and tuned in to professional games on television. While some parents chatted away on the sidelines or dropped children off for practice, he chose to stay and observe. Whenever possible, he participated in informal scrimmages in order to better understand what the children go through in games.

He has also placed an emphasis on understanding–through talking with people from other countries–on what it is like to grow up playing the game. He has tried to broaden his team's experiences by having them watch more games and practice at home to better duplicate the experience of young players in other countries. His enthusiasm and constant studying have taught him patience and to learn from his mistakes. These have been valuable assets in taking his team to the top.

Even with significant experience, he believes that the rate of the team's growth will eventually outstrip his ability to coach them. He feels that they will then be best served by being coached by an experienced player or professional youth coach.

SILENCE IS GOLDEN

"When I first started coaching, I felt the need to coach the girls through every step of the game," says parent coach Paul Friedman of Montclair, New Jersey. "I was talking them through skills and tactics, yelling lots of stuff, most of which I later discovered they couldn't hear. Being a parent coach can be draining, especially if you overcoach, like I did. Often, I'd come home exhausted, with a sore throat from yelling too much.

"One Sunday changed all that, though. I was coaching in my usual verbal style. My older daughter was serving as my 'assistant coach' for the day. 'Dad,' she said at one point, 'calm down. You're too intense. They're doing just fine.'

"I was stunned. I kept quiet, and that allowed me to realize that learning happens without constant prodding from a parent or coach. Certainly, children need to be taught, but they also need to experiment and experience the game on their own. As in many aspects of life, I needed to understand that children gain knowledge independently, without a parent having to tell them about every step on the way. Having never played the game myself, I didn't realize this or see their evolution as soccer players in the long view.

"The girls are progressing just fine without my constant yelling, and I don't need throat lozenges any more."

adidas

5

GIRLS' SOCCER

19. a recipe for success 161
20. guidance for girls .167

CHAPTER 19

a recipe for success

MAKING SOCCER A POSITIVE EXPERIENCE

It is an exciting time for a girl to be playing soccer in the United States. There are abundant opportunities to play and enjoy the game at all levels, from recreational to Select teams to high-level club and college play. Unlike their male counterparts, American women far surpass the rest of the world, both in quality and numbers of participants. Since its formation in 1985, the U.S. Women's National Team has dominated international competition.

"It is a bit of an understatement to say that the U.S. women are the best in the world," confirms April Heinrichs, women's soccer coach at the University of Virginia in Charlottesville, head coach of the U-16 Girls National Team, and captain of the 1991 U.S. Women's National Team that won the inaugural Women's World Cup. "They have the best sponsorship, equipment, and players. They are continually challenged, though, to prove that they are the best. The rest of the world is using the U.S. women as a benchmark."

Girls can play soccer just for fun, or they can shoot for the stars. For those with aspirations, there is a bright future. According to *Soccer America*, a national weekly magazine, women's college soccer is on the rise. In 1998, 600 colleges fielded women's soccer teams.

College opportunities set U.S. women's soccer apart from other countries, where soccer is not widely offered to women. Another factor unique to this country is Title IX, the federal law passed in 1972 mandating equal opportunities for girls' sports. (It prohibits sex discrimination in educational institutions that receive any federal funds.) Title IX created a climate of entitlement and acceptance. Although there are still disparities between sports opportunities for males and females (it is estimated that after more than 25 years, girls still have only half the opportunities of boys to play in school athletic programs), conditions—and attitudes—have, in fact, drastically improved since passage of the law.

Today, more than 30 million women play soccer in 85 countries around the world. Although some countries are making significant advances, the women's level of competition in many of these countries is surprisingly undeveloped when compared with the superior level that the men's game enjoys. In England, for example, where the sport was invented, the governing body of soccer did not begin formal administration of the women's game until 1993.

International women's soccer is emerging, though. Brazilian women have demonstrated some of the flair that marks their men's game. China, which challenged the United States in the 1996 Olympic final, is strong, especially considering that its program was disbanded for two years after losing in the quarterfinals of the 1991 World Championships. The Scandinavian countries are solid; Norway, which won the 1995 World Cup by beating the United States, represents the only blemish on a perfect Championship and Olympic record. To illustrate the rise of other countries, Heinrichs predicted before the 1999 Women's World Cup that any one of 10 countries could win.

the makeup of a good player

Three vitally important traits that girls need to develop to be successful at soccer are aggressiveness, intensity, and competitiveness. They can, in many cases, be the deciding factors in a game. If players are totally matched in skill, it is these qualities that provide the winning edge.

Aggression in soccer should be viewed positively, and in this case, it should be seen as synonymous with assertiveness. Keeping this in mind will help you emphasize it and endorse it in your daughter wholeheartedly. To develop aggression, it can be constructive for girls

GIRLS AND SPORTS

Sports participation by girls in the United States has steadily increased over the past three decades. In 1971, 1 in 27 girls participated in high school sports. In 1997, that figure was 1 in 3. Early involvement in sports goes a long way toward keeping women physically active, and healthier, their entire lives. Research reveals that girls who play sports reap both physical and social benefits. Here is a compilation of those benefits from the Women's Sports Foundation, a national organization headquartered in East Meadow, New York.

- One to three hours of exercise a week over a woman's reproductive lifetime (the teens to about age 40) may bring a 20 to 30 percent reduction in the risk of breast cancer, and four or more hours of exercise a week can reduce the risk by almost 60 percent.
- High school sports participation may help prevent osteoporosis (loss of bone mass).
- Physical activity appears to decrease the initiation of high-risk behavior, such as cigarette smoking, in adolescent girls.
- 80 percent of women identified as key leaders in Fortune 500 companies participated in sports during their childhood.
- Women who are active in sports and recreational activities as girls have greater self-confidence and self-esteem than those who were sedentary as children.

to play soccer with boys. Even in casual play, the level of both skill and aggression of all players will nearly always rise to the level of players around them. Encourage girls to play with their brothers or among a mix of neighborhood boys and girls. Playing with older and more aggressive girls is equally useful.

Appropriate aggression often needs to be explained to children. When you praise your child for being aggressive on the field, explain why. A lot of children get understandably confused. They are not allowed to be aggressive at home or with peers, yet they are encouraged and praised for aggressiveness on the soccer field. Stress the appropriateness of soccer aggression.

Imagery is useful to help develop aggression and avoid confusion. Have your daughter imagine that she is shedding her nice self and putting on her aggressive self as she crosses the field's sideline. You can also have her visualize how she is going to go in strong for tackles. Set goals, such as winning a certain amount of tackles or headers in a week. Help your child literally learn the feeling of aggression. Encourage her to throw her body around freely. It's a physical freedom as much as it is an emotional freedom.

Whatever you do, remember that, particularly with this trait, it's best to take small steps forward rather than suddenly expecting her to be aggressive.

intensity

Intensity is a state of mind about any endeavor. It is desire. It is striving for personal excellence. It refers to a player caring enough to put in the maximum amount of energy into everything she does. It is about exhibiting hustle, talking on the field, making tackles, and being aware of what's happening beyond the ball and what other players are doing. Literally, intensity is about being up on the toes, not caught flat-footed, with the willingness and readiness to demand of the body everything it can give. It does not necessarily take years or perfect skills to develop intensity. An 8-year-old player can display it as well as a 15-year-old.

Intensity takes confidence. This confidence is something that takes active encouragement from both coaches and parents. Girls must be taught not to fear physical contact and that it is okay to initiate it. Girls will "mix it up," if they feel safe. Adults must reinforce this skill, showing patience and support. One concrete measure is to have girls switch positions a lot since some positions lend themselves more to physical contact (such as defense). This will allow girl players a range of experience with intensity.

It's important to remember that players should practice like they play. Practices should be run with intensity, and some parts, like scrimmages, should be run with maximum intensity. The best way to achieve an intense practice is to ensure that a competitive edge is added to the activities, such as one-versus-one tournaments, or any activity that works in a restricted area and requires close control. This forces a high frequency of physical contact and fast play.

competitiveness

While competition should not be emphasized with soccer players younger than age 10, it is definitely a part of the game as children grow older. Anson

coach's corner

The first long-term coaching assignment I had was working with girls. In fact, since 1987, I've trained at least 30 girls' teams (ages 5 to 18) and coached several of them on a long-term basis. When girls come to play for me, they have some differences from boys, most of which are there because of parental or societal views. For example, it has to be especially instilled in girls that it is okay to be aggressive, and their parents often have to be convinced that it is not damaging or unhealthy to play in bad weather.

In 1998, I decided to embark on an experiment. I worked closely with the club in my town to ensure that a U-8 (under age 8) girls' team be fielded and trained as seriously as the U-8 boys. I knew there were preconceived notions about how it would work out, but I wanted to give the girls the same opportunity as the boys.

Although the town had enough U-8 boys try out to form three teams, we barely got enough girls for one U-8 team. But the team we did field exceeded even my own expectations. They had an almost 100 percent attendance rate for both practices and games. Their discipline, attitude, and achievements all gave me great satisfaction. I have learned that they respond to a coach like a coach does to them. If you treat them like soccer players, they will go out and work as hard, if not harder, than any of the boys' teams.

I didn't think these girls would progress as rapidly as they did with things like doing homework practice and experimenting with advanced moves like Cruyff turns.

The message to me is clear: Don't set limits. Let the girls set the pace. The message to parents is similar: Treat your daughters as you would your sons, and be conscious of the fact that you may not be.

Dorrance, the highly successful women's soccer coach at the University of North Carolina in Chapel Hill and former U.S. Women's National Team coach, has devised the widely quoted "competitive cauldron," a system of instilling competitive instinct into his women players. In his book, *Training Soccer Champions*, he details how an intensely competitive atmosphere is created by keeping methodical, written records in practice in which scores and rankings of teammates are kept, and even posted. This open competition creates the intense atmosphere that Dorrance feels is instrumental for player development.

Dorrance's constant exposure of his players to competition helps them get over any initial reluctance and teaches them that this trait is highly valued. His system seems to work. The University of North Carolina's women's soccer team is the most successful soccer program in the nation—men's or women's.

This competitive cauldron is not for the faint of heart. Of course, in the youth game, care must be taken to nurture this intense competition and to understand that it may not be appropriate for all players. Also, Dorrance stresses what he calls the balancing act. As discussed in other parts of this book, humor, lightheartedness, and the realization that soccer is only a game should always remain part of the equation.

Peers helping peers is useful in this regard. In Dorrance's system, he stresses that the veteran players are a strong influence on the newcomers. This is applicable to youth soccer, and focusing on this is often overlooked in a sport where the leaders are usually the adult coaches. Encouraging more experienced youth players to take leadership roles and mentor younger players would be great for all athletes and would undoubtedly produce better players.

Dorrance uses some of the following training methods to foster competition among his players, including goalkeepers.

- One-versus-one competition; this is the crux of competition, since all confrontation in games comes down to dueling against one other opponent
- Other small-sided competition, such as four versus four, with, for example, two veteran players and two newcomers
- Two versus two in a heading competition
- Shooting competition, with the emphasis on shooting when fatigued, such as after some fitness training

In Dorrance's system, playing time is based on extensive, objective evaluation of the results of practice. Most of all, it duplicates the competitive aspect necessary for games. How can you ask a player to come through on game day with a fierceness that she has not experienced in practice?

learn to love the game

April Heinrichs believes that allowing girls to develop a sheer love of the game will keep them at it. She advises parents of a daughter to just "let her play."

"Americans tend to look for external motivation, prodding, or excuses," says Heinrichs. "There are so many wrong reasons why people play: in the hope of college scholarships, because their parents want them to, or their friends are doing it. What ensures that a girl stays with it is her passion, desire, and work ethic. You can't make a child have those. You can't genetically engineer that or spoon-feed it to an athlete.

"My entire self-esteem was built on being a good soccer player. It's the game that gave it to me. It was not until I was 25 years old that I was able to say of my life and my soccer, 'Hey, these could be two separate things. Soccer probably got me through years of personal development. It certainly got me over the hump.'"

"The fact that soccer is a team game is the first and foremost benefit for girls," says Heinrichs. In great preparation for life as an adult, it allows girls the forum to express leadership (soccer naturally produces leaders) and work with peers, both in overcoming failure and celebrating success. "I had the team to pick me up; I picked them up. If you are having a bad day, the team picks you up, emotionally and physically. On a good day, you share your contributions. You get feedback from peers. Success, feedback, and achievements–all of these things were given to me by the team. When people finish playing, it's not the awards they most remember or the games they won or the goals they scored," says Heinrichs. "It's their peers they recall."

"Soccer is a great avenue to express yourself," Heinrichs adds, but cautions that a girl must find the right team on the right level of play. Then, as a parent, you have to let go. "If a girl gets five good years, that's great. She will always say, 'I played soccer.' If she gets 15 years, then it's in her blood."

guidance for girls

HELPING THEM SUCCEED IN SOCCER AND LIFE

More than seven million girls ages 6 through 18 in the United States play soccer, which is more than 40 percent of all young people playing the game. This is an extraordinary statistic when compared to the much lower female-to-male participation ratio of most other sports. Why has soccer developed such a female following? It is a combination of timing and the nature of the game. When the youth soccer movement took off in the 1970s, the social climate was changing in favor of more equal opportunities for girls in sports. Also, soccer is a skill-based game—as opposed to strength-based—which, in a sense, equals the playing field between girls and boys.

girl athletes

While soccer may seem to level the playing field, girl athletes are still not treated the same as boy athletes. There is usually always an undertone, subtle or otherwise, that they are not quite like the boys. Equality will have arrived when they are not considered girl soccer players but, rather, just soccer players.

People often talk about women playing soccer differently. They say that the game and players look different. Of course, there are always some differences, such as speed and power. But if a player has coordination and skill and is comfortable with the ball, she will look like a soccer player. There is no gender attached. Conversely, while an uncoordinated, awkward physical state is often associated with girls, both boys and girls look equally raw when they begin playing. The expression still remains, though: "That child plays like a girl."

Some referees work girls' games differently than boys', stopping more frequently for supposed infractions in girls' games or taking breaks at the quarters when they may not for boys'.

Some referees allow girls to use their arms to protect their breasts if the ball is coming toward their chests. Some even tell the girls at the beginning of the game that they will allow this. This would usually be ruled a hand ball, which is a foul. If they play the ball properly on the chest, there should be no danger of injury. Is there a similar rule for boys when a ball is heading toward their crotches? Of course not. They learn to move their bodies and take the ball high on the insides of their thighs. You may want to check your league for any such discrepancies. Bring up any problems in writing to your club or league.

Refereeing girls' soccer can be different than refereeing boys' in other ways. Some referees more readily call off a girls' game than a boys' game for a wet field or other bad weather. Some referees don't allow girls to be as physical as boys. There may be less tolerance by referees in girls' games for hard tackling, pushing, or pulling. This can change the pattern of girls' play; constant whistles to signal fouls often send the message to girls to lighten up, making them tentative or timid.

Watch some boys' games to see if the referees treat them differently than they do the girls. If they do, politely ask why they seem more cautious with the girls. Even if they deny it, you'll get them thinking about it. This can serve to heighten their sensitivity to the issue.

Parents sometimes express different attitudes as well. You can hear them on the sideline, gasping over hard tackles and other aggressive moves during a girls' game. On the flip side, the same maneuvers in a boys' game may bring out a "That's my boy" comment. Rather than criticize another parent for being overly concerned, praise the aggressive behavior as a natural part of soccer. For example, counter the gasps and groans with, "Good hustle" or "Nice tackle."

There are other indications, even early on, that girls are treated differently. The amount of running and sprinting in soccer practice is sometimes less for girls; heading is often introduced later and pursued less aggressively.

Because of the way some parents and society still treat girls, they are generally less physical. While they may touch shoulders, they are less likely to barge (an English term for making strong physical contact). Soccer training often consists of having players spring up and sprint from different positions such as their knees, lying on their backs, and so on. Girls are sometimes more reluctant to get down on the ground. They have been saddled with the old distaste of getting dirty.

While boys can be fashion conscious, too, girls seem to be more so, even on the soccer field. Girls should not wear makeup or jewelry when playing soccer. This sense of the importance of clothing or looks ties into the fear of getting dirty. A coach may make a point to do something in the beginning of practice that requires girls to get dirty right away. This way, the issue of getting dirty is over with early in the practice..

Parents can also help put a girl at ease with the elements. Take your daughter out in the rain and mud, slosh around, and have fun with it. Before she sets out to play soccer, tell her that it looks like a day in the dirt.

While parents may be enthusiastic to correct inequalities in the way girls are treated, care must be taken concerning coaches, referees, and other parents. If people perpetuate any inequality, it is almost certainly unconscious on their parts. Don't overcompensate by ramming the message down people's throats. This is especially true of the girls themselves. A tough-as-nails approach is probably just as unreasonable as heading for shelter at the first signs of a light sprinkle.

MOM'S VIEW

"You can't be a professional soccer player. Choose something you can major in at college." That was the stinging response to my daughter after she answered her fifth-grade teacher's inquiry about career choices. The teacher's comment, however, did not stop half the boys in the class from saying they, too, hoped to become professional athletes.

This comment reveals that our society still does not fully accept the idea that women can aspire to be professional athletes. This career choice is just as valid as any other, which is why girls need extra support in their athletic endeavors. Research has shown that, by far, one of the most powerful aspects of this support is positive role models.

My daughters can look to both of their parents, who are still competitive athletes. My older daughter, Yael, can state her career goal with confidence because of two role models in her life. One is the legendary distance runner Grete Waitz, who has been a dear friend of ours for nearly 20 years. Her other role model is America's premier female soccer player, Mia Hamm. When Yael looked to Mia Hamm as her hero, we wrote letters to the soccer star until we received her autograph, which now sits among Yael's soccer trophies.

The beauty of it all is that my daughters, too, have become role models. My younger daughter, Shira, is known by even high school players for her skill at juggling a soccer ball. Yael has delighted younger girls' teams with frequent skills demonstrations.

No matter what your daughter's level of interest or ability, it pays to give her total sup port. Seeking out role models shows that you respect her activity.

coaching girls and boys

There is no denying that there is a difference between coaching girls and coaching boys. This does not refer to what a coach should do, but often to the situation the coach inherits from society.

The beauty of soccer is that it offers an opportunity for true equality. Its skills are not particularly strength-dominated. Kicking a ball hard or far, for example, is more about timing than strength. The true differences between the sexes, then, lie more in attitude.

Allowing that these are mass generalizations, a few observations of common behaviors can be made. Girls are analytical. They digest and rationalize what a coach says and does. Boys may just take it at face value. Girls are more apt to cry if a coach yells or reprimands them. Boys may scowl at a half-time dressing down by the coach, whereas the girls absorb and analyze it. Girls take it all more personally.

There are two styles of teaching: command and cooperative. An example of command style is to say, "When I say go, you stand here, and you there, and pass the ball." Cooperative would be to say, "We need to learn how to pass better. I am dividing you into two groups. Each group has five minutes to create a game that develops this skill."

Many coaches use just the command style. It is useful for a coach to adopt both styles when coaching either boys or girls. Coaches should not be afraid to be more demanding and commanding with girls. Just because every request is not prefaced with a "please" does not mean that the coach is being rude or mean. Girls need to realize that sometimes you just have to do what the coach says.

If a girl complains that a coach is tough, first determine whether there is validity in her complaint, then reinforce the coach's efforts. "Coach is asking you to play hard, and that's okay." Don't be reluctant to tell a girl to "gut it out" when the going gets rough.

Sometimes, girls' coaches are more apt to cancel practice for inclement weather. Make sure you let the coach know that you expect practice to be held unless the conditions are unreasonable. Always encourage your daughter to attend practice with a good attitude. Stress the commitment and the toughness it builds.

Unequal attitudes may exist among coaches in other areas. Often, when a coach goes out on the field to see a boy who is injured, his objective is to keep that boy in the game. Some coaches much more readily take out a girl if she is injured. Again, if you approach the coach to discuss this or other such matters, always do so in a nonargumentative way.

Despite your natural parental instincts, avoid running onto the field if your child is injured. Technically, it is against the rules. The coach should be equipped to handle the situation. In terms of minor injuries in general, they are part of the game. Boys are socialized to accept them more readily than girls are. Try to take a positive, relaxed attitude toward a cut, bruise, or other minor injury.

The various sensibilities of girls and boys can be valuable in their own way. The challenge is not to make everyone uniform; the challenge is to understand the differences and how best to work with them to ensure that both girls and boys get the benefits of all approaches.

getting through puberty

Welcome to one of the biggest roller-coaster rides in parenting—negotiating your daughter's puberty. With all of the physical, social, and emotional ups and downs of puberty, the true blessing of being a female soccer player is the focus, direction, and meaning it can give a girl and her family during this often rocky ride.

Puberty is a particularly difficult time for athletic girls because all of its issues are magnified by participation in sports. In addition to adjusting to puberty's physiological changes (which are designed to help her make babies, not score goals), a girl is pulled by conflicting emotional and social forces. Times may have changed, but not enough to provide a secure atmosphere for most girl athletes. In fact, girls drop out of sports at a rate six times higher than boys do, many of them during this time.

Before puberty, girls and boys are fairly equal from a physical point of view, says Mona Shangold, M.D., director of the Center for Women's Health and Sports Gynecology in Philadelphia. Exercise benefits both girls and boys in terms of strengthening their muscles, including their hearts.

With puberty comes physical changes in girls. As they make more estrogen, girls stop growing taller. (In fact, girls who enter puberty at a younger age stop growing sooner and tend to be shorter as adults). Estrogen also contributes to a rounder shape and added fat to breasts, hips, and thighs. Since girls must carry this added fat during sports participation, they must work harder at any given level of performance, adds Dr. Shangold.

There are some athletic benefits to added estrogen during puberty. Estrogen gives girls stronger, thicker, and thus, more durable bones. Testosterone levels rise slightly, which helps strengthen bones and allows for the possibility of greater muscle strengthening.

Puberty has no effect on skills development. Skill can increase as long as any athlete, girl or boy, puts in the practice. In terms of the menstrual cycle, there need be no special considerations or changes in girls' sports participation. After all, women athletes have excelled–and even won Olympic medals–during all phases of their menstrual cycles.

Athletic girls experience some developmental differences that sedentary girls don't. Athletic girls tend to experience their first menstrual periods (called menarche) at a later age. The average age at the onset of menarche in the United States is 12½ years. Among athletic girls, it is 13½ to 15½. Experts are not sure what the cause and effect is; it is not even clear whether there is one. Does exercise delay menstruation, perhaps by promoting thinness and thus low body fat? Or does the fact that it is delayed make a girl a better athlete? Probably some of both, according to Dr. Shangold, which makes the issue even more confusing.

A delay in the menarche is not medically harmful as long as menstruation occurs by age 18. Dr. Shangold concludes that delayed puberty, irregular periods, and amenorrhea (the absence of menstruation) should be evaluated, but that girls should continue to exercise. If girls or their parents are concerned about this issue, they should consult a doctor, preferably one with experience treating female athletes.

On the other side of the coin, much has been written about the early onset of puberty and menstruation in girls. This phenomenon is increasing, as the start of puberty is coming at increasingly younger ages. Lack of physical exercise is cited as one of the possible reasons. Experts stress that physical activity and sports is an extremely important health benefit for young girls.

You can help ease a girl through any physically or socially difficult time, including puberty, and keep her active by taking the following steps.

Get ready for the ride. Times such as puberty may be difficult, but they will be smoother if you accept their inevitability and their transitory natures as well.

Communicate. Resist any urge to take the silent approach. Encourage your daughter to talk about her feelings. Talk about your own experience. Reassure her that the changes she is going through do not have to hamper her soccer. After all, the entire U.S. Women's National Team went through puberty and made it.

Seek out others. Encourage your daughter to find a role model or someone in whom she can confide–an older girl, accomplished player, or female coach.

Bring in the coach. Enlist the help and advice of a coach, preferably one with experience with girls at various ages and stages.

Set goals. Keep her focused on a long-term goal, such as a soccer trip or special camp, to get her through difficult periods.

Bring on the reading material. Consider a subscription to a specialty publication such as a women's sports magazine, or inquire about information from organizations like the Women's Sports Foundation, a national organization headquartered in East Meadow, New York.

Get the right gear. Invest in comfortable and well-made women's soccer gear, including a sports bra for comfort. (For more information on soccer gear, see chapter 3.)

Watch what she eats. Pay special attention to nutrition, particularly avoiding fad diets.

Play more than soccer. Encourage cross-training and conditioning. A little variety in sports and exercise can add freshness, and conditioning exercises can help a girl avoid injuries and take her to new levels in soccer.

playing together

Mixing the sexes on sports teams is a much debated question, and there are valid arguments on both sides—and plenty of controversy.

Some girls have no choice but to play on boys' teams. Towns that have inadequate or insufficient teams for girls must, by law, allow girls to join boys' team. When there is a choice, however, the issue becomes complicated. John Ouellette, national coach of the American Youth Soccer Organization (AYSO), believes that playing with boys is detrimental to girls' soccer development and can discourage girls from playing. (The AYSO recommends that girls play with girls from the age of six on.)

It's not that girls do not have the physical and athletic ability to compete with boys, says Ouellette. "It's that the boys intimidate the girls."

Ouellette has seen evidence that giving girls their own programs radically increases the number of girl players. During a three-year span in one Utah area, for example, one division grew from 3 girls' teams to 37.

On the other hand, Ouellette is a strong supporter of coed play in casual soccer and in controlled environments, where the girls can be protected. He says that probably 80 percent of the women on the U.S. National Team played informally with boys and men at one time or another.

There are other sides to the argument. Almost from the beginning level, boys play a different game than girls. From an athletic point of view, it is a faster, tougher game. Some soccer experts think allowing girls to compete in these games improves their skills.

While Ouellette's concerns for the emotional and physical safety of girls and for the growth of female soccer lead him to strongly support girls playing only with girls, he offers this advice for parents whose daughters are considering playing on boys' teams.

- Be honest in evaluating your daughter's skill level. Look at both her physical and emotional readiness. Seek evaluation by someone else to get an independent judgment.

- Carefully evaluate the prospective boys' team and program. Ask yourself if it will provide your daughter with what she needs, such as a faster and more physical game.

MOM'S VIEW

My husband and I have come to a new chapter in our 12-year-old daughter's career. For the first time, Yael is playing for a boys' team, the Montclair Mavericks.

Yael's history with the players on the team began several years ago, when she first practiced with them informally in casual scrimmages of girls and boys that were organized by her dad. From the beginning, it was clear that this was a different game, one in which her level of play, and thus her enjoyment, rose to new heights. She said that the boys were more serious about soccer than the girls whom she played with, and serious play was her priority.

Eventually, because she blended well with the team, the coaches invited her first to participate in a series of their formal practices and then to be a guest player in some of their games.

Near the end of her last season in girls' soccer, Yael's team split apart. There was no other appropriate girls' team, and she (and we) preferred not to leave the town and the coaches. Her coach discussed with us the possibility of her trying out for a boys' team. It was then brought up with the board of directors, who have control over the team, and was subsequently approved.

Yael went through three tryouts with the team, scored in the top five, and made the team.

The Maverick players and coaches have been great. They've been enthusiastic and they treat her with respect. While she has much to gain from them, it is clear that she has brought a new dimension of skill, finesse, and physical fitness to the team.

Best of all, she is enjoying the game. She plays with more enthusiasm and doesn't complain. She is happy and relaxed. Ironically, she says there is less pressure. The stress of being the star on the girls' team is finally off her. Now she is just one of the team.

There are surely risks, but every possible situation entails risks. Sometimes, the greatest risk is the one not taken. But we did our homework before making the move. And every time she and her teammates slap high fives, we believe that we all made the right choice.

- Stay closely involved. Observe practices, games, and coaches. Make sure proper and age-appropriate skills are taught and ensure that emotional and physical protection are provided by coaches.

Whether or not boys and girls play together, parents should ensure that the message comes across loud and clear: Playing separately or together, both on and off the soccer field, everyone should be treated with respect and equality.

adidas
adidas
adidas
adidas
adidas

6

OFF THE PLAYING FIELD

21. the total soccer education 177
22. the soccer family 184

the total soccer education

OTHER WAYS TO BECOME A BETTER PLAYER

A professional player races up the sideline, feints, turns, and deftly dribbles by a defender. As he attacks the near post, drawing the goalkeeper out, he passes the ball, and his teammate taps it in for a goal.

Feint. Dribble. Pass. Goal.

You might guess that these marvelous demonstrations of skill are the result of years spent on the practice and playing field. But that answer is only partly right. One of the little-known secrets of soccer is that some of the best skill-building takes place in the backyard, up against a schoolyard wall, or even in front of a TV.

Yes, your child will learn key elements of the game from listening to coaches and competing in real games. But practicing by himself, playing casually with friends and family, and watching games can have profound effects on his development.

casual play

Individual practice, pickup games, and family soccer all offer an array of benefits to your child simply because they're not organized. Playing on his own, without the direction of adults, he is more inclined to experiment and think creatively. He has more leeway and a greater sense of independence. He can choose when and how to play and what skills he wants to develop.

Casual play also offers your child a chance to enhance his relationships with both friends and siblings. And when you join in, you can be actively involved in your child's sport, providing a safe physical and emotional environment that is filled with encouragement.

You do not have to be an expert in the game to play with your child. You do not even have to be particularly able to play. It's perfectly acceptable to make mistakes. And if you're uncomfortable kicking the ball around, you can serve as a facilitator, tossing or fetching the ball, setting up targets and goals, and finding other players and directing small groups.

Below is a list of casual play games that your child can try. The games are designed for as few as two players of any level, up to and including high school, and each game develops specific skills.

Juggling competition. Count how many times a player can juggle (keep the ball in the air by using various parts of his body except his hands and arms) the ball before it touches the ground. Each time the ball hits a part of his body, it counts as one juggle. This game develops ball control.

Soccer golf. Designate "holes" such as cones or trees around your yard, and count how many kicks it takes a player to reach each one. Record scores and chart how much he improves from game to game. This exercise develops the skills of kicking chips (passes or shots that are lofted into the air by kicking the ball below its center) and short, accurate passing.

Cone knockdown. Have several players, each with a ball, stand in a circle with several cones placed in the middle. All players simultaneously kick the balls back and forth, attempting to knock down cones with each shot. The person who knocks down the last cone wins the round. This game develops short, sharp passes and shots.

Two-on-two heading. Divide the players into two teams of two people each. The teams should stand about 10 yards apart, facing each other, with markers set behind one group to act as a goal. (The younger the children, the closer together the teams should be.) One teammate tosses a ball to the other,

CASUAL PLAY IN A DAILY ROUTINE

You don't need to set aside a specific time for casual soccer play. In fact, you don't even need to try specific games. There are many ways to make soccer activities a spontaneous part of your child's daily routine, starting with these.

- Let your child take a ball to school. He can dribble to or from the bus stop and, while well out of the way of traffic, play soccer games while waiting for the bus.
- Keep soccer balls in the car. Bring them out during family get-togethers, trips to the grand–parents', a day at the beach, and other times.
- Keep balls around the house. Soccer players instinctively touch and dribble if they see a ball. You may want to slightly deflate the ball to facilitate indoor play.
- Blow up balloons and use them inside or outside the house to encourage young children to practice heading and juggling. For a higher-level player who can benefit from honing his skills, a tennis ball can be used as well.
- Use your imagination. Make soccer part of everyday tasks. Just as budding baseball and basketball players pitch or shoot paper balls into trash cans, your child can roll up socks and chip (kick them in the air) them into a clothes hamper.

who attempts to score by heading the ball between the goal markers. The defending team acts as goalkeepers, trying to stop the ball. After one turn, the two sides change roles. This game develops heading and goalkeeping skills.

Shoot. Have two players kick a ball against the side of a brick building. Once the first player kicks, the second must kick the ball on the rebound before it stops moving or passes him. Every time a player misses, he is assigned a letter of the word *shoot*. The first person to spell the entire word loses. The game develops shooting skill and reaction time.

Follow the leader. Give each player a ball and designate one of the players as the leader. The leader dribbles the ball around the field and does turns, feints, or other moves, and the other players must do whatever the leader does. The game develops dribbling and helps players learn to look up while dribbling.

Keep-away games. These games entail keeping the ball away from the other team by using any soccer moves. Always stack the odds in favor of the passers (six players versus two, or four versus one, for example) in order to focus on the passers completing a maximum number of passes. You can add restrictions such as using the left foot only or keeping the ball below head height. These games develop all soccer skills.

Sharks and fishes. Create the boundaries of a large rectangle with cones or markers, and divide the players into two groups. Station one group at one end of the field and give each player a ball. Station the other players in the middle of the field. The players with the balls (fishes) must try to dribble across the field without losing the balls. The players without balls (sharks) must try to take away the balls and kick them away from the opposing players. The game develops dribbling (maintaining control of the ball while running) and tackling (defensive techniques in which the feet are used to knock the ball away from an opponent or to interfere with a play).

Headers and volleys. Gather a minimum of three people. One starts in goal, while the other two work together to score, either by heading the ball or kicking volleys (balls that are in the air). No other type of scoring counts. If a player misses a shot or scores with a shot other than a header or volley, he replaces the goalkeeper. If the keeper is scored on with a header or volley, he loses a point and remains in goal. The players who are trying to score start with five points each, while the first keeper starts with six points to make the game fair.

watch and learn

It seems hard to understand at first. How can your child improve his skills by watching someone else play the game? But the truth is, watching soccer is a great way to learn. Children expand their knowledge and add to their appreciation of the game when they see others play. They develop aspirations to improve when they watch a high-level player use fancy moves. And they learn by imitating. One demonstration speaks louder than a thousand words.

Watching soccer also completes the educational picture. When children see higher-level players using the same basic skills that good coaches and trainers spend many hours teaching them, the light clicks on and they develop a new understanding of what they are learning.

MOM'S VIEW

My daughters, Yael and Shira, developed their soccer skills by doing a lot of homework through the special soccer relationship they have with their dad.

Despite never having played soccer before our daughters got involved, he has taken to the field with joy and enthusiasm. Over time, he has spent hours watching professional youth coaches and soccer games, reading soccer materials, and using the athletic instincts he gained from being a national-class road runner. He and the girls all tap the ball to the bus stop and spend evenings in a variety of parks, sometimes choosing their venue based on the proximity of the postplay ice cream parlor.

When the girls need instruction in more difficult skills, their dad has not hesitated to trade meals, favors, or even a small fee for the services of a local, young professional coach or experienced player. This also provides role models for the girls. In turn, their dad has learned from watching these sessions.

As a result of all of this, the girls have a special bond with their dad. Through mere practice, they also have skills that dazzle onlookers. They have thoroughly enjoyed the challenge, for example, of counting and creating astounding juggling records. At age 10, Yael could juggle the ball 1,784 times consecutively; by age 8, Shira was up to 421.

It is one thing for a child to learn individual skills, and quite another for him to put them together or use them in a game. A child could be taught a Cruyff turn (a deceptive direction change), for example, and practice it for hours. But he can only learn when and where to make that move in the context of the game by seeing it done.

Also, witnessing failure has its value. There is nothing like seeing a top player make a mistake in front of an audience to make it memorable for your child. When your youngster sees that a move or choice was incorrect, it's likely that he will remember the event when he plays.

You can facilitate his watching the game in several ways. You can encourage him to pay attention and guide him with comments ("Did you notice how nicely she passed?" or "Even though he didn't succeed, did you see that great run he made with the ball?"). Positive comments are important. If your child tends to see coaches or parents yell or make negative comments or display negative behavior or body language like throwing up their arms in disgust, he will imitate this counterproductive behavior.

Try some of these other techniques to help your child.

Talk about what he sees. Let him describe the action to you. Follow up after the game with an activity, such as backyard practice, or for young children, even a written composition or artwork.

Identify a list of skills. Have him count the number of one-touch passes (when a player passes the ball immediately after receiving it) in a specific time frame, for example, or identify set plays (pre-designed plays that teams enact when they have control of the ball after a stoppage of play). You can even have him make cards marked with the numbers 1 to 10. He can hold up the cards to award style points.

Predict who will score. Ask him to guess who will score first, how that goal will be scored, and in which half.

Count the passes. Ask your child to count the number of consecutive touches that each player makes before passing. Because holding on to the ball for too long is a common error among young players, seeing how relatively quickly the ball is moved among high-level players helps your child understand that soccer is a team game.

Watch one player in his position. This is especially useful for higher-level players. Your child can focus on where the player goes in different situations and what skills he uses. Your child can also try to predict the direction of the next move that the player will make.

THE ROAD TO GREATNESS

"Everybody wants to win, to be on a successful team. What makes a player successful, though, is what she does when no one is looking. What does she do when club competition is over or the high school season ends? A team may train only twice a week. What does she do on the other days?" says April Heinrichs, women's soccer coach at the University of Virginia in Charlottesville, head coach of the U-16 Girls National Team, and captain of the U.S. Women's National Team that won the first Women's World Cup in 1991.

television

In the past few years, worldwide professional soccer has become a regular feature of TV broadcasts. Special games such as the World Cup are shown on network TV. Throughout the week all year long, cable stations broadcast soccer games, many of which are played by teams in the world's best leagues.

Professional soccer is everywhere, and merely having the television on during these games can have a remarkable effect on your child's understanding of the sport. From consistent television viewing, he can learn about the skills and strategies of high-level soccer, gaining knowledge that can't be taught in any other way.

Be aware, however, that television cannot replace certain features of seeing a game in person. While television cameras can bring the action closer to the viewer, they tend to "ball watch," restricting the coverage of what players are doing when they don't have the ball. For a true education, the options are greater when watching a game in person. During a live game, your child can get a much broader view of play and focus at different times on action on and off the ball.

videos

There are dozens of soccer videos on the market, targeted to every skill level. Video viewing can be an excellent supplement to a child's soccer education, provided that you choose the right tapes. Here is some advice on selecting soccer videos, from Richard Kentwell, president of Reedswain, a catalog company that specializes in videos and books for soccer coaching and instruction.

Buy skills videos first. While videos of soccer matches can be exciting and informative, the how-to aspect of skills videos is more useful. There are a number of classics in the skill-video category, such as the series of Coerver Fundamentals, which focuses on ball skills.

There are also videos that specialize in one aspect of the sport, such as goalkeeping–an important topic for an instructional video because this position often gets less attention from coaches. Another specialty is a series of videos for girls and women (but applicable to all players) by Anson Dorrance, the renowned women's soccer coach at the University of North Carolina in Chapel Hill and former U.S. Women's National Team Coach.

Look for game-action videos. A good video of this type demonstrates the skills found in a game situation and is structured as "whole, part, whole." That is, the game situation shows the skill in the context of competition, then the skill is isolated and demonstrated, then it is shown in the game again.

Pick a video that has lasting value. It is important to select a challenging video that will have value for your child over the long term. If you're not sure what to buy, speak to a knowledgeable salesperson about your child's abilities and the skills he'd like to learn, then ask for a recommendation. You can also ask an experienced coach, preferably one who knows your child's abilities.

Don't worry about overall length. In a skills video, longer isn't always better. A longer video may just repeat many skills and tips. It's the quality of the material, not the quantity, that makes a good video.

Watch in bits and pieces. The recommended way to view a video is to look through it once in its entirety to get the flavor. Then, break it up into segments. Do not try to digest the entire video at once.

books and beyond

When it comes to reading about soccer, you have several choices. The sports section of your local bookstore is likely to contain a large selection of soccer books, and though most are meant for coaches and are instructional, parents and players can gain from them as well.

Just as with videos, the soccer-book category has its classics. One of these is *Training Soccer Champions* by Anson Dorrance.

If you prefer magazines, *Soccer America* for adults and *Soccer Jr.* for children are popular. Even looking through soccer-equipment catalogs can be useful. These are often fun to peruse and use as wish lists of desired gear. They can be educational as well, teaching children about the variety of soccer equipment.

Does your child prefer high-tech over the printed word? Then you might want to consider soccer software. There now are programs on CD-ROM that allow you to design and develop your own training sessions, including exercises and tactics. These can be purchased from the same companies that sell videos and books.

coach's corner

Growing up, soccer was very much a part of my family's life. I watched my first soccer game at age one, though I do not remember it. As I grew older, I would spend Saturday nights watching a popular TV show called "Match of the Day." My sisters and I, who each supported a different team, would come down to the television wearing our team colors. This was family time. Even my Mum watched, often while doing her knitting.

The most complete sensory experience, however, was watching a game in person. I still feel the thrill and excitement of going to the stadium, passing through the turnstiles, seeing all the colors, and hearing the noise. The fans, wearing their opposing sets of colors. The players, highlighted by the camera flashes as they came onto the field. The beauty of a well-prepared field with green grass and white lines. The sounds—the crowd, crunching shinguards, and the crack of a hard-hit ball. All are equally powerful.

The experience of watching soccer is tribal, with the singing and chanting. And witnessing teams do battle is like living history. In fact, watching soccer teams dueling it out is gladiatorial. It can probably be traced back to the Romans.

CHAPTER 22

the soccer family

PUTTING IT ALL TOGETHER

You stand nervously along the sidelines, unable to sit in the lawn chair that you brought. It's just another game, you tell yourself, but as usual, that thought doesn't lessen the anxiety.

"Looking good!" you call out to your child, who is among the masses heading for that coveted object. As she plays, you shout encouragement: "Way to go!"

You pace the field, following the action up and down. You exchange comments—mostly game analysis—with a few other parents. A goal is scored by the opposing team. You wince. Your team's goalkeeper sags in defeat. And so do you, although you yell out weakly, "Nice try."

Soccer parents. They are a special breed. They speak their own language. They are deeply involved in this game—sometimes too deeply. Whether boisterous or quiet, soccer-knowledgeable or soccer-ignorant, they all share something in common: They want to do right by their children, to encourage them.

Perhaps one of the most valuable aspects of youth soccer is the relationship that it can build between parents and children. Most children love their parents to be involved in their lives. When handled appropriately, the mutual rewards of a shared parent/child soccer experience are unique and invaluable.

Children and parents can practice together, share in a dinnertime discussion of soccer, or watch it on television or on videos. Soccer gives children a chance to view their parents in a different role. In this rare instance, parents are generally not authoritative (that is the coach's role); they are supportive. Children can show mastery over their parents, which they take enormous pleasure in doing. This is something that a secure parent recognizes as a valuable rite of passage in a child's life.

Parents playing the game themselves is a relatively new angle. Moms or dads, for instance, might consider organizing a league of their own. This is just what happened in Montclair, New Jersey, in the fall of 1998. A mom who was watching practice kicked a runaway ball back to her child's coach.

"That's pretty good," he told her. "Too bad you don't play."

"Too bad there's no soccer team for mothers," she replied.

From that conversation was born Soccer Moms in Training, a class of women who sweat it out each week under the instruction of their children's soccer coaches. Each

MOM'S VIEW

Organized sports were the bedrock of my youth. I loved them all, and I never viewed playing them as anything but fun. Basketball, baseball, and football were my favorites, along with playing tennis with my father. There were few high school teams for girls in these activities, and certainly no dream of a future career. In my early adulthood, I took up road running, in which both my husband and I still avidly participate, but there are not many appropriate opportunities for young children in that sport.

Because I enjoyed sports so much as a child, I was delighted when my older daughter came to us when she was eight years old and asked to play soccer, like her girlfriend. From the moment she joined the other players on the field on that sunny day, I could see that this was the perfect game. Soccer is a blend of the athleticism and grace of every sport I have enjoyed. Unlike my childhood, my soccer-playing daughters are not "just tomboys." They are like millions of others, boys and girls, having fun and experiencing everything that sports has to offer, including having dreams. My older daughter benefits from the confidence and determination to fulfill her current goal: to become a professional soccer player.

Wherever soccer takes them, parents can, and should, play an active role. Our children know that we are there with them: coaching, cheering, and carrying the water bottles.

week, they get better. Most of all, they remark on how much better they understand and respect what their children do on the soccer field.

the best experience possible

Being involved in your child's soccer is a great way to express some of the best aspects of parenthood. Here are some tips on how to be a supportive influence.

- Take an interest in all aspects of your child's soccer, such as training, competition, and team relationships.
- Ensure that your child arrives on time for practice and games and is appropriately dressed.
- Show support by practicing with your child.
- Always seek to find the positive aspects of her soccer playing.
- Be well-informed. Learn the rules of the game and the many intricacies associated with a sport that you probably didn't grow up playing.
- Do not push your child, or engage her in inappropriate competition, such as serious play at a young age.
- Be equally involved. While dads are traditionally more sports-oriented than moms, it is important for both girls and boys that moms be active, too.
- Be unconditionally loving, and communicate that love, no matter what

SIDELINE ETIQUETTE

A cacophony of sound can be heard along the sidelines of every youth soccer game, no matter what the age or level of play. While it is natural to get caught up in the emotion of the game, parents should avoid yelling specific instructions and issuing commands in the heat of battle. This can be extremely confusing for a child, and possibly contrary to the coach's instructions, making it all the more upsetting for her.

Here are some other rules of etiquette for spectators.

- Do not run up and down the sidelines shouting. If you want to follow the action, make sure that you do not distract the players or block the view of other spectators.
- Do not direct comments to the referee or linesmen. Unless they are praiseworthy, do not direct comments to members of the opposition.
- Do not stand near the goals. In many youth leagues, standing behind the goal is prohibited.
- Stand, or sit, at least three to five yards back from the sidelines (touchlines). Again, this is a rule in many youth leagues.
- Model good sportsmanship by applauding exceptional moves by the opposition.

the circumstances. Either say it outright, or show it: "I love you for who you are, not what you do."

it's a family affair

Soccer is a wonderful activity for the entire family. Whether it is playing or watching, there is something for everyone.

Rather than focusing on what the game lacks for various family members, concentrate on what it can have. A soccer game or practice can be an excellent vehicle to set aside family time.

Make the soccer ritual a complete one. Invest in a video camera or a good camera and take photos of your child. Let a sibling try a hand at the camera as well.

Surround soccer occasions with other activities. Organize the other team families for a postgame celebration or outing. Bring a picnic or go out for ice cream or a meal. If the game is away, explore the local sights or events, such as museums or a town center. Even a mall gives some family members something to look forward to, especially if they are teenagers.

Invite your extended family to games to experience the atmosphere and the excitement. To get them even more involved, find them a role, such as transporting players, photographing, or videotaping.

siblings and soccer

The family soccer experience extends to siblings, whether they choose to play the game or not. You can help facilitate a healthy outcome to "sibling soccer" if you keep in mind some tips.

MOM'S VIEW

I looked forward with excitement to my first parent-child soccer game. Finally, I thought, a chance to truly share in my daughter's soccer experience.

As the group of adults mixed in with 10-year-olds ran up and down the field, I was filled with confidence. "I can do this," I said to myself. Then, in an instant, something happened that shattered my illusions.

The ball came my way, flying high in the air. I distinctly remember the black and white design on which my eyes focused, while out of my peripheral vision I encountered a sight that filled me with terror. In full sprint were a mass of players coming at me—and that coveted ball.

Good student that I am, I heard the lessons in my head: Settle the ball, then look for the pass. Right. As soon as it landed, I quickly kicked it away, not caring where it went as long as the descending horde stopped coming toward me.

I have not viewed youth soccer players the same way since. I now appreciate their bravery and skill even more than before. I look upon them with awe and respect, and I understand the pressure that they face.

Despite the abject terror of that one moment, I did have fun. When I woke the next morning, my body sore and bruised, I was a different soccer parent. I could see the game through my children's eyes.

If siblings choose to play:

- Encourage, but do not force, one of your children to mentor the other. Siblings, whether younger or older, can serve as the best possible role models. It gives a child an enormous sense of confidence and pride to be able to influence siblings.
- Allow for the fact that competition between siblings is natural.
- Resist the temptation to compare siblings, and discourage them from comparing. Remember that the benchmark for success is hard work and enjoyment, not talent or achievements.
- Learn to juggle the attention. If schedules conflict, try not to always send the same parent with the same child. Enlist carpools or other family members to assist you in flexible scheduling.
- Pace yourself. Do not spend so much energy on an elder child's soccer that you run out of interest–and thus, time and attention–for a younger sibling.

If siblings choose not to play soccer:

- Do not force them to be involved in their siblings' soccer. They will gravitate toward soccer if they choose.
- Help them find their own sport or activity on which to focus.

- Recognize and support their unique talents, such as chess or art. Avoid being consumed with soccer.
- Do not insist they go to games. Give them a good alternative, like a fun activity or place to visit while you are at soccer games. Explain, however, that there may be exceptions, such as away games or important competitions, which you may want the entire family to attend.

an active lifestyle

Life is an energy pie, according to David E. Martin, professor of physiology in the department of cardiopulmonary care sciences at Georgia State University in Atlanta, who has worked with a number of Olympic athletes. Each of your child's activities is a piece of that pie: soccer, schoolwork, socializing, and other endeavors such as music lessons or other sports. No matter how many slices you cut, there is only so much pie. If you or your child is trying to load on too many activities, then fatigue, staleness, and burnout can be the unfortunate results.

While understanding the many benefits of the youth soccer system, be aware of its potential drawbacks. The imbalance of training and competition can be troublesome, particularly for younger children. If you feel that your child's schedule is too rigorous, cut back and focus on fewer activities.

Much of this book offers suggestions to help families achieve a healthy soccer and lifestyle balance. If you make an effort to protect your child from burnout–by ensuring that she is in a well-balanced soccer program, gets sufficient rest, and is well-nourished, and by taking family time outside of soccer–youth soccer can be a very rewarding experience for both you and your child. Children who have achieved balance in their lives get the most pleasure out of soccer. They look forward to practice and games, and they usually exhibit high energy levels. While they may feel tired after playing, it is a good tired. They are enthusiastic, and they look forward to playing again. In the end, that deep satisfaction and anticipation is what we really want them to get out of the game.

laws of the game

The goal of soccer is very simple: Put the ball into the opposing team's net more times than they put the ball into your net. Following is an explanation of the field positions in soccer, as well as the laws of the game.

general guidelines and team composition

Each team comprises the following:

- **Goalkeeper, goalie, or keeper:** This player is unique in that he may use his hands within the penalty area to keep the opposing team from scoring. The keeper is the only player legally allowed to touch the ball with his hands.
- **Defenders:** Their primary role is to take the ball away and start the attack in their team's favor. Their secondary role is to close down the space and the attack of the opposing team.
- **Midfielders:** They play both offense and defense. The midfield (middle ground) is the link between the offense and the defense.
- **Forwards:** They finish the attack and try to score. They must be willing to come back and aid in the midfield or defense to start an attack. Often, forwards are required to help defend corner kicks and free kicks and help at other times when their team's defense is under heavy pressure.

Other than the goalkeeper, the players' positions are determined by different tactics. All players must develop offensive and defensive skills, and every player has the potential to be a scorer. There is no such thing as a fixed space or position in soccer. Players may interchange positions according to the flow of the game.

A ball and open space to play are the only essentials. In organized youth practices and leagues, however, shinguards are mandatory for safety. Although there are laws in international soccer to penalize certain types of play, many U.S. youth leagues have their own interpretation. Two examples are contrary to international law: lying on the ground while kicking a ball can be ruled as "dangerous play" in the youth game. Also, some referees allow girls to protect their chests from the ball by using their arms.

laws of the game

International soccer is governed by FIFA (the international soccer federation). They've boiled the game of soccer down to 17 laws, which are presented here in an adapted version. For a complete set of the laws, contact any of the national youth soccer organizations or check the Internet (see the resource list on page 207).

DIFFERENT WAYS TO PLAY THE GAME

The U.S. Youth Soccer Association (USYSA) recommends the following standards for different age groups. *Note*: Field dimensions given here are the minimum required by the USYSA.

AGE	FIELD DIMENSIONS (YD.)	PLAYERS PER TEAM	BALL SIZE	GAME DURATION (MIN.)
UNDER 6	25 × 20	3	#3	32, NO GOALKEEPER
UNDER 8	50 × 30	4	#3	48, NO GOALKEEPER
UNDER 10	70 × 50	8	#4	50, GOALKEEPER OPTIONAL
UNDER 12	100 × 50	11	#4	60
UNDER 14	100 × 50	11	#5	70
UNDER 16	100 × 50	11	#5	80
UNDER 19	100 × 50	11	#5	90

law 1: **the field of play**

The soccer field is rectangular, not more than 130 yards in length (minimum 100 yards) and not more than 100 yards in width (minimum 50 yards). At each end is a goal, a penalty area, a penalty spot, and a goal area. There is a semicircular arc extending over the center top of the penalty area. This arc is 10 yards from the penalty spot and marks the minimum distance that other players must stand away from the penalty-shot taker. The halfway line divides the field equally in two. Corner arcs are in each corner of the field. This is where the ball must be placed for corner kicks.

law 2: **the ball**

The ball is made of leather or synthetic material. Its circumference can be between 27 and 28 inches, and its weight can be between 14 and 16 ounces for a full-size (#5) ball. The referee must decide a ball's appropriate pressure and is at liberty to replace the ball at any time.

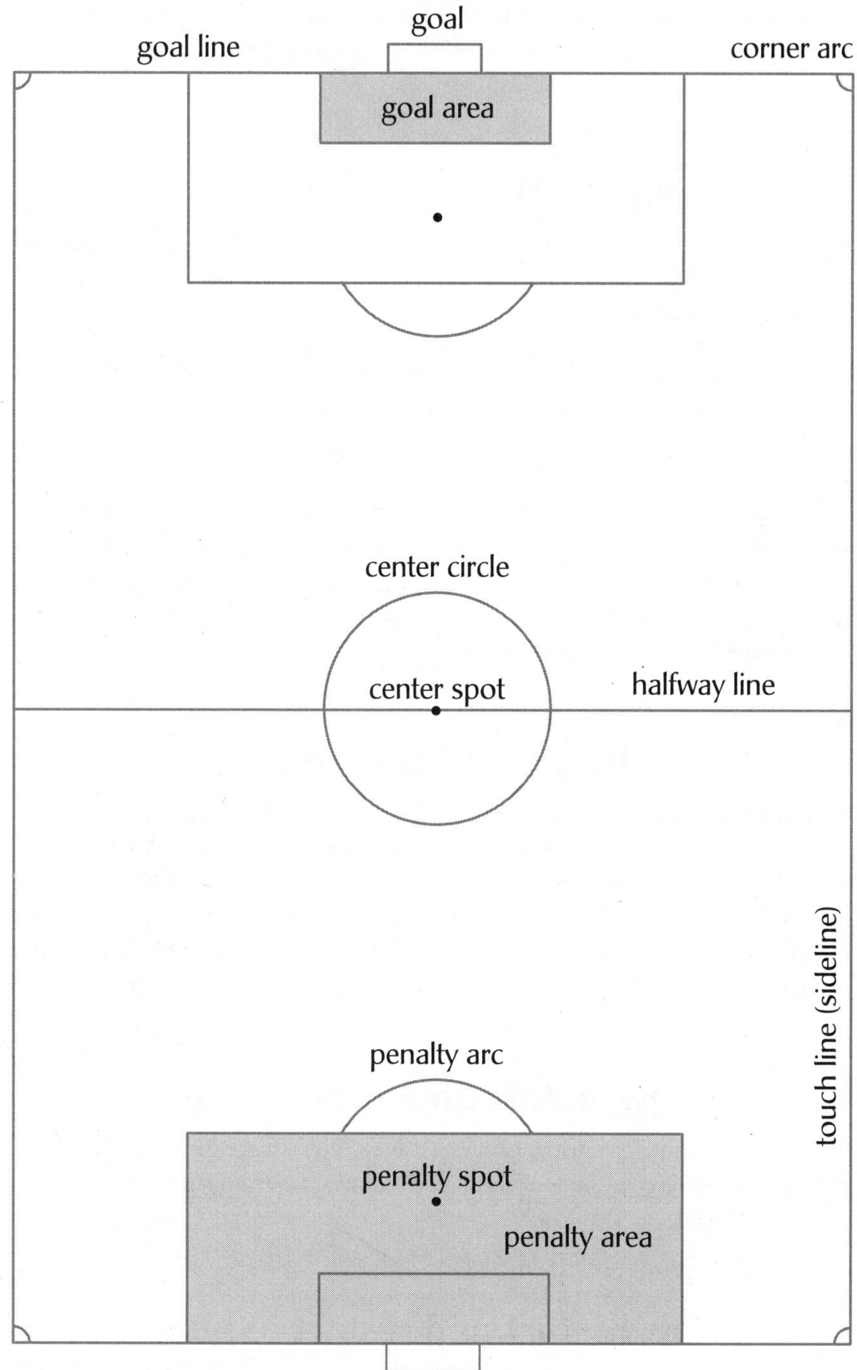
goal
goal line
corner arc
goal area
center circle
center spot
halfway line
touch line (sideline)
penalty arc
penalty spot
penalty area

law 3: **number of players**

A team is composed of 11 players (10 outfield players and a goalkeeper, U-12 and older). A match may not start if either team consists of fewer than 7 players. It is possible that a team of 7 would face a team of 11. Substitution rules are determined by local leagues.

law 4: **players' equipment**

Players should not wear anything that might injure themselves or another player. For this reason, referees will inspect players and have them remove watches and jewelry. The goalkeeper must wear a distinguishing jersey. Shinguards are mandatory. Clothing should not restrict movement, and cleats should be worn when applicable.

law 5: **the referee**

The referee is completely in charge of the game. He keeps the time and the official score. The referee is responsible for administering punishment for rule infractions and misconduct. The referee may halt the game for injury or cancel the game to protect the safety of the players, such as for inclement weather or poor field conditions or for any infringements of the Laws. All decisions by the referee are final.

law 6: **assistant referees**

There are two assistant referees (linesmen). Their duties, subject to the decision of the referee, are to indicate when the ball is out of play, which side gets the ball, and whether the ball should be put back in play by a throw-in, corner kick, or goal kick. Linesmen also assist in substitutions and misconduct that has occurred out of view of the referee. They may also signal offside. A linesman communicates this information by use of a flag.

law 7: **duration of the game**

An adult game consists of two 45-minute halves. Youth soccer game time rules vary according to age group. Games may differ in duration according to competition and tournament rules.

law 8: **start and restart of play**

The winner of a coin toss chooses which goal it will attack in the first half. The other team takes the kickoff from the center spot (center of the field) to start the game. After a team scores, the other team restarts play with another kickoff from the center spot.

A dropped ball is a way of restarting the game after a temporary stoppage such as one caused by an injury or infraction. For dropped balls, the referee drops the ball at the site of the stoppage. After it bounces, the ball can be played.

law 9: **the ball in and out of play**

The ball is out of play only when it has fully crossed one of the field boundaries. It is still in play if it bounces off a goalpost, a corner flag, or an official. Play is stopped when the referee blows his whistle.

law 10: **method of scoring**

A goal is scored when the entire ball crosses the line between the two goal posts. The team that scores the most goals wins. If zero or an equal number of goals are scored, the contest is a tie.

Many leagues have rules that provide for breaking ties. These options range from sudden-death over-time to overtimes of set time lengths to penalty-kick shootouts.

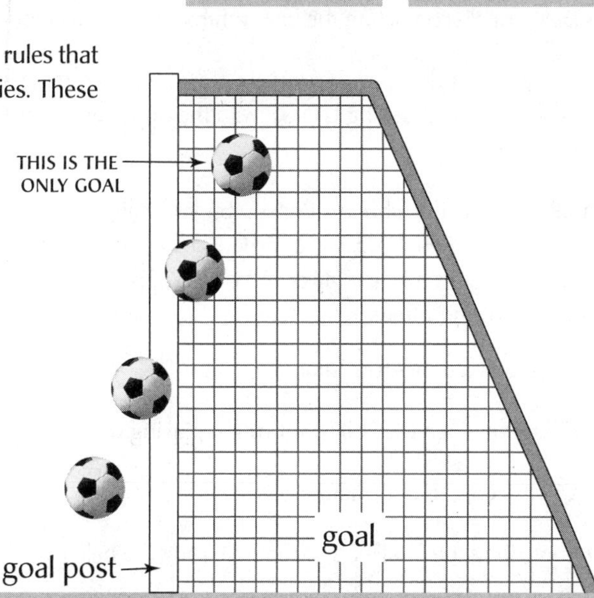

law 11: **offside**

A player is considered offside if he is nearer the opponents' goal than both the ball and two opposing players at the moment the ball is played forward by another member of his team. A player is not in an offside position if he is in his own half of the field, if he is level with the last defender, or if the ball was received directly from a goal kick, corner kick, or throw-in.

A player is not penalized for being offside unless, in the opinion of the referee, he is seeking to gain advantage or is interfering with play or an opponent. An indirect free kick is awarded to the opposing team when a player is offside.

law 12: **fouls and misconduct**

A direct free kick is awarded to the opposing team at the point of the foul for the following offenses.

- Kicking, or attempting to kick, an opponent
- Tripping an opponent
- Jumping at an opponent
- Charging an opponent in a dangerous manner
- Spitting at, striking, or attempting to strike an opponent
- Holding or pushing
- Deliberately contacting the ball with hands or arms (applies to all players except the goalkeeper)
- When tackling, making contact with the opponent before making contact with the ball

Should any of the above offenses be committed by the defensive team in the penalty area, a penalty kick is awarded to the attacking team.

An indirect free kick is awarded to the opposing team at the point of the foul for the following offenses.

- Playing in a dangerous manner
- Charging when the ball is not within playing distance
- Obstructing an opponent
- Preventing the goalkeeper from releasing the ball from his hands
- Delays by the goalkeeper

- If a defensive player deliberately plays or throws in the ball to his goalkeeper and the goalkeeper plays it with his hands

A caution (yellow card) is issued to a player if he:

- Shows dissent (by word or action) with a referee's decision
- Enters or re-enters the field without the referee's permission
- Displays unsporting conduct
- Displays persistent infringement of the Laws of the Game
- Disregards the required distance during restart of play with a free kick or corner kick

An indirect free kick is awarded for the last three infractions.

A player can be ejected from the game (red card) for:

- Serious foul play
- Violent behavior
- Spitting at another player or anyone else
- Denying a goal, or the opportunity to score a goal, to an opponent by deliberately handling the ball (this doesn't apply to the goalkeeper in his own team's penalty area)
- Denying a goal-scoring opportunity to an opponent by using an offense punishable by a penalty kick or a free kick
- Use of foul or abusive language
- A second yellow-card offense

law 13: **free kick**

Free kicks are either direct or indirect. For both direct and indirect free kicks, the ball must be stationary when the kick is taken. The kicker cannot touch the ball a second time until it has touched another player.

A direct free kick can be kicked directly into the goal without the assistance of another player. For an indirect free kick that goes into the net to be considered a goal, it must first be touched by another player other than the kicker.

On free kicks, the opposing team must be at least 10 yards away, unless standing on their own goal line. For a team taking a free kick from its own penalty area, the opponents must be outside the penalty area and at least 10 yards away.

law 14: **penalty kick**

A penalty kick is awarded to the attacking team when the defending team commits a foul that warrants a direct free kick inside its own penalty area. This type of kick results in the greatest advantage for the attacking team because it pits the kicker against the goalkeeper. The penalty kick is taken from the penalty spot. Other players must stand at least 10 yards away from the penalty spot and be outside the penalty area. The person taking the kick cannot play the ball a second time until it has been touched by another player. If the ball rebounds off the goalkeeper or goalpost into the field of play, it is live.

law 15: **throw-in**

A throw-in is a method of restarting play. It is awarded when the entire ball passes over the touch line (sideline), either on the ground or in the air. The team that did not kick it out of play throws the ball in from the point where it crossed the touch line. The ball is in play immediately when it enters the field of play. The thrower may not touch the ball again until it has touched another player. A goal cannot be scored directly from a throw-in.

law 16: **goal kick**

A goal kick is a method of restarting play. A goal kick is awarded when the entire ball, having last touched a player of the attacking team, passes over the goal line, either on the ground or in the air. A defending player kicks the ball from anywhere within the goal area. Opponents remain outside the penalty area until the ball is in play. The ball is in play when it is kicked directly beyond the penalty area. The kicker cannot play the ball again until another player touches it.

law 17: **corner kick**

A corner kick is a method of restarting play. A goal may be scored directly from a corner kick. A corner kick is awarded when the entire ball, having last touched a player of the defending team, passes over the goal line, either on the ground or in the air. The ball is placed in the nearest corner arc and is kicked by an attacking player. Defending players must be at least 10 yards away from the corner arc. The ball is in play when it is kicked and moves. The kicker cannot play the ball again until another player touches it.

glossary

Attacker	A player whose job it is to move the ball toward the opponent's goal in order to score or to create a scoring opportunity
Back heel	A ball played using the back of the foot
Back pass	A pass that a player makes backward toward his goal; often, this pass is made back to one's own goalkeeper
Ball familiarization	The practice of making a player comfortable with a soccer ball through constant touches of the ball
Bending the ball	Striking the ball with an off-center kick so that it travels in a curved path; also known as a banana kick
Bicycle kick	An expert move that is made by throwing the body up into the air, with the legs moving as if pedaling a bicycle; the player kicks the ball backward over his head
Block tackle	A tackle using the inside of the foot behind the ball and from a standing position
Boots	The English term for soccer cleats
Caution	An action taken by the referee against a player for one of several offenses, ranging from delaying the restart of play to unsporting conduct; the referee's action entails issuing a yellow card to the offender
Center forward	An attacking player who generally operates in the opposition's half of the field
Center spot	A mark at the center of the halfway line used for kickoffs
Change (the field)	Passing a ball from one side of the field to the other; also called switching the field
Charge	Allowed intentional conduct between players; this contact must be shoulder to shoulder with arms close to the body, and is permitted only while the ball is near enough to play; it must be intended to gain possession of the ball; it is only permitted when at least one foot of each player is in contact with the ground; if the charge is not performed in this manner, it may be ruled a foul
Chest control	Receiving the ball on the chest, in the area of the sternum

Chip pass	A lofted or high pass, often with backspin
Classic	A system of youth league play used in certain parts of the United States
Clearance	When defending players send the ball far away from their goal
Conditioned game	A practice game in which the coach imposes a variety of restrictions, such as one or two touches
Contain	A method used by the defense to restrict a member of the opposition to an area of the field
Cooldown	The practice of slowly curtailing physical activity after playing. This should include stretching to ensure flexibility and prevent injury
Corner flag	A flag used to mark each of the four corners of the field
Corner kick	A method of restarting play in which a kick is taken by a member of the attacking team when the ball goes over the goal line after last touching a defensive player; it is taken from the corner nearest to where the ball went out of bounds
Cover(ing)	A defensive player who guards a member of the offense who does not have the ball or is in anticipation of getting the ball; it also refers to one defender who supports, or takes over, for another defender
Cross	A ball, usually a lofted pass, played across the face of the goal
Crossbar	The part of the goal that is parallel to the ground and directly over the goal line
Cruyff turn	A turn used for change of direction and to deceive an opponent; named for Johan Cruyff, the famous Dutch player who popularized it
Cushioning the ball	Use of any body part other than the hands to absorb the impact of the ball with the aim of controlling it
Dangerous play	Any play that is likely to endanger any player; it results in an indirect free kick for the opposing team; an example is kicking the leg too high in the air in order to play the ball
Dead ball	A ball that is not in play
Defender	A player whose key responsibility is to stop the attacking team

Direct free kick	A free kick awarded for a personal foul; a player takes the kick from the site of the infraction and may score directly from this type of free kick
Distribution	The various individual techniques used by a player to pass the ball to teammates; it is generally used to describe this task when performed by a goalkeeper
Diving header	Using the head to strike the ball as a player throws himself toward the ball or is falling toward the ground
Down the line	A ball played parallel to the touch line toward the opposition's goal; a commonly used tactic for throw-ins
Dribble	To maintain control of the ball while running
Drop ball	A method of restarting play normally used after an injury stops play, or after play has been stopped without the ball going out of bounds; the referee drops the ball at the site of the stoppage; one bounce must occur before the ball can be played
Drop kick	A distribution method used by the goalkeeper; it is done by dropping the ball from the hands to the ground and then striking the ball immediately after it bounces
Dummy run	A run by a player without the ball to draw defenders away from the ball carrier
Far post	The goalpost farthest from the ball
Feint	A deceptive move meant to fake out an opponent
Field player	Any player other than the goalkeeper
FIFA	Acronym for Fédération Internationale de Football Association, which is the international governing body of soccer
Finish	To score a goal
Football	The word used for soccer throughout much of the world outside of North America
Forward	Any player used primarily as an attacker; usually plays in the opposition's half of the field
Free kick	A kick from a stationary position that is awarded to a team that has been fouled; there are two types of free kicks, direct and indirect
Give-and-go	Also known as 1-2 and wall pass; a pass to a teammate, who one-touch passes the ball back into space for the player to run to

Goal A goal is scored when the entire ball crosses the goal line, between the goalposts and under the crossbar; a goal is also the structure (posts, crossbar, and net) at each end of the field into which the ball is played to score

Goal kick A method of restarting play in which a kick is awarded to the defending team when the ball is played over the goal line by the attacking team; it is taken from anywhere in the goal area; the ball is only in play from a goal kick after it passes out of the penalty area and onto the field; the opponents remain outside the penalty area until the ball is in play

Goal line The two boundary lines located at the ends of the field

Goal mouth The area in front of the goal

Goalpost The vertical or upright posts that are perpendicular to the goal line.

Goalside The position that a defender takes when marking a player, between his goal and the opposing player

Grid A clearly marked four-sided area commonly used for training

Half-volley A kick made immediately after the ball bounces on the ground

Hand ball With the exception of the goalkeeper, use of any portion of the arm from the shoulder down, to control the ball; doing this results in a foul being called and a direct free kick

Header Using your head to pass or control the ball

Indirect free kick Awarded for violations of playing rules such as offside, delay of game, and misconduct; from this type of free kick, a goal can only be scored when touched by two players.

Instep The portion of the foot to the side of the shoelaces; the inside of the foot

In swing A pass, cross, or shot that curves toward the goal

Javelin throw A method of distribution by the goalkeeper; a catapult-style throw

Jockeying The act of slowing down an attacker where a defender may fake tackles and try to disrupt the attacker's dribbling; used to provide other teammates with time to recover and get into defensive position

Juggling	Keeping the ball airborne using any body surface except for the hands and arms
Kickoff	Used to start play at the beginning of each half and after a goal has been scored; a goal may be scored directly from a kickoff, which is taken from the center spot
Laces drive	A shot, pass, or clearance with the laces area of the foot
Laws of the Game	Seventeen rules, established and maintained by FIFA (the international soccer federation), that govern soccer
"Man on"	A call to make a player aware that he is being closely marked by an opposing player or that an opponent is rapidly approaching
Man-to-man marking	A defensive system in which each defender is responsible for guarding a specific opponent
Maradonna turn	A turn used to change direction and elude an opponent; named for Diego Maradonna, the famous Argentinian player who popularized it
Marking	Guarding, or defending, an opponent
Midfielders	The players responsible for linking play between attackers and defenders
Narrowing the angle	A goalkeeper advancing to block an attacker, thereby decreasing the size of the area of the goal in which an attacker can direct a shot. Also referred to as closing down the angle.
Near post	The goalpost nearest the ball
Nutmeg	Passing or pushing a ball between another player's legs
Obstruction	Blocking an opponent with the body; this is penalized by an indirect free kick, unless the obstruction is done within playing distance of the ball, in which case it is legal
Offside	A player is in an offside position if he is nearer to his opponent's goal line than both the ball and the second-to-last opponent; he is not offside if he is on his half of the field or is level with the second-to-last opponent or level with the last two opponents; an indirect free kick is awarded to the opposing team to be taken from the place where the offside occurs
Offside trap	A defensive technique to put attacking players in an offside position; this usually involves defenders quickly moving away from their own goal to create a situation

in which attackers are positioned illegally in advance of the ball

Off the ball — Anything happening away from the immediate area of the ball

Olympic Development Program — ODP; the official program of the U.S. Youth Soccer Association in which players represent their states

One-touch pass — A pass in which the ball is played with a player's first touch

1–2 — Also known as give-and-go and wall pass; a pass to a teammate, who one-touch passes the ball back into space for the player to run to

Out swing — A kick that swerves away from the goal

Overhead kick — Also named the bicycle kick

Overlapping players — Players making forward runs off the ball to help the ball carrier; creates space for a new pass or to distract defenders

Parry — A goalkeeper's use of any body part, usually the hands, to deflect the ball from the goal

Pass — Playing the ball to another player by striking it with various areas of the body

Penalty area — The large, lined rectangular area in front of the goal where the goalkeeper may handle the ball. Also referred to as the 18-yard box because of its dimensions

Penalty kick — Awarded to the attacking team for any personal fouls or intentional handling of the ball by the defense inside the penalty area; the direct free kick is taken from the penalty spot, 12 yards from the goal-line, and with the exception of the goalkeeper and the player taking the kick, all other players must be at least 10 yards from the penalty spot and outside the penalty area

Pinny — A lightweight colored vest worn over clothing and used to delineate one team from another; also referred to as a scrimmage vest

Pitch — The term used in some countries for a soccer field

Plant foot — The nonkicking foot, or the foot remaining on the ground

Poke tackle — Stealing the ball from an opponent by toeing the ball away

Premier — A system of youth league play used in certain parts of the country

Punching the ball	A goalkeeper technique, where the ball is punched clear of the goal
Punt	A goalkeeping distribution technique; the ball is dropped from the hands and then kicked with the laces
Push up	To move the defense out toward the offensive half of the field
Recreational	A system of youth play, usually not involving tryouts
Red card	A small red card held up by the referee; one serious infraction or two yellow cards within the same game will cause a red card to be issued; examples of these infractions include serious foul play, violent behavior, or foul or abusive language; a red card results in a player's ejection from the game
Referee	The official in charge of the game
Referee's assistants	Two officials whose duties are to indicate when the ball is out of play or when a team is offside; which side is entitled to a corner kick, goal kick, or throw-in; and when a substitution is desired; they may alert the referee to any and all things that the referee cannot see; the final decision rests with the referee
Save	A player's successful prevention of a goal, usually associated with a goalkeeper
Scissors kick	A kick made by a player while off the ground in which the ball is struck by one foot as the legs make a scissors-like motion
Scrimmage	A practice game; also called a friendly
Scrimmage vest	A lightweight colored vest worn over clothing and used to delineate one team from another; also referred to as a pinny
Select	A system of high-level play
Set play (set piece)	When a stoppage in play results in one team having 100 percent control over what happens next; restart situations include free kicks, throw-ins, corner kicks, kickoffs, penalty kicks, and goal kicks
Shielding	Keeping an opponent away from the ball by using the body
Shot	A kick, header, or any intended deflection of the ball toward a goal by a player attempting to score a goal
Side volley	A shot, pass, or clearance made by striking the ball while

it is in the air, using various parts of the leg or foot, and sending the ball across the body

Slide tackle A tackle in which the defender slides and makes contact with the ball

Small-sided game A game that includes only a few players per team

Stopper A defender who usually plays in front of the sweeper

Strike Use of any body part (except the hands and arms) to hit the ball

Support Being in any position to help another player, such as helping out a teammate on the ball by moving to an open area or to a position to receive a pass

Sweeper A defensive player who roams behind the other defenders and has no specific marking duties; he is the last line of defense before the goalkeeper

Swerve pass A pass that follows a curved path because of the way the ball is struck with the side of the foot

Switch (the field) Passing a ball from one side of the field to the other; also called changing the field

Tackle A defensive technique using the feet to take the ball away from an opponent

Take on To beat and get past a defender using skill or speed

Takeover While dribbling, a player exchanges the ball with a teammate by leaving it for that player to run up and take control of the ball

Target players Usually, forwards who are the target of passes and crosses; usually play with their backs to the goal on which they are trying to score

Team transition When a team shifts from a defensive situation to attack or vice-versa

Through pass A pass designed to go between two defenders in order to take them out of the play, releasing one's own player into space

Throw-in A method of continuing play after the ball has crossed the touch line; players must have their feet on or behind the touch line, must maintain contact with the ground, and must use a two-handed throw made from behind the head; a goal cannot be scored directly from a throw-in

"Time"	A frequently used term during play made by one's teammate to signal to a player that he has time or space (defenders are not nearby)
Tip save	Use of the fingertips by the goalkeeper to deflect the ball away from the goal
Toe poke	Use of the toe to strike the ball
Touch	Contact that a player has with the ball while it is in his possession; for example, a player who "three touches" the ball, receives it, touches it again, and then kicks it away; touch also describes a player's ability to control the ball well
Touch line	The line that defines the outer edge of the longer sides of the field; also referred to as the sideline
Trap (trapping)	The process of receiving a soccer ball; the word *trap* is combined with a body part to identify how control is gained of the ball, such as thigh trap, chest trap, and sole-of-the-foot trap
Travel	A system of youth league play used in certain parts of the United States
Volley	Striking the ball in midair with either foot
Wall pass	Also known as 1–2 and give-and-go; a pass to a teammate, who then one-touch passes the ball back into space for the player to run to
Warmup	In order to prepare for any aspect of playing, players participate in gradual physical exercise, such as light running and stretching, and even mental preparation
Wingers	Forwards who play on the wings/sides/flanks of the field
World Cup	The official World Championship of soccer; it is sanctioned by FIFA and held every four years
Yellow card	A small yellow card held up by a referee to inform all participants and spectators that an infringement of the rules dictating a caution has occurred
Youth license modules	Three U.S. Youth Soccer Association age-specific courses (U-6, U-8, U-10) for coaching accreditation
Zone defense	A defensive system; defenders mark a designated area instead of tracking players across the field

resources

The following are the three major youth soccer administrative agencies and one major coaching organization in the United States. Addresses, toll-free numbers, and Web sites are included if you'd like additional information.

U.S. Youth Soccer Association (USYSA): With a registration of more than 3 million players from under age 6 through age 19, USYSA covers the entire country through state associations in all 50 states. It is the youth division of U.S. Amateur Soccer, and includes high-level play through the Olympic Development Program. Its programs and publications serve all aspects of the game, from coaching to administration to refereeing. For disabled players, call your USYSA state association to inquire about programs in your area, or ask the national office for information about Top Soccer.

U.S. Youth Soccer Association
899 Presidential Drive, Suite 117
Richardson, TX 75081
(800) 4 SOCCER
www.youthsoccer.org

American Youth Soccer Organization (AYSO): It has a registration of more than 625,000 youth between the ages of 4½ and 18, plus almost 92,000 volunteer coaches and 47,000 volunteer referees. AYSO stresses participation for all players and recreational play. Its programs and publications serve all aspects of the game, from coaching to administration to refereeing. For disabled players, ask about the VIP Program for Kids with Special Needs.

American Youth Soccer Organization
P.O. Box 5045
Hawthorne, CA 90251
(800) USA-AYSO
www.soccer.org

Soccer Association for Youth (SAY): It serves 80,000 members and includes players from ages 4 through 18. Members operate their own local programs. It provides training and publications for all aspects of the game.

Soccer Association for Youth
4050 Executive Park Drive, Suite 100
Cincinnati, OH 45241
(800) 233-7291
www.saysoccer.org

National Soccer Coaches Association of America (NSCAA): For youth, high school, college, and professional coaches. Membership includes a bimonthly newsletter, *Soccer Journal*.

National Soccer Coaches Association of America
6700 Squibb Road, Suite 215
Mission, KS 66202
(800) 458-0678
www.nscaa.com

magazines and publications

Soccer America: A weekly newspaper with a bimonthly section on youth soccer. The focus is on international, professional, and collegiate soccer. A subscription includes the *Soccer America Yellow Pages*, an annual national youth soccer camp directory, an annual college scholarship directory, and monthly national and international youth tournament calendars.

Soccer America
P.O. Box 23704
Oakland, CA 94623
(800) 997-6223

Soccer America Yellow Pages: With more than 200 pages, this is the definitive source for national and regional youth soccer organizations, tournaments, coaching, and soccer products. Published by *Soccer America*.

Soccer Jr.: A magazine for youth soccer players. Published six times a year, it provides a broad soccer experience, beyond practices and matches, with a worldwide view of the sport. Special editions include "Soccer for Parents," a supplement that comes out twice yearly.

Soccer Jr.
27 Unquowa Road
Fairfield, CT 06430
(800) 829-5382

catalogs

Eurosport
Hillsborough, N.C.
(800) 934-3876

Reedswain
Spring City, Pa.
(800) 331-5191

Soccer Learning Systems/SLS
San Ramon, Calif.
(800) 762-2376

Soccer Madness
Sunrise, Fla.
(800) 447-8333

TSI Soccer
Durham, N.C.
(888) TSI-1001

internet

Soccer has a massive representation on the Internet. There are sites for players, leagues, clubs, and organizations. There are also educational sites on topics such as sports medicine and nutrition.

You can further explore any of the topics in this book on the Internet. Just go into a search engine to look for any number of topics. The addresses below are suggested by Al Sinclair, president of New Jersey Youth Soccer, who has conducted national clinics on the topic of soccer on the Internet. Although the sites listed here are stable, Sinclair points out that, just like the rest of the Internet, many soccer sites are not. As with any area of the Internet, Sinclair recommends that parents explore the sites themselves before turning over access to children.

www.soccercity.net: An extensive site on all aspects of the game

www.fifa.com: The Web site for FIFA, the international soccer federation

www.us-soccer.com: The Web site for the U.S. Soccer Federation

www.socceramerica.com: The largest soccer Web site in America. It includes the entire *Soccer America Yellow Pages*

about the authors

Gloria Averbuch is the author of seven books on exercise, health, and fitness. She most recently wrote *On the Run: Exercise and Fitness for Busy People*, co-authored with Grete Waitz (Rodale Press, 1997), and *The New York Road Runners Club Complete Book of Running and Fitness*, co-authored with Fred Lebow and currently in its fourth printing (Random House, 1997). She is a contributing author to *Women's Soccer: The Game and the 1999 FIFA Women's World Cup* (Universe Publishing, 1999). She broadcasts sports events and health and fitness information on radio, including "Fitness Features," which airs regularly on WABC in New York City.

Averbuch, who holds a youth soccer coaching license, is a staff member of Ashley's Soccer Camp and Soccer Domain, an indoor sports facility in Montclair, New Jersey.

She is a lifelong athlete and currently a competitive masters runner. She is married to former national-class marathoner Paul Friedman, who serves as a part-time youth soccer and sports conditioning coach. They are the parents of daughters Yael and Shira, both of whom are high-level soccer players.

Ashley Michael Hammond is the owner of Ashley's Soccer Camp and Soccer Domain, an indoor sports facility in Montclair, New Jersey. His soccer programs include thousands of players a year and are conducted in dozens of towns. His company donates thousands of dollars a year to soccer programs and scholarships.

Hammond is also the high school boys' soccer coach at Montclair Kimberly Academy, a U.S. Department of Education National Blue Ribbon School. He has won a number of prestigious scholarships and awards for excellence in teaching, including the New Jersey State Student Teacher of the Year award for 1994. He is a contributor to *Games and Great Ideas* (Greenwood Press, 1995).

Hammond, who began playing soccer seriously at age 10, is a former player for a professional team in his native England. He is a British- and American-licensed coach and a certified referee. He lives with his wife, Meg, and her three children in Montclair, New Jersey.

index

<u>Underscored</u> page references indicate boxed text. *Italic* page references indicate illustrations or photographs. **Boldface** text denotes main subject headings.

A

ACL injuries, 119–20, <u>120</u>
Active-isolated stretching, 33
Advanced players, 67–77
  coaching, <u>75</u>
  commitment issues, 77
  rules, 73–74
  self-motivation indicators, 67–68
  skills for
    chest control, *68*
    dribbling, 69
    heading, 71
    jockeying, 72–73
    passing, 68–69
    shooting, 69, 71
    slide tackle, 72, *73*
    tackling, 72
    turns, 69
  summer camps for, 140–41
  tactical instruction, 73–77
Aggression
  fostering, in girls, 162–63
  in girls' vs. boys' games, 168
  as part of soccer, 7, 162–63
Alignments, of players on field, 74–75
American Camping Association, 138
American College of Sports Medicine, fluid intake guidelines, 105
American Youth Soccer Association (AYSO), 7, 8
  coed play discouraged by, 172
  description and address, 207
Anemia, 99
Ankle injuries
  fractures, 117–18
  ligament injuries, 117
Anorexia, 104
Anterior cruciate ligament (ACL) **injuries**, 119–20, <u>120</u>
Artificial failure, 52
Assistant referees, 192
AYSO. *See* American Youth Soccer Association

B

Back
  muscle pulls, prevention of, 123
  stretch, *36*
Back-heel pass, 68
Back passing, 68, 73
Balance, physical, *11*, 12
Balance, in soccer lifestyle, <u>76</u>, 188
Ball control, *53*
  expert players, <u>79</u>
  intermediate players, 64–65
  novice players, 52–53
  as part of learning hierarchy, *11*, 12
Ball distribution, *11*, 12, 14
Balls, soccer
  fear of, <u>65</u>
  sizes, <u>20</u>, <u>190</u>
  sleeping with, <u>44</u>
  types, <u>20</u>
  USYSA law, 191
Banana pass, 81, *81*
Baseball, for cross-training, 111
Basic skills, 11–12, 43–44, <u>74</u>
Basketball, for cross-training, 110
Beckenbauer, Franz, 4
Beginner players, 43–48
  basic skills development, 43–44
    parent involvement in, 44, 46–47
  fun for, 48
  introducing gear, <u>44</u>
  sample lesson plan, <u>45</u>
  "swarm ball," 55–56
Best, George, 4
Bicycle kick, 82, *82*
Blanco, Cuauhtemoc, <u>70</u>
Blanco move, <u>70</u>
Block tackling, 62, *62*

Bloody nose, 123
Bone health, in girls, 104
Boys' vs. girls' games
  coaching discrepancies, 169–70
  refereeing discrepancies, 164, 167–68
Brain injury, heading and, 123–24
Bras, sports , 22, 172
Brazil. *See also* Pelé
  soccer culture of, 5
  women's soccer in, 162
British Universities North American Club (BUNAC), 140
Bulimia, 104
BUNAC, 140
Butterfly stretch, *36*

C

Calcium
  adolescent athletes and, 98
  female athletes and, 99
Calf stretch, *37*
Calorie needs, of young athletes, 99
Camps, soccer, 136–42
  accreditation and quality of, 140
  elite camps, 141
  guidelines to help assess, 138–40
  higher-level camps, 140–41
  international staff at, 140
  locating, 138
  safety issues, 137, 138–40
Captains, team, 84
Carbohydrate-rich snacks, 104
Casual play exercises, 177–79
Catalogs, 208
Cautions to players (USYSA law), 195
Chest control, 68, *68*
Chest pass, 68
Chondromalacia, 119
Clark, Nancy , 99
Classic play level, 130–31
Cleats, 16, 17, 56
Clinics, off-season, 141–42
Clothing, 18–19
  cold-weather, 19, 21–22
  hot-weather, 22
  neatness of, to promote pride, 56
  sizes, 15–16
Coaches
  communicating with, 26, 28
  gender of, 26–27
  licensing, 24, 27, 79, 150
  parents as, 150–57
  qualities to look for, 27, 75
  as role models, 26
  training and background of, 24
Coaching
  advanced players, 75
  expert players, 79
  fairness issues, 151
  game day tips, 155
  games for skills development, 178–79
  girls, 164, 169–70
  overcoaching, 157
  parent meetings, guidelines for, 155–56
  personal stories, 13, 50, 84, 144, 148, 164
  sample lesson plan, 45
  tactics to avoid, 52
  teaching concepts (A-Z), 151–55
Codes of conduct, for
  parents/guardians, 156
  players, 156
Coed play, 172–73, 173
Cold weather
  clothing for, 19, 21–22
  need for dietary fat during, 98
College soccer, 145–47
  planning for, in high school, 146–47
  for women, 161
Communicating
  parent to child, 65
  parent to coaches, 26, 28
  parent to referees, 29
  player to player, 83
Competition
  in Games Based Approach, 14
  intensity of, 149, 163
  intermediate players, 66
  level of, 87, 130, 133
Competition play level, 130–31
Competitiveness, development of, 165
Concentration, 148, 148
Concepts of game, introducing, 56
Concussions
  mouthguards to prevent, 124
  symptoms of, 123

Conditioning. *See also* Fitness
body strength and, 114
importance of, 111, 113–15
parents helping with, 113
serious, for older players, 113–15
water workouts for, 114–15
year-round, 111, 112, 113
Cone knockdown (game), 178
Cooldowns, 33–34
Cross-training, 108–11
baseball, 111
basketball, 110
cycling, 110
dance/gymnastics, 111
hockey, 111
martial arts, 111
racquet sports, 111
running, 110–11
swimming, 111
Cruyff, Johan, 4, 70
Cruyff turn, 61, *61*, 70, 180
Culture, soccer and, 4–5, 6, 80
Cycling, for cross-training, 110

D

Dance, for cross-training, 111
Decision making
holding up the ball, 66
intermediate players, 64–65
Deep-water running, 114–15
Defenders
description of position, 189
expert-level abilities, 85
Dehydration, 107
Discomfort, physical, 149
Diving header, *72*
Diving techniques (goalkeeper), 93
diving parry, *91*
practice exercises
diving high jump, 93
"Ray Amato Splash," 93
Dorrance, Anson, 164–65, 182
Dribbling, 50, 69
Drinking. *See* Fluids
Dummies. *See* Feints

E

Eating disorders, 104
Ejection from game (USYSA law), 195
Elimination games, 52
Emotional health, of goalkeepers, 86
Energy bars, 106
Energy in play, 149, 163
England
history of soccer and, 3
personal childhood stories, 6, 63, 87
soccer culture of, 5, 80
Equipment. *See* Gear
Etiquette, for spectators, 186
Exercises
conditioning, 113
stretching, for warmup, *34–39*
water workouts, 114–15
Expert players, 78–85
abilities of players, 79, 81
abilities of team, 79
captains, team, 84
fitness, importance of, 78
on-field communication, 83
skills for
feints, 83
passing, 81
shooting, 81
sliding, 83
swerve pass, 81, *81*
summer camps for, 140–41
tactical instruction, 83–85
fluidity of position, 85
man-to-man marking, 85
offside trap, 83, 85
set plays, 85
Eye injuries, 125
Eyewear, protective, 125

F

Fairness, in coaching, 151, 152
Fake moves. *See* Feints
Families, of players, 184–88
fitness support, 113
games, family time and, 186
parent-child bonds, 180, 184–85
parent-child games, 187
siblings, 186–88
Fartlek, 110
Fatigue, iron deficiency and, 99
Fats, dietary, 98
Fear, of ball, 65

Feints, 59
in dribbling, 69
expert players, 83
Maradonna turn, 69
stepover, 69
stutter step, 69
during turns, 69
Field alignment of players, 74–75
Field awareness, 65
Fields, soccer
diagram of, *191*
dimensions of, by age group, 190
hazards on, checking for, 23, 118
player communication on, 83
shortages of, in U.S., 7–8
USYSA law, 191
FIFA
goalkeeping ruling, 89–90
laws of the game, 189–96
soccer ball, official size, 20
Web site address, 209
First-aid, for
bloody nose, 123
fractures, 117, 118, 119
tooth knocked out, 124
First-aid kits, 118
Fitness
as benefit, 8
conditioning, 111–15
cross-training to enhance, 108–10
demands of game, 109
expert players, importance to, 78
to lessen injuries, 125
loss of, during off-season, 112, 113
psychological, 147–49
year-round, 111, 113
Flat-footedness, 116
Flicking, 61, 93
Flinching, 65
Fluidity of position
advanced players, 74–75
expert players, 85
intermediate players, 65–66
Fluids
dehydration signs, 107
importance of, 105
postgame recovery and, 104
sports drinks, 105
tips for using, 105–6
Follow the leader (game), 179
Foods. *See also* Nutrition; Snacking
Food Guide Pyramid, 98
glycemic index of, 102
for halftime, 102
meal suggestions, for game day, 103
serving sizes, for athletes, 99
suggestions for the road, 103
Foot dominance
player development and, 54
in shooting, 59
training both feet, 54
Foot pass, 50–51, *51*
back-heel, 68
outside-of-the-foot, 68
Foot problems
accessory navicula, 116–17
heel injuries, 117
overpronation, 116
Seaver's syndrome, 117
Footwear
cleats, 16
indoor soccer shoes, 16
injury prevention and, 125
sneakers, 16–17
turf shoes, 16
Forwards
description of position, 189
expert players, 85
Fouls (USYSA law), 194–95
Fractures
ankle, 117–18
leg or arm, 119
shinbone, 118–19
Free kick
awarded for fouls, 194–95
USYSA law, 195
Frog stretch, *37*
Fun
in conditioning program, 113
in Games Based Approach, 9–10
at higher skill levels, 50
importance of, 9–10, 48, 57

G

Game day
coaching tips for, 155
meal suggestions for, 103
tips for, 46

Game duration
- player age and, 190
- USYSA law, 192

Games, for skills development, 178–79
Games Based Approach, 9–14, 10
Gear, 15–24
- essential, for games, 19
- organizing and labeling, 19
- shopping for, 15
- types
  - cleats, 16, 17, 56
  - clothing, 18–19
  - cup, to protect testicles, 122
  - eyewear, protective, 125
  - footwear, 16–17
  - goalkeeping, 19–21, 89
  - mouthguards, 124
  - shinguards, 17
  - soccer balls, 20
  - socks, 17–18
  - sports bras, 22, 172
- USYSA law, 192

Girls. *See also* Girls' soccer
- eating disorders and, 104
- injuries more common to
  - anterior cruciate ligament injury, 120
  - chondromalacia, 119
- menarche, delayed, in athletes, 171
- nutritional needs of, 104–5
  - calcium, 104
  - iron, 99, 104
- physical changes, at puberty, 171
- sports bras and, 22

Girls' soccer
- coach, gender of, 26–27
- coaching, 164, 169–70
- players, number of, in U.S., 167
- refereeing, 167–68
- team support, value of, 166
- traits needed to succeed
  - aggression, 162–63
  - competitiveness, 163, 165
  - intensity, 163
  - love of game, 165–66

Girls' vs. boys' games
- coaching discrepancies, 169–70
- refereeing discrepancies, 164, 167–68

Gloves, goalkeeper's, 20–21
Glucose, 102–3
Gluteal muscle stretch, *35*
Glycemic index, 102–3, 102
GOAL (practice exercise), 92
Goalkeepers, 86–93
- abilities needed by, 86
- advanced players
  - abilities of, 93
  - exercises for, 93
- beginner players
  - abilities of, 86–87
  - exercises for, 90–92
- coaching, 89–90
- description of position, 189
- emotional health of, 86
- gear for, 19–21, 89
- individuality of, 86
- injury risk for, 88
- intermediate players
  - calls used, 92
  - exercises for, 92–93
- kicking skills overlooked, 89
- novice players, 56–57
- parental support, 88–89
- personal childhood story, 87
- training, special, 88

Goal kick (USYSA law), 196
Goalmouth scramble, 60
Groin muscles
- exercise for strengthening, 115
- pulls, 121
- stretches for, *36–37*

Guarding the ball, 51–52, *52*
Gymnastics, for cross-training, 111

H

Halftime, foods for, 102
Half-volleys, 82
Hamstring stretch, *34*
Headers and volleys (game), 179
Heading, *55*
- advanced players, 71
- brain injuries and, 123–24
- diving header, 71, *72*
- intermediate players, 60–61
- novice players, 54–55
- safe, guidelines for, 124

Head injuries
- bloody nose, 123
- concussion, 123

Heat exhaustion, 107
Heat stroke, 107
Heel injuries, 117
Hiding on the field, 66
Hierarchy of soccer skills, 11–12, 14
High school level. *See* Expert players
High school soccer, 145
college soccer and, 146–47
preparing for, 145
preseason training and practice, 145
Hips
exercise for strengthening, 115
injuries to
hip joint inflammation, 122
slipped capital femoral epiphysis, 122
stretch for, *39*
History of soccer, 3–4
Hockey, for cross-training, 111
Holding up the ball, 66, 72
Hook turn, 52
Hot weather
clothing for, 22
fluids during, 105–7
Hughes, Charles, 76, 111

I

Indoor play, 142
Injuries, 116–25
ankle, 117–18
dental, 124
eye, 125
groin, 121
head, 123–24
heel, 117
hip, 122
knee, 119–21
neck, 122–23
prevention of, 109–10, 125
shin, 118–19
shoulder, 122
spine, 122–23
testicle, 121–22
Inner-city programs (U.S.), 5
Inside-of-foot turn, 52
Inside-of-left-foot swerve pass, 81
Inside-of-the-foot pass, 50–51, *51*
Instruction. *See* Coaching; Teaching concepts
Intensity of play, 149, 163
Intermediate players, 58–66
competition issues, 66
decision making, 64–65, 66
rules, 62
skills development
ball control, 58, 64–65
block tackling, 62, *62*
Cruyff turn, 61, *61*
dribbling, 59
fluidity of position, 65–66
heading, 60–61
holding up the ball, 66
jockeying, 66
juggling, 61
laces drive, 60, *60*
shooting, 59–60
tackling, 61–62
throw-ins, *64*
trapping, 59
turns, 61
tactical instruction, 62–64
International soccer federation. *See* FIFA
International women's soccer, 161–62
Internet resources, 209
Iron
adolescent athletes and, 98
female athletes and, 99, 104
deficiency, symptoms of, 99

J

Jackets, warmup, 19
Javelin throw (goalkeeping), *90*
Jerseys
team, 18–19
training, 18
Jockeying, 66, 72–73
Juggling, *53*
intermediate players, 61
novice players, 53–54
personal story, 63
Juggling competition (game), 178

K

Keep-away games, 179
Keepers. *See* Goalkeepers

Kicks. *See also* Volleys
exercises for goalkeepers, 92–93
importance of, for goalkeepers, 89
types of
corner kick, 196
drop kick (goalkeeping), 93
free kick, 194–95
goal kick, 196
penalty kick, 196
Knee injuries, 119–21
anterior cruciate ligament injury, 119–20, 120
chondromalacia, 119
Osgood-Schlatter disease, 119–20
torn knees, 120
Knowledge of game, 148–49

L

Laces drive, 60, *60*
Laws, FIFA, summary of, 189–96
Learning methods (informal), 177–83
casual play, 177–79
TV soccer broadcasts, 181
videos, 181–82
watching others play, 179–80
Leg crossovers, 115
Leg scissors, 115
Levels of play, 129–35
appropriate, determining, 87, 130, 133
categories
classic, 130–31
independent Select, 132
Olympic Development Program, 132–33
premier, 131
recreational, 129–30
Select, 131–32
Levels of skill
advanced players, 67–77
beginner players, 43–48
expert players, 78–85
intermediate players, 58–66
novice players, 49–57
Licensing, of coaches, 24, 27, 150
Lifestyle, 76, 188
Ligament, ankle, injury of, 117
Linesmen, 192
Lower-back stretch, *36*
Low-fat foods, children and, 98

M

Magazines, soccer, 208
Major Soccer League (MLS), 4
Man-to-man marking, 85
Maradonna, Diego, 69, 70
Maradonna turn, 69, 70, 74
Martial arts, for cross-training, 111
Meals, for game days, 103
Menarche, delayed, in athletes, 171
Menstruation
anterior cruciate ligament injury and, 120
calcium and, 104
onset delayed in athletes, 171
Mental skills development, 147–49
Midfielders
description of position, 189
expert players, 85
Misconduct (USYSA law), 194–95
MLS, 4
Motor skills, *11*, 12
Mouthguards, 124
Muscle glycogen replenishment, 104
Muscle pulls, in back, preventing, 123

N

Nancy Clark's Sports Nutrition Guidebook, 99
NASL, 4
National Collegiate Athletic Association (NCAA)
clearinghouse, 147
scholarships, 146
soccer first recognized by, 4
National Soccer Coaches Association of America (NSCAA), 208
Navicula pad, 116–17
NCAA, 4, 146, 147
Neck
injuries, 122–23
stretch for, *38*
North American Soccer League (NASL), 4
Norway, women's soccer in, 162
Nose injuries
bloody, 123
broken, 123

Novice players, 49–57
introducing
concepts, 56
positions, 56
rules, 56
positional awareness, 55–56
skills for
ball control, 52–53, *53*
dribbling and passing, 50–51
goalkeeping, 56–57
heading, 54–55, *55*
juggling, 53–54, *53*
shielding, 51, *52*
shooting, 54
turns, 52
NSCAA, 208
Nutrition, 97–107
adolescent training diet, 98
effect on soccer performance, 101
fluid intake, 105–6
girls' needs, 104–5
needs of young athletes, 98–99
supplements, 106
tips, 100, 102

O

ODP. *See* Olympic Development Program
Offside (USYSA law), 194
Offside trap, 83, 85
Olympic Development Program (ODP), 131, 132–33, 146–47, 207
Olympic Games, soccer debut at, 4
One-touch play, 83
Open-the-gate stretch, *39*
Osgood-Schlatter disease, 119–20
Out of bounds (USYSA law), 193
Out of play (USYSA law), 193
Outside-of-right-foot swerve pass, 81
Outside-of-the-foot pass, 68
Outside-of-the-foot turn, 52
Overcoaching, 157
Overtraining, 125

P

Pants, warmup, 19
Parent-child games, 187
Parenting
advanced players, 77
beginner players
coaching, 44, 46
fun for, 48
preparing child, 47–48
camps, choosing, 138–40
coaches, communicating with, 26, 28
girl players, 171–73
goalkeepers, 88–89
mental fitness, nurturing, 147–49
nutrition, 97–107
parent/child bonds, 184
perceptions, girls' vs. boys' games, 168
pressure to win, misguided, 144
programs, finding, 23–26
role in tryouts, 134, 135
skills development, fostering 177–83
tips for
being supportive, 185–86
games, before and after, 46
gear introduction, 44
keeping soccer in perspective, 76
organizing gear, 28
Parents, as coaches, 150–57
advancing, 156–57
for beginner players, 44, 46
fairness, 151, 152
first steps, 150–51
overcoaching, 157
teaching concepts (A-Z), 151–55
team parents, dealing with, 155–56
Parry, diving (goalkeeping), *91*
Passing
advanced players, 68–69, 73
back pass, 73
drop pass, 73
expert players, 81
inside-of-the-foot pass, 50, *51*
novice players, 50–51
one-touch play, 83
swerve pass, 81, *81*
Pelé, 4, 143
Penalty kick (USYSA law), 196
Performance Conditioning for Soccer Newsletter, 109
Personal skills, enhanced, 14
Personal stories
coaching, 13, 50, 84, 144, 148, 164
communicating with coach, 28

English childhood soccer, 6, 63, 87
soccer as childhood obsession, 47
Physical exam, preseason, 125
Players
number of, in U.S., 4, 167
number on team
by age group, 190
USYSA law, 192
Playing levels. *See* Levels of play
Playing up, 135
Popularity, of soccer, in U.S., 3
Positional awareness
beginner players, 55–56
novice players, 55–56
as part of learning hierarchy, *11*, 14
of self, 14
of team, 14
Positions
descriptions of, 189
expectations of, expert players and, 85
fluidity of, 65–66, 74–75, 85
introducing, with novice players, 56
Positive thinking, 147–48
Postgame
nutrition for, 102, 104
quick-release foods for, 102
tips for parents, 46
Practice sessions, skill games for, 178–79
Premier play level, 131
Preseason training (high school), 145
Programs, organized
guidelines for choosing, 10, 12, 23–29
coaches, 27
sample questions to ask, 24
what to observe, 24–26
for inner-city youth, 5
locating, 8, 207–9
options, 26
qualities of excellence, 25
Protein, athletes' need for, 98
Psychological fitness, 147–49
Puberty, girls and
parenting tips, 171–72
physiological changes, 170–71
Punishment, by coaches, 113
Pushups, as punishment, 113

Q

Quadricep muscles
strengthening, 115
stretching, *35*
Quick-release foods, 102

R

Racquet sports, for cross-training, 111
"Ray Amato Splash," 93
Recreational play level, 129–30
Recreational vs. serious play
coach transitions, 44, 46
divide between, 7
Red card, reasons for, 195
Referees
abuse of, 27–29
advanced players as, 74
communicating with, 29
girls' vs. boys' games, 167–68
role of, 28
training for, 29
USYSA law, 192
Relaxation, importance of, 147
Restarting the game
corner kick, 196
goal kick, 196
throw-in, 196
USYSA law, 192–93
Rules
introducing, to novice players, 56
laws of the game, 189–96
Running
conditioning and, 114–15
as cross-training sport, 110–11
deep-water conditioning, 115–16
amount of, during games, 109, 111
as part of practices, 58

S

Safety, 23, 125, 154
SAY, 89, 207
Scholarships, soccer, 145–46
Scissors kick, 82, *82*
Scoring (USYSA law), 193
Seaver's syndrome, 117
Selection process, emotions and, 66
Select play level, 131–32
Self-positional awareness, *11*, 14

Serious players, qualities of, 143
Set pieces, 75–77, 85
Set plays, 75–77, 85
Shadowing, 66, 72–73
Sharks and fishes (game), 179
Shielding, 51–52, *52*
Shinguards
mandatory, 189
to prevent ankle injuries, 117
proper fit, 17
types of, 17
Shin injuries
fractures, 118–19
shinsplints, 118
stress fractures, 118
Shinsplints, 118
Shoot (game), 179
Shooting
advanced players, 69, 71
expert players, 81
intermediate players, 59–60
novice players, 54
side volley, *71*
Shorts
constriction from, 18
knit vs. woven, 18
Shoulder injuries, 122
Shoulder stretch, *38*
Shuffling (goalkeeping), 92
Siblings, 186–88
Sideline etiquette, 186
Side volley, *71*
Situps, 113
Skill games, 178–79
Skill levels. *See* Levels of skill
Skills. *See specific skills*
Skin protection, from sun, 121
Slide tackle, 72, *73*
Sliding, 83
Slipped capital femoral epiphysis, 122
Slow-release foods, 102
Snacking, 100–101, 104
Soccer
history of, 3–4
reasons for choosing, 8
watching
as learning tool, 179–81
as sensory experience, 183
Soccer America (newspaper), 208
Soccer America Yellow Pages, 8, 208, 209
Soccer Association for Youth (SAY)
description and address, 207
goalkeeping, comments on, 89
Soccer balls. *See* Balls, soccer
Soccer camps. *See* Camps, soccer
Soccer golf (game), 178
Soccer Industry Council of America
field shortages, 7–8
statistics from, 4
"Soccer in the Streets," 5
Soccer Jr. (magazine), 208
Soccer Start program (USYSA), 5
Soccer Tactics and Teamwork, 76, 111
Socks, 17
Software, soccer, 182
Spectators, etiquette for, 186
Spine
congenital deformity of, 123
injuries to, 122–23
Sports bras, 22, 172
Sports drinks, 105, 106
Sports glasses, 125
Standards, by age groups
ball size, 190
field dimensions, 190
game duration, 190
players per team, 190
Standing a player up, 72
Statistics
girl players in U.S., 167
physical activity, in a game, 109, 111
players in U.S., 4
Stepover, 69
Stress fractures. *See also* Fractures
calcium deficiency in girls and, 104
shin, 118
Stretching
active-isolated, 33
exercises for
buttocks, *35*
calves, *37*
groin, *36–37*
hamstrings, *34*
hips, *39*
lower back, *36*

neck and shoulders, *38*
quadriceps, *35*
trunk, *38*
importance of, 32–33
Stutter step, 69
Styles of play, exposure to, 75, 179–81
Sunburn protection, <u>121</u>
Supplements, nutritional, <u>106</u>
Support tips, for parents, 185–86
"Swarm ball," 55–56
Swerve pass, 81, *81*
Swimming, for cross-training, 111

T

Tackling
for advanced players, 72
slide tackle, 72, *73*
Tactical instruction
for expert players, 83–85
necessity of, 11
plays
fluidity of position, 85
man-to-man marking, 85
offside trap, 83, 85
set play, 85
throw-in, 62–64
Teaching concepts
advice for coaches, 151–55
Games Based Approach, 9–14
learning hierarchy, 11–12, 14
tactical instruction, 11
Team nature of soccer, 166
Team positional awareness, 14
Teams for parents, 184–85
Teeth
first-aid for knocked-out, <u>124</u>
protection with mouthguard, <u>124</u>
Testicular injuries, 121–22
Thighs, inner, strengthening, 115
Throw-in
tactical use of, 62–64
technique, *64*
USYSA law, 196
Ties, breaking, 193
Tip save (goalkeeping), *91*
Title IX, girls' sports and, 161
Torn knees, 120
Total player concept, *11*, 14
Town play level, 129–30
Town select play level, 130–31
Training Soccer Champions, 165, 182
Trapping, 59
Travel foods, <u>103</u>
Travel team play level, 130–31
Trips
abroad, 141
in U.S., 142
Trunk stretch, lateral, *38*
Tryouts
high school, 145
league, 133–35
parental role, <u>134</u>, 135
Turns, 52, 69
Maradonna turn, 69
stepover, 69
TV soccer broadcasts
1999 Women's World Cup, 4
1998 World Cup, 4
as learning tool, 181
Two-on-two heading, 178–79

U

Umbro Conditioning for Football, <u>111</u>
United States youth soccer
compared with England, <u>80</u>
compared with other countries, 4–5, 7
enthusiasm for game, <u>13</u>
Games Based Approach, 9–14
growing pains, 7
inner-city programs, 5
levels of play, 129–35
popularity of, 3, <u>14</u>
positive elements of, 5–6
U.S. Amateur Soccer, 207
U.S. Soccer Federation
coaching licenses offered, 24, <u>27</u>, 79, 150
inner-city youth funding, 5
Web site address, 209
U.S. Soccer Sports Medicine Book, <u>109</u>
U.S. Women's National Team, 5, 161
U.S. Youth Soccer Association (USYSA)
description and address, 207
guidelines on safe heading, 124
on heading and head injuries, 124
Olympic Development Program, 131, 132–33, 146–47, 207
Select (all-star) play level, 131–32

U.S. Youth Soccer Association (USYSA) *(continued)*
- Soccer Start program, 5
- standards for age groups, 190

V

Videos, soccer
- personal, for college recruiters, 146
- tips on selecting, 182
- types of, 182

VIP Program for Kids with Special Needs, 207
Visualization, 148, 148, 163
Vitamins, 106
Volleys
- bicycle kick, 82, *82*
- expert players, 81–82
- half-volleys, 82
- scissors kick, 82, *82*

Volunteer coaches, 44, 46, 150–57

W

Wall ball (goalkeeping), 92
Wander, Jeff, 90
Warmups
- components of, 31
- stretching
  - active-isolated, 33
  - exercises, *34–39*
- tips for, 31–32

Water consumption. *See* Fluids
Water workouts, 114–15
- deep-water running, 114–15
- leg crossovers, 115
- leg scissors, 115

Weather extremes, clothing for, 21–22
Weight lifting, 114
Weight-loss dieting, 99
Winning and losing
- coach's perspective, 144
- as part of soccer education, 14

Women, as coaches, 26–27
Women's soccer
- equal opportunities law, 161
- international scene, 161–62
- on the rise, 5, 161

Women's Sports Foundation, 172
Women's World Cup
- 1991 inaugural Cup won by U.S., 161
- 1999 games shown on TV, 4

World Club Championship, 4
World Cup
- effect of, on other countries, 5
- 1974, Cruyff turn, 70
- 1986, Maradonna turn, 70
- 1998, Blanco move, 70
- 1998 games broadcast live, 4

Y

Yellow card, reasons for, 195
Youth license modules, 24, 27, 130, 150, 205
Youth soccer. *See* United States youth soccer